Praise for *Seeing Jesus*

"In *Seeing Jesus*, Hudson not only helps us view Christ through the quirky, surprising, and even bizarre lenses of our spiritual ancestors, but he also invites us to question the ways we remake Christ in our own image today. Equal parts visual album, historical inquiry, and opportunity for personal spiritual *examen*—wholly intriguing!"

—Sarah Arthur, editor of *At the Still Point: A Literary Guide to Prayer in Ordinary Time*

"This wise, witty, fun, thought-provoking, and erudite book includes fascinating details throughout. Whether you're a skeptic or a believer or a little bit of both, you will enjoy this wonderful ride through history, encountering charlatans, saints, and ordinary people who've laid claim to extraordinary visions of Jesus."

—Ann Spangler, bestselling author of *Sitting at the Feet of Rabbi Jesus*

"Robert Hudson's fascinating new book is a feast for the eyes, the mind, and the heart. His beautifully crafted prose and well-chosen artistic representations inspire even as they challenge us to keep our eyes open for our own divine 'sightings.' This is a book of profound human pondering and deeply spiritual significance."

—Terry Glaspey, author of *Discovering God through the Arts* and *75 Masterpieces Every Christian Should Know*

"Robert Hudson's lively, open-hearted, open-minded reflections on the lives and claims of Christian mystics invite believers to consider what these impassioned, intuitive, Spirit-driven people may have to teach us about how we live in the company of saints, surrounded by clouds of witnesses."

—Marilyn McEntyre, author of *Caring for Words in a Culture of Lies* and *Dear Doctor: What Doctors Don't Ask, What Patients Need to Say*

"Robert Hudson coaches readers to hike high among the spiritual pillars of old and the moderns. As a good guide, he knows where we may stumble and where we need to pause. With sure prose and storytelling, Hudson enlivens anecdotal histories of the sinner-saints who have laid claim to this gift: seeing Jesus."

—Cynthia Beach, author of *The Surface of Water* and *Creative Juices*

SEEING
JESUS

Also by Robert Hudson

The Poet and the Fly: Art, Nature, God, Mortality, and Other Elusive Mysteries

The Further Adventures of Jack the Giant Killer

Kiss the Earth When You Pray: The Father Zosima Poems

The Monk's Record Player: Thomas Merton, Bob Dylan, and the Perilous Summer of 1966

The Christian Writer's Manual of Style, 4th Edition

The Art of the Almost Said: A Christian Writer's Guide to Writing Poetry

Thomas Dekker's Four Birds of Noah's Ark: A Prayer Book from the Time of Shakespeare

Companions for the Soul (with Shelley Townsend-Hudson)

Making a Poetry Chapbook (chapbook)

Proof or Consequences: Thoughts on Proofreading (chapbook)

Beyond Belief: What the Martyrs Said to God (with Duane W. H. Arnold)

SEEING
JESUS

VISIONARY ENCOUNTERS FROM THE FIRST CENTURY TO THE PRESENT

ROBERT HUDSON

BROADLEAF BOOKS
MINNEAPOLIS

Published in association with the literary agency of Credo Communications, LLC, Grand Rapids, MI 49525; www.credocommunications.net.

Cover design: Gearbox Studio

Print ISBN: 978-1-5064-6575-3
eBook ISBN: 978-1-5064-6576-0

Printed in Canada

To
Glenn and Julie Warners
Bryan and Linda Whittemore
Shelley Townsend-Hudson

You don't want to walk and talk about Jesus,
You just want to see his face.

—Keith Richards / Mick Jagger (1972)

In all faces is seen the Face of faces,
veiled, and in a riddle.

—Nicholas of Cusa (1453)

CONTENTS

1. You Just Want to See His Face 1

PART ONE: DISCIPLES

2. The Doubter: Thomas..19

3. The Stranger Within: Cleopas, His Companion, and Mary...........32

4. "On the Right Hand of God": Stephen, Paul, and Ananias...........46

5. *VOOM!* John of Patmos..58

PART TWO: ASCETICS

6. Demons and a Dream: Anthony of Egypt and Martin of Tours 77

7. God's Grouch: Jerome 91

8. Apocryphal Visions: The Gnostics...105

PART THREE: MYSTICS

9. The Shadow of Living Light: Hildegard of Bingen 119

10. "Repair My House": Francis of Assisi...131

11. "All Shall Be Well": Julian of Norwich 144

12. "It Is Full Merry in Heaven": Margery Kempe 157

PART FOUR: TRAILBLAZERS

13. Quakers, Shakers, and Groundbreakers: George Fox, Jacob Boehme, Public Universal Friend, Mother Ann Lee, Emanuel Swedenborg, and the Spanish Mystics 171

14. To Imagine Is to See: William Blake 190

15. "I Know You, and I Don't Know You": Sojourner Truth 200

16. Revival Fires: Lorenzo Dow, Charles Finney, and Joseph Smith 213

PART FIVE: MODERNS

17. "Keep Your Mind in Hell": Silouan the Athonite 231

18. "O God—If There Is a God": Sadhu Sundar Singh 243

19. Inner Locutions: Mother Teresa 254

20. Tortillas and Televangelists: Maria Morales Rubio and Oral Roberts 265

Epilogue: The Face of Faces 277

Acknowledgments 283

Appendix: Visions of Jesus—A List 285

Notes 289

Selected Bibliography 311

1

YOU JUST WANT
TO SEE HIS FACE

"And then I saw it . . . the face of Jesus."

She was a traveling evangelist, a chalkboard artist, one of several who were popular in evangelical circles at the time. She had stopped by our small suburban Chicago church to present a weekend series of inspirational talks.

The first thing you noticed was how unformidable she seemed: small, square built, sixtyish, with dark, somewhat dowdy hair and thick-rimmed glasses. She looked as if she could be someone's great-aunt in an old photograph.

But with nothing more than a handful of colored chalk, she worked magic. Talking all the while, she brought to life colorful scenes from the Bible—Adam and Eve in the garden; Jesus as a shepherd; and most dramatic of all, the crucifixion, which, as I recall, she could transform with a few rapid hand strokes into a joyously radiant resurrection.

This was the mid-1960s, and I was eleven or twelve years old. My parents had insisted that I attend these "chalk talks," which our church billed as "revival meetings," though they were nothing like the more vigorous affairs that go by that name in the rural South.

Although much of what happened during that weekend is lost to me now, one memory stands out as among the most haunting of my childhood. With the intensity of a Hebrew prophet and the utter sincerity of, say, someone's great-aunt, she described her experience of seeing the actual face of Jesus. It was one of those moments that make you catch your breath. Everyone in that room hung on her words. She was so earnest, so inspiring.

When she was younger, she explained, she'd stood at her screen door gazing out at the trees in her backyard and weeping because of her sins. She prayed a simple prayer of repentance, and in a flash, Jesus appeared. His face filled her vision, blinding her to every other sight. Whether she said it was for minutes or hours, I don't remember, but with an expression of infinite compassion, that face hovered before her, conveying forgiveness and acceptance.

Even after the initial flash, the face lingered. The image grew gradually smaller during the days that followed until it hovered only in one corner of her eye. For a month, or maybe it was a year, she could see that face in miniature, floating at the edge of her field of vision, constantly watching, sometimes stern when temptations assailed but always loving and kind. What a blessing, she exclaimed, that as a new Christian, she could think no thought and do no deed unperceived by that tender gaze.[1]

As I said, I was a preteen at the time, impressionable, insecure, naive. I was gripped by her presentation but cautious . . . and the fact is, I didn't believe her.

And may God forgive me, I still don't.

❋ ❋ ❋

My skepticism surprises me. After all, a passable history of Christianity could be written with nothing more than a catalog of those who claimed to have had such visions. The book you are holding now, in fact, peeks into a few select chapters of that history.[2] Consider Paul the apostle, whose encounter with the risen Christ is the one against which all others are measured: blinded by that holy presence and stunned by that overpowering voice—"knocked off his ass," as a mischievous friend of mine likes to say. In an instant, that brief experience changed the Pharisee into a follower, and the follower changed history.

Nor was Paul alone. By my rough count, the Gospels and the Book of Acts offer detailed accounts—with names attached—of at least forty people who set eyes on the living, resurrected Jesus, who gazed into his eyes, spoke with him, touched his wounds. Paul suggests that hundreds of anonymous others saw him as well before he ascended to heaven.

But here's the problem. Some theologians insist that the apostolic era marked the end of such visitations and that Jesus would not reappear until the end of time, at the second coming. In the interim, Jesus promised to dispatch the Holy Spirit in his place[3]—*sensed* as a presence rather than *seen* as a person. So if Jesus himself, whether sensed or seen, can return willy-nilly long after ascending to heaven, as some people claim, then why is the Holy Spirit even needed? In nearly every century since then, we find tales of Christians who claim to have seen Jesus's face or heard his voice or both. The faithful would surely remind me that God can do whatever God wants, that Jesus can reappear whenever and wherever he pleases. God is God after all. And furthermore, they might add, what right do I have to doubt anyone's word?

Dismissing such claims out of hand would be easy were it not for the fact that many of the most influential Christians in history are among their number: Jerome, Francis of Assisi, Mother Teresa, and more. And it seems as if a new book is published every few months by someone now living who claims to have seen Jesus under some unusual circumstance and by some special dispensation. Hadn't Jesus promised his disciples, "I will not leave you as orphans; I will come to you"?[4]

But another problem arises. Why does Jesus appear only to a select few? Why sometimes to the most devout and sometimes to the least? Or more personally, why to a chalk talk evangelist and not to me?

The more recent the claim, I confess, the more intense my skepticism. How much easier it is to believe that one of the Desert Fathers saw Jesus in a vision under a fiery sun after praying and fasting for weeks on end than to believe that a well-fed, well-heeled, late-night televangelist—with a mansion and a private jet—did. Although both the desert monk and the televangelist may be *convinced* of the genuineness of their experience, in modern claims, I often smell a rat. I sense a certain amount of manipulation going on—just before the collection plate is passed. For a small contribution, some televangelists will happily share Jesus's direct and specific will for your life. One TV preacher used to sell the handkerchiefs with which he wiped the sweat from his forehead while on his ecstatic conference calls with God. Their direct line to heaven is their authority. They peddle their visions. They are special, they claim, because God has singled them out for an intimacy the rest of us lack.

In my twenties, I knew a man, a respected Pentecostal leader, who claimed he could read the actual words of God like ticker tape moving across the inside of his closed eyelids. The more I got to know him, the more I came to think he was either deluded or the most willfully evil person I'd ever met. Over time, the messages he received conformed less to the biblical commandments and more to this man's own compulsion to control others.

My cynicism is obvious.

* * *

But part of me holds back. Deep down, I would love nothing more than to glimpse that face, even for a moment. I wish I could have stood in Jerusalem to see what Jesus looked like. Would I dare to glance into his eyes? Would his voice be as high and lilting as Lincoln's is supposed to have been? Or low and booming, like Dylan Thomas reading "Do Not Go Gentle into That Good Night"?

When I think about that voice, my inner ear hears the grand cadences of the King James Bible. How could Jesus *not* have spoken these very words: "Suffer little children, and forbid them not, to come unto me: for of such is the kingdom of heaven"?[5] Our English-biased ears are attuned to such poetic diction. We may be amused by the country preacher who is convinced that God wrote the Bible in King James English, but when it comes to the voice of Jesus, I think most of us unconsciously assume it must have been very close to "Suffer little children . . ." Jesus spoke Shakespearean. How could he *not* have?

But no, Jesus spoke to a largely illiterate people in their own Aramaic tongue, an earthy argot of everyday working folks: fishermen, net menders, merchants, tax collectors, prostitutes, slaves. He didn't speak the mellifluous language of Queen Elizabeth's time, nor were his cadences those of twenty-first-century America either—he spoke neither KJV nor NIV. Even the Gospels in their original language offer only a Greek translation of his words. The fact is, we will never know just how different that voice was from the voice we think we know, because Jesus's ancient Galilean dialect of Aramaic is no longer spoken, though scholars know its general sounds and rhythms and inflections. But even if they could reproduce the spoken language perfectly, still, that individual voice—its texture and tonality—is irretrievable.

We know, for instance, that Jesus could speak in a loud voice, as when he called out to those who were thirsty to come to him and drink, or when he called Lazarus from the tomb, or when he spoke in agony from the cross.[6] But that gives us little to go on. Most people can speak loudly when necessary. As an open-air preacher, Jesus knew how to be heard.

In his vision in Revelation, John of Patmos goes further. He says that the voice of Jesus sounded "like a trumpet" and "like the sound of rushing waters."[7] But that was a magnificently visionary Jesus who held seven stars in his right hand and had a two-edged sword sprouting from his mouth.[8] How odd it would have been if, after stepping out of the clouds, he'd spoken in a normal voice—a newscaster voice, a café barista voice.

Another hint is found in the Synoptic Gospels, all of which state that Jesus "taught as one who had authority," the word *taught* being often translated as *spoke*.[9] That may be the most telling detail of all. We detect a firmness in that phrase as well as a certain fullness of timbre. It's suggestive, though even that doesn't make it Shakespearean. What we assume to be poetry in Jesus's speech was probably more akin to clarity and resolve. A teacher's voice.

Still, let's face it—hearing Jesus deliver the Sermon on the Mount in Aramaic would have been like watching a foreign film without subtitles. We wouldn't have had a clue.

✻ ✻ ✻

Although we know a great deal about the character of Jesus from the Gospels—his words and actions and especially his effect on those around him—we find nothing about his appearance. The most indisputable fact is that none of our images of him, whether in classic works of art or in films, bear the least resemblance to what he must have actually looked like. For instance, instead of a long robe, he probably wore a knee-length tunic cinched at the waist with a belt. I suspect his olive-brown skin, broad Middle Eastern features, unkempt appearance (by modern standards), close-cropped hair (yes, men wore their hair short then), trimmed beard, and most likely, small stature would take us aback. You may remember the outrage in 2001 when a forensic anthropologist named Richard Neave sculpted a head of a typical Galilean from Jesus's time based on archeological data and an actual skull, offering a glimpse into what Jesus might have looked like. People said he looked more like an anxious Neanderthal than the Son of God.[10] In her book *What Did Jesus Look Like?* author Joan E. Taylor suggests that Jesus may have looked like any number of men depicted in second-century Egyptian mummy portraits (figure 1.1).[11]

Had Jesus looked markedly different from the average person of his time—for instance, were he extremely tall or muscular,

Figure 1.1. A mummy portrait from Faiyum, Egypt, ca. 150 (Altes Museum, Berlin)[12]

unusually fair-haired or light-skinned—the gospel writers would surely have mentioned it. Such details would have been essential in assuring us that Jesus was set apart in some way from those around him, lending him greater authority. The writers would have noted such facts if only to convey to the reader that Jesus was a real person, particular and unique. After all, on a few occasions, the physical appearance of other people in the Bible is described; Moses was handsome, Samson and Absalom both had long hair, King David was ruddy, Zacchaeus was short.

The dusky shade of Jesus's complexion is probably what makes the accounts of his transfiguration so startling. Matthew's gospel says his face "shone like the sun," and Luke's states simply that "the appearance of his face changed."[13] Later, in John's vision in Revelation, that face "was like the sun shining in all its brilliance."[14] Those are the only direct references to Jesus's face in the Bible. Powerful images but still unrevealing.

If we could have encountered the earthly Jesus, we antiseptic moderns would have noticed one thing immediately: he would have smelled bad, especially by our modern standards. It feels blasphemous to say it, but it's true. No country in history has been as clean scrubbed and sanitized as modern America. The culture in which Jesus lived was aware of soaps and perfumes, but they were expensive, which Judas was quick to point out when he criticized Mary of Bethany for anointing Jesus's feet with what the KJV calls aromatic "spikenard."[15] Peter most certainly did not apply antiperspirant before a long day of fishing, nor did Paul shower after hours of net mending or trekking from city to city.

Still, Jesus was no dirtier or smellier than anyone else in first-century Israel, so no one would have noticed or cared. If transported to some modern American cities, though, he might well be arrested under the antihomeless statutes, driven to the edge of town, or placed in a temporary shelter. I'd like to think that some of our urban churches would take him in, give him a meal and a bed. But honestly, if he were to show up anonymously at my own front door at dinnertime, I would feel uneasy and ask him to leave. My wife and daughters, bless their hearts, would not.

✳ ✳ ✳

But if I can't be transported back to the Jerusalem of Jesus, dare I ask God for a vision of the kind Charles Finney or Sundar Singh had? Could I ask for his face to fill my vision as it filled the eyes of the chalk artist?

The idea excites me. But only momentarily.

Then a sort of panic sets in. What if such a vision turned out to be like John's on Patmos or Julian's in England? Overwhelming, all-consuming, life-altering, even life-threatening? As you'll see, many of the visions in this book were of precisely that kind . . . moments of no return. Do I really possess the courage to invite such a vision into my life?

Despite years of church attendance, years of editing the work of Christian writers, years of "professing Christ as my personal savior," as the evangelicals say, I have the vague feeling that an actual *personal* encounter with a life-size, flesh-and-blood, anciently alien Jesus would be a shattering experience. I'm not talking about a sentimentalized, meek-and-mild, King James Version of him or a modern, sanitized interpretation of his appearance—like the flowing-haired saintly image in that famous portrait by Warner Sallman (figure 1.2), a copy of which must hang in every Protestant church in the United

Figure 1.2. Warner Sallman's iconic portrait *Head of Christ* (© 1941, 1968, Warner Press, Inc., Anderson, Indiana. Used with permission.)

States, or that other hugely popular portrait of Jesus by Heinrich Hofmann in 1889 (figure 1.3). Theologian Paul Tillich once wrote, "An apple of Cezanne has more presence of ultimate reality than a picture of Jesus by Hofmann."[16]

I'm talking about the Aramaic-speaking, rough-hewn, odiferous, road-soiled, itinerant Jesus who nonetheless would be able to look straight through me just as he looked through the woman at the well, whose every fault and vice were visible to him, leaving me vulnerable and shivering.

Nor is it a coincidence that the direct, unwavering gaze of Jesus would make me every bit as uncomfortable as the intense look of a desperately homeless person on the streets of my hometown of Chicago. It would make my heart race. A convicting gaze. An unblinking and slightly overlong gaze. If indeed we are to treat the poor and hungry and naked and imprisoned as though they were Jesus in disguise, then there is a deep

Figure 1.3. Heinrich Hofmann's famous idealized conception of Jesus—a detail from his painting *Christ and the Rich Young Ruler* (1889)

significance in the comparison. The question is not so much "Dare I look into those eyes?" as "Dare I look away?" Is it possible (to paraphrase Tillich) that there is more presence of ultimate reality in the face of one homeless person than in all the sermons in all the world? Say amen, somebody.

So . . . a part of me longs to see that face, and a part of me is terrified at the prospect.

✳ ✳ ✳

According to conventional wisdom, God sometimes denies us our desires as a sort of loving discipline. After all, the Bible writers ask us to believe without seeing: "Faith is the substance of things hoped for, the evidence of things not seen," says the writer of Hebrews.[17] So perhaps God disciplines us by not answering our prayer—our desire—to see the face of Jesus.

Or, by contrast, is it my skepticism, my innate lack of faith in such reports, that keeps me from having a similar experience? A friend of mine once said that only people disposed to believing in UFOs will ever see one. Deniers never do. Similarly, I'm skeptical about ghosts. Despite knowing people who claimed to have seen them, I doubt they exist, at least in the form that many people believe.

For instance, consider this story: Late one night a restaurant owner took me on an after-hours tour of his reputedly haunted old restaurant. After telling me tales of the hauntings that had taken place there, he squired me up to a dimly lit banquet hall on the second floor, where the chairs and tables were covered with dusty sheets. We stood there, mute, for what seemed a long time, though it was no more than a minute. Then he whispered, "There! Do you see her? The ghost of a little girl . . . staring at us!"

I saw nothing, though I admit my heart thumped. I'm not immune to adrenaline surges at such times.

"I don't see anything," I said, straining my eyes into the dark.

"There, by that chair in the corner. She's looking right at us. You see her?"

I paused, summoned my courage, then walked over to the shadowy corner. I pointed. "Here?"

I expected my host to say something like "Well, now you've scared her off," but he only said, "No. Sorry. I guess I didn't see anything."

After the tour, he and his wife explained to me—vehemently— that my "big problem" was that I lacked imagination, at which point I thought, *Is that what this was about? Was I supposed to play along and just pretend I saw ghosts? This was all a game, right?*

Which leads me to this question: Is that what claims of seeing Jesus are about? Are we supposed to play along and pretend we believe what Christians across the centuries have claimed? Sometimes it feels like that. When churchgoers claim that God has spoken to them, using such language as "God spoke to my heart," we never respond by saying, "Hogwash." We're respectful. Empathic. We suspend our disbelief, much as we do when we read fantasy novels and fairy tales. So maybe I'm the problem. By not believing in ghosts—by lacking imagination—perhaps I disqualify myself from seeing them.

But Jesus is different. I believe he exists. Although I'm skeptical of those across the centuries who claim to have seen him, or at least sincerely believe they have, I'm intrigued by the possibility. Some of them, I hope, were not just metaphorically squiring us through the haunted old religious restaurants in their heads.

But how do we know? How are we supposed to understand such experiences—and such people? How do we make sense of them? How do we separate the special from the specious? Must we believe everyone's claim unreservedly, or may we doubt, test their veracity, or even laugh out loud at the absurdity of some? Are we ever allowed to say, "Hogwash"? These questions are at the heart of this book.

✳ ✳ ✳

I approach each story with those questions in mind. This book strives to be an informal narrative history—or perhaps I should say an *anecdotal history*, with one fascinating story after another. Wherever the historical record allows, I have tried to allow each person to tell the story of Jesus's appearance in his or her own words.

And that word *story* is pivotal in "making sense." This is a book of stories and a book *about* stories—about famous Christians of the past. And in the process, I tell a few stories of my own. By using the word *story*, though, I don't mean to imply that these claims of seeing Jesus are necessarily fictitious. Nor do I imply that they are factual either. Whether they are truth or fiction, one fact remains: you don't need to believe in ghosts to enjoy a ripping-good ghost story.

Everywhere we look, good stories and bad stories abound, the true and the false, and we tell them apart, instinctively, not just by their adherence to facts but also by their content, their emotional core, the message they convey, the heart truths they contain. Think of Job: Are we required to accept the story of his sufferings as a historical fact to believe that it is in a deep sense true? Or the parables of Jesus: Does the story of the Good Samaritan lose its validity if the incident was made up to make a point? Is Jesus a liar if that story is just . . . a story?

Jesus explained how to distinguish between true things and false things (he was talking about prophets at the time, but it applies to storytellers as well); he said, "Ye shall know them by their fruits."[18] My hope is that the same will hold true for the storytellers in this book.

When the literalness of a claim is in doubt, we'll look at its fruits, at how each visionary encounter with Jesus changed the person and how that experience affected others at the time and for centuries afterward. We'll take each story of seeing Jesus at face value, neither believing nor disbelieving and claiming no more for them than the person claimed for himself or herself, and we'll weigh the fruitful and unfruitful encounters as if in a balance. Perhaps we'll especially relish the *unfruitful* ones because the existence of false claims suggests that true ones might also be possible.

As the Sufi poet Rumi once wrote, "Counterfeit only exists because there is such a thing as real gold."[19]

PART ONE
DISCIPLES

2

THE DOUBTER
Thomas

Since we have no idea what Jesus looked like, how would we even recognize him if we passed him on the street? For that matter, how did any of the people in this book, in the midst of their unusual experiences, know it was really Jesus and not, as Ebenezer Scrooge said of Jacob Marley's ghost, just an "undigested bit of beef . . . a fragment of underdone potato"?[1]

I think about this because I once met a genuine counterfeit Jesus, and I confess, he was pretty convincing.

I was in graduate school at the time. In the late 1970s, all sorts of cults and offbeat religious movements were in the news—Moonies, Eckankar, Scientology, the Way—and large university campuses were lodestars for zealots of all stripes.

One day, our campus was in an uproar. A young man dressed in dirty robes had arrived looking as though he'd just stepped off the set of some biblical epic, complete with a rope belt, sandals, long hair, and a scraggly beard. He seemed to be in his late twenties but looked surprisingly weathered. His feet and hands were dirty. Behind him trailed three or four other ragged-looking men in similar attire—disciples, no doubt—and a couple of women.

The robed man climbed onto a bench in the courtyard outside the student union, and he began to preach. He claimed to be Jesus returned to earth in the flesh. Except for his unusual claim, the wisdom he dispensed was conventional, biblical even, though at certain points, he expressed a fair amount of vitriol over what had become of the church since the first century. Modern pastors, he felt, were the Pharisees of our time. Even false Christs share at least one thing in common with the genuine one, I suppose—they go after the religious establishment like a terrier after rabbits.

Not one to suffer false prophets lightly, a local Southern Baptist preacher mounted a nearby bench, and as he literally thumped a Bible with his free hand, he denounced the young man as a mocker, a blasphemer, one possessed by demons.

It was drama of the highest order, amusing at times, intense, theatrical, a little embarrassing due to the extreme emotions it brought out in the actors. It occurred to me that the young man may have been pranking us or was a paid actor in some sociological research experiment. If so, he was extremely well prepared.

Sadly, if one were to judge the performances solely on the basis of compassion, gentleness, and charisma, the false Jesus would have won hands down. Instead of responding to the preacher with vituperation, the young man listened, argued gently and effectively, and edged closer to the preacher, seemingly delighted with the harassment. Then, while the Baptist minister paused to catch his breath, the self-proclaimed Jesus loudly forgave the minister for his unbelief. He called on God to heal him of his blindness . . . and he embraced him. Or at least he tried to. The minister squirmed from his grasp, somewhat pugnaciously, and I don't remember much about the chaos that ensued.

A day or two later, I happened to be standing in that same courtyard with a young woman named Ginny, whom I was dating at the time. She was the daughter of a prominent minister. The robed young man had returned, and an even larger crowd had gathered to hear him, though mostly for amusement. On this day, the visitor was sparring not with Southern Baptists but with rowdy frat boys who bellowed snatches of hymns to drown out the would-be Jesus's sermon: "Onward, Christian soldiers, marching as to war . . ."

Finding himself shouted down, the man realized his message would not be heard that day. So, hopping down from his bench, he pronounced a general curse upon the crowd, shouting something about a "wicked generation" and "hardness of heart," and proceeded to shove a path through the crowd, like Moses parting the collegiate sea.

His path, as it happened, led directly to Ginny and me. Still pronouncing curses, he walked toward us. He stopped suddenly. Looking into Ginny's eyes, he reached out a hand, placed it on her head, and said gently, "But you, I see, have the faith of a child." He was right, though without knowing it. She did have a deep and beautiful spirit, and she is today a prominent minister herself.

And jarring my shoulder, he brushed past us. Whether Ginny was bemused or shaken I don't recall.

Only later did it occur to me what I should have said, calmly, without rancor: "I won't believe you until I put my fingers in the nail holes in your hands and reach my hand into the wound in your side." This Jesus would certainly have picked up on the cue and denounced me as a "Doubting Thomas"—which is what I would have hoped for because at that point, the argument would have been entirely on my side.

Unlike the real one, counterfeit Jesuses do not stand up well to Thomas . . . the Doubter.

✳ ✳ ✳

You see, I identify with Thomas's "show-me" brand of belief—his mistrust when the disciples told him that Jesus had been resurrected and his refusal to believe it until he could actually touch those wounds for himself. I think he was on to something . . . something we would do well to heed. While the apostle Paul says that the Christian's faith is in "things unseen"[2] because those things are eternal, the problem is that not everything that's unseen is worth having faith in. In the religious communities I've been a part of, I've witnessed the less-than-positive effects of an overzealous faith in the wrong unseen things—conspiracy theories, end-times panics, crackpot enthusiasms, supposed miracles, devotion to unworthy leaders, adherence to specious doctrines, and general flimflam—and often with tragic results. Every cult in the world only exists because its followers believe in things that are unseen.

When Jesus tells Thomas that they who believe without seeing are blessed, he's not talking about a blind faith in just anything; he's talking about one thing only—himself—about having a discerning trust that a specific Person is real.

✳ ✳ ✳

The scene is familiar. On Sunday evening, the day of Jesus's early morning resurrection, Jesus appears to the disciples in a locked room—locked, according to John's gospel, because the disciples were fearful of being arrested. That detail is significant, for it indicates that Jesus not only was raised from the dead but is able to appear in a room that is sealed off from the outside. His appearance is doubly miraculous . . . a feat of wall walking.

But Thomas is not present. Why? We don't know. Like the other disciples who, after the crucifixion two days earlier, fled out of fear, Thomas too may have hidden, but somewhere other than the locked room. When the disciples later tell him that they've seen Jesus alive again, he refuses to accept it: "Unless I see the nail marks in his hands and put my finger where the nails were, and put my hand into his side, I will not believe."[3]

A week goes by. The disciples are back in the same room, which is again securely locked, but this time Thomas is with them—and when Jesus appears, he singles Thomas out and says, "Put your finger here; see my hands. Reach out your hand and put it into my side. Stop doubting and believe."[4]

Thomas, convinced at last, responds, "My Lord and my God!"[5]

Forever after, Thomas has been saddled with the epithet Doubting Thomas—"Stop doubting," Jesus said. How many thousands of sermons have used him as a prop to illustrate Jesus's next words: "Because you have seen me, you have believed; blessed are those who have not seen and yet have believed."[6]

So when we think of Thomas, a vaguely unfavorable image comes to mind, an image of a somewhat stubborn skeptic, even a cynic, who only accepts what his senses tell him. Of all the disciples, he seems to be the most dubious about the reports of Jesus's resurrection, whose faith was so weak that he demands physical proof. In one of Emily Dickinson's crisp phrases, "Thomas' faith in anatomy – was stronger than his faith in faith."[7]

Artists portrayed Doubting Thomas as early as the fifth century, and by the time of the Renaissance, he had become a favorite subject for the likes of Rubens, Dürer, Caravaggio (figure 2.1), and Rembrandt (figure 2.2). I've long been struck by Caravaggio's interpretation because Thomas does not seem to be looking at the wound in Jesus's side; instead, he's looking beyond Jesus, as if blind, and trusting only the touch of his finger as it explores that exposed gash—a stark and deeply psychological portrayal. Seeing isn't believing. Touching is. In the end, Thomas is usually portrayed as someone who needs to be taught a lesson. "Okay," Jesus seems to say, "if you're going to be that way about it, here—poke these wounds."

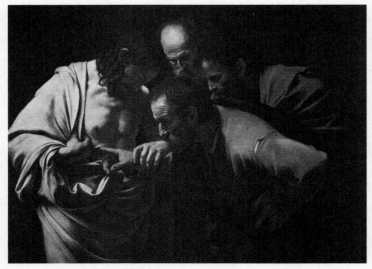

Figure 2.1. Caravaggio's powerful chiaroscuro painting *The Incredulity of Saint Thomas* (ca. 1602)

Figure 2.2. *The Incredulity of Saint Thomas* (1652), a pen-and-wash sketch by Rembrandt

✳ ✳ ✳

Thomas is nearly absent from the first three gospels: Mark, Matthew, and Luke list him by name in the roll call of the disciples, but that's all. Not a peep otherwise. John's gospel, by contrast, takes a special, if not always positive, interest in Thomas. Three stories are featured.

In the first, Mary and Martha send for Jesus, hoping he might heal their sick brother, Lazarus. Jesus prepares to return to them in Judea, though he informs the disciples that he knows, as if by telepathy, that Lazarus has already died. The disciples object to the plan, reminding him that he was nearly stoned to death when he last visited there, though Thomas, unperturbed, says to them, "Let us also go, that we may die with him."[8] Thomas's faith at that point seems unshakable.

The next story takes place in the upper room the night before the crucifixion. After telling the disciples about his own imminent death and resurrection, Jesus tells them that he is going to "prepare a place" for them and that he will "come back" to take them with him. "You know the way to the place where I am going," says Jesus.[9]

Thomas takes this somewhat layered metaphorical language literally and replies, "Lord, we don't know where you are going, so how can we know the way?"[10] (Poet Malcolm Guite calls Thomas the "courageous master of the awkward question"![11])

Jesus responds, "I am the way and the truth and the life. No one comes to the Father except through me."[12]

Again, Thomas is not lacking in faith; rather, he's aware that he's missing a subtext somehow, that he's not quite up to speed.

In the final story, the one in which Thomas touches Jesus's wounds, Thomas is not so much "the Doubter" as "the Empiricist," demanding proof for the claims made by the other disciples. But why? Is his faith that shallow? Is he so simpleminded that he failed to pick up on the hints that Jesus dropped not just in the upper room but all throughout his ministry? Hadn't Jesus told them he'd return? Or is Thomas jealous that he was left out?

As unorthodox as it may seem, I suspect that by asking for reliable physical evidence—not just hearsay but the kind that would stand up in a court of law—Thomas is exhibiting more faith than the rest of the disciples put together. He's doing what Jesus had repeatedly taught them to do—to be wary.

Although Matthew's gospel mentions Thomas only in the list of disciples, it does so precisely at the moment when Jesus sends them into the world to cast out evil spirits and heal the sick. Jesus warns them that they'll meet resistance, that they'll be "like sheep among wolves." So he advises them to be "as shrewd as snakes"[13]—or, according to the King James Version, as "wise as serpents." On an earlier occasion, Jesus warns them to "watch out for false prophets," and here is his test for spotting them: "By their fruit you will recognize them."[14]

Much later, and more ominously, when the disciples ask Jesus to explain his references to the "end of the age" and what signs will foreshadow his imminent return, he responds, "Watch out that no one deceives you. For many will come in my name, claiming, 'I am the Messiah,' and will deceive many. . . . If anyone says to you, 'Look, here is the Messiah!' or, 'There he is!' do not believe it. For false messiahs and false prophets will appear and perform great signs and wonders to deceive, if possible, even the elect. See, I have told you ahead of time. So if anyone tells you, 'There he is, out in the wilderness,' do not go out; or, 'Here he is, in the inner rooms,' do not believe it."[15]

Put simply, Jesus admonished his followers to be alert to the many frauds that would appear *before* his return. No wonder Thomas asked for proof. Jesus had told them to be cautious, as shrewd as snakes, and not to believe everyone who says, "Here he is, in the inner rooms"—which presumably included locked rooms. My hunch is that Thomas had such an overpowering faith in Christ's return that he didn't want to make the mistake of accepting a substitute, responding to a false alarm. Rather than doubting, he was displaying tenacious obedience.

Modern theologians, who study these things, would explain that with those admonitions, Jesus is talking about the end times, when he would return in majesty to judge the world. Clearly, they would argue, he was not talking about his immediate resurrection on the third day. But I would counter that the disciples were not clear about much of anything—let alone theology—in the days right after the resurrection. Furthermore, why should we expect clarity from the disciples when, two thousand years later, theologians are still parsing Jesus's words?

For me, the question is, Why were the other disciples so accepting, so trusting? Hadn't they heard the same admonitions as Thomas?

Here's another question: Why would Thomas focus on Jesus's wounds rather than his face? Don't we usually identify people by their faces? According to scientists, we have a remarkable ability to discern familiar faces, being able to distinguish among as many as five thousand from memory. It's a human superpower.[16]

This is whimsical speculation on my part, but Thomas may have had a good reason for distrusting faces; perhaps he knew how people were often mistaken for each other on the basis of facial features alone. You see, Thomas was a twin. In fact, he is the only person in the Gospels who is referred to that way. His name was Didymus—*Thomas* and *Didymus* being, in fact, the same name in two languages: Aramaic and Greek. And both names mean "twin."

The identity of Thomas's twin is unknown, though presumably, he or she survived into adulthood because had the sibling died in infancy, it's unlikely that anyone would have remembered it or found the fact important. Thomas is referred to as "Thomas the twin" three times in John's gospel. Even if his twin was fraternal, a sister perhaps, rather than identical, it raises an interesting possibility, for even fraternal twins can look much alike. My own two oldest daughters, born four years apart, are often mistaken for twins.

So Thomas might have suspected that the disciples had mistaken Jesus for someone else—an imposter of the kind that Jesus had warned them about . . . a false prophet, a false messiah. Just because someone looks like Jesus does not mean he is Jesus. No, says Thomas, show me the wounds in his hands and side—show me the proof that this is the same man who was violently anchored to the cross—and that will settle the matter.

* * *

Among the apocryphal books written in the first centuries after Christ (we'll look at some in chapter 8) is a short Gnostic document called the Gospel of Thomas, which purports to be a kind of commonplace book of the apostle's reminiscences of Jesus's teachings. The sayings include many that are also recorded in the Canonical Gospels, but it also contains others that seem alien to the Jesus we've come to know.

I have no idea what to make of that book, nor have scholars determined whether its sayings were actually collected by the apostle's followers. Still, I'm intrigued by its alternate version of Jesus's famous statement in John: "Because you have seen me, you have believed; blessed are those who have not seen and yet have believed."[17] In the Gospel of Thomas, Jesus says to him instead, "Know what is in front of your face, and what is hidden from you will be disclosed to you. For there is nothing hidden that will not be revealed."[18]

This Gnostic version certainly doesn't have the poetic ring of John's version, nor the same delicate balance in phrasing, but it shifts the emphasis in an intriguing way. No longer does it imply that Thomas is a doubter, a naive skeptic. Rather, it suggests that by closely observing the reality before him, the actual physical presence of Jesus, Thomas—and by extension, all of us—is better able to understand those unseen things. We might rephrase Dickinson's thought this way: "Thomas's faith in anatomy *is* his faith in faith." It's not a matter of weighing the seen things *against* the unseen, as if they were mutually exclusive, forming an incontrovertible dualism. Instead, the seen things, the facts known to our senses, contain the unseen. Reality is the revelation. The world as it is, is the mystery.

✳ ✳ ✳

I've grown to like Thomas because he's someone I understand, someone who thinks like an ordinary person does when confronted with extraordinary circumstances. When he hears a wild story, he's as dubious as most of us would be. When he confronts Jesus face-to-face—the reality before him—he sets his doubts aside . . . and believes.

Still, we differ from Thomas in one important way. All we have is the unseen Jesus, the one hidden from our sight. We haven't looked into that actual face, touched the wounded hands and side, so the best we can hope for is to be one of the blessed who believe without seeing.

Or . . . perhaps not.

Perhaps we see that face all the time and touch those wounds daily without realizing it. Could *that* be the hidden truth that the Gospel of Thomas speaks of? Whenever we see the reality of "what is in front of our faces"—the suffering, the afflicted, the persecuted, the oppressed in the society around us—we see the living person of Jesus; we see his wounds . . . especially his wounds. Whenever we buy a sack lunch for a homeless person on the street corner or visit a friend in the hospital or listen with compassion to a depressed coworker, whenever we counsel someone dealing with emotional devastation, whenever we stand up for the victims of violence and oppression, whenever we sit by the bedside of a dying family member or send a check to a charity, we are touching the wounds of Jesus, putting our fingers in his side. He said, "Whatever you did for one of the least of these brothers and sisters of mine, you did for me."[19]

So I think back to the imitation Jesus at the beginning of this chapter, and I wonder . . . if I'd been able to talk with him and he'd been able to tell me honestly about his past, about the emotional scars that had led him to believe that he was the resurrected Christ, or even if he could have talked openly about the mockery and persecution he faced on college campuses—from Southern Baptists and frat boys—then perhaps I really *would* have seen the genuine Jesus in him. If only he could have let someone touch those wounds. That's the downfall of many would-be Jesuses; they think they must be perfect, that they must be people without wounds.

Our problem is not so much that we doubt Christ is alive; our failure, rather, is that we refuse to see the reality of his presence before our face every day. He goes unseen. This, I think, is the message of Thomas the Doubter: "You will never believe that Jesus has returned from the dead until you touch his wounds for yourself"—the wounds of your family members, or your neighbors, or the next person you meet . . . the wounds of the entire world. They belong to Jesus.

3

THE STRANGER WITHIN

Cleopas, His Companion, and Mary

Here's a thought . . .

If Luke's gospel were our sole account of Jesus's resurrection, I think our Easter celebrations would look quite different, maybe even something like this:

On Easter Sunday morning, we would gather in the sanctuary, and after everyone has been seated and the organ prelude has ceased to resonate in the rafters, the congregation would grow quiet, knowing what to expect. It happens this way every year.

At first, distant voices are heard at the front of the church. The door at the side of the altar opens, from which a young man and woman emerge. Talking animatedly, they begin pacing up the center aisle. They are discussing the recent events in Jerusalem—the crucifixion . . . the fear . . . the scattered followers. But also this: Certain friends—Mary Magdalene, Joanna, and a few other women—had gone to the tomb with spices that very morning only to find that the body had vanished. Who can explain it? Then, out of nowhere, according to the women's tale, two men in "shining garments"[1] appeared, or "in clothes that gleamed like lightning."[2] So terrified were they that they fell to the ground, and one of the gleaming men asked, "Why do you look for the living among the dead? . . . He has risen!"[3]

"Could it be true?" the young man and woman wonder aloud. "Is he alive?"

By this time, they've reached the back of the sanctuary, where they turn and, still talking, walk back up the aisle toward the front. But unbeknownst to them, a third person has joined them, strolling a few steps behind, listening, head down, hands clasped behind his back.

The couple continues their conversation . . . about those shining figures and how the women rushed back to the disciples with the news. Though the disciples thought they were imagining things—overwrought and unreliable—Peter, at least, was alarmed. So he and the women raced back to the tomb, and sure enough, all that remained were the linen wrappings the body had been buried in.

By this time, the two travelers—plus one—have reached the front of the sanctuary, and the stranger speaks at last: "So what are you talking about?"

Startled, they turn. They gaze at him.

"You haven't heard?" the woman exclaims.

"Tell me," says the stranger.

So the man and the woman take turns telling the story over again: the prophet . . . the crucifixion . . . the burial . . . the hope for the redemption of Israel . . . the women . . . the empty tomb . . . the angels. "What does it all mean?" they ask.

The stranger ponders, then replies, turning toward the congregation so that everyone can hear, "How foolish you are, and how slow to believe all that the prophets have spoken! Did not the Messiah have to suffer these things and then enter his glory?"[4] Still speaking to everyone in the pews, he explains that the Scriptures, from Moses to the prophets, were a slow-motion revelation about the inevitable advent of the Messiah. And the Messiah had come. *That's* what it all means!

The young couple, intrigued but still baffled, invite the man to join them for a meal now that they've reached their destination. The stranger accepts. The trio then climbs the shallow steps to the altar, where a loaf of bread and three goblets of wine are waiting, as if for Communion. The stranger takes the bread in his hands, blesses it, and turning to the couple (and to us in the congregation), breaks it into three pieces—one for each of them. A look of astonishment comes over the faces of the man and woman.

"Is it you, Lord?" asks the woman, trembling, her knees nearly buckling beneath her.

And the man, bowing his head, says, "Rabboni."[5]

At this point in the pageant, the stranger vanishes—poof!—in the proverbial puff of smoke, or at least as well as that can be stage-managed during a Sunday-morning worship. Every church performs this bit of business differently, I imagine, though in most, the stranger, unnoticed by the couple, simply walks quickly out the door to the side of the altar, through which the couple had entered a few minutes before.

Then, making everyone jump in their seats (it never fails), the organ erupts into the boisterous opening chords of "Christ the Lord Is Risen Today," and at the end of each line, everyone belts out the refrain: "A–a–a–a–a–alleluia!"[6]

✳ ✳ ✳

Such would be our Easter service based on Luke's gospel alone. That version does indeed begin with the women going to the tomb. Finding the body gone, they see the angels, rush back to the disciples, and return to the empty tomb with Peter. But then the narrative shifts. In Luke, the resurrected Christ doesn't appear to the women or to Peter or to the disciples at that point; he appears to a man named Cleopas and an unidentified companion. (See figure 3.1.) For the purpose of my imaginary Easter pageant, we'll say that this person is Cleopas's wife. Most scholars believe that the "Clopas" mentioned in John's gospel[7] is identical to Luke's Cleopas; slight variations in the spelling of proper names are common in the Gospels. Furthermore,

Figure 3.1. German Expressionist Karl Schmidt-Rottluff's woodcut *The Road to Emmaus* (1918)—one of the few representations that leaves one of the travelers (on the left) gender neutral. Notice the intriguing detail that only two shadows are cast on the road.

John's gospel adds that Clopas's wife, who was present at the crucifixion, was named Mary.[8] She may even have been one of the unnamed women at the tomb with Mary Magdalene that morning.

Luke's gospel says that Cleopas and Mary are walking to the village of Emmaus, about seven miles from Jerusalem. Why? We don't know, though this was certainly not a pleasure trip; like many of Jesus's followers in those dangerous days after the crucifixion, they may have been fleeing the authorities. As Jews, they wouldn't have traveled the day before—Saturday, the Sabbath—but would have waited until Sunday morning. And clearly, before leaving, they'd heard the news about the empty tomb.

The obvious question is, How is it even possible that Cleopas and Mary *didn't* recognize Jesus? They'd known him personally, seen him, heard him. The seven-mile trek to Emmaus would have taken nearly two hours, and their lengthy discussion—about the prophets' foreshadowing of the events in Jerusalem—must have lasted for at least half that time.

Some writers suggest that the pair didn't recognize Jesus because his face was obscured by a hood or a scarf or the folds of his cloak. Or Cleopas and Mary were walking slightly ahead or behind the stranger—at an off angle—so they couldn't see his face. Those theories seem ludicrous to me, for it is human nature to want to see the face of the person with whom we're speaking—especially if that person is a stranger, to say nothing of one who seems to have appeared out of nowhere. And darkness cannot be blamed because the passage says the three of them arrived at Emmaus just as evening was falling.

Some commentators suggest that the newly resurrected Jesus must have looked different, mysteriously transformed and unrecognizable somehow. But to Cleopas and Mary, this stranger didn't seem mysterious or out of the ordinary at all. He looked normal, human—he just didn't look like Jesus.

Beyond that, there's the matter of voice. Even if the face were obscured, how could Cleopas and Mary not have recognized the voice? According to researchers, our voices are as varied as our fingerprints,[9] and we humans have an impressive ability to recognize the voices of the people we know. While "earwitness" testimony in the courtroom is notoriously unreliable when it comes to strangers' voices, it is acceptable evidence when it comes to the voices of those familiar to us. And it's not just the sound of the voice; it's the phrasings, the cadences, the patterns of thought, the use of favorite words and expressions. So if Jesus's resurrected body *was* transformed somehow, then his voice must have been transformed as well.

This raises some thorny questions: If Jesus neither looks nor sounds like Jesus, is it really Jesus? (To flip the old adage on its head, If it doesn't walk like a duck or quack like a duck, is it a duck?) If it *is* Jesus, how could he have been unaware that Cleopas and Mary had failed to recognize him? Why did he wait so long to reveal himself? Was it a prank? Was he going along with it as a joke? Or had he purposely disguised himself, hiding his face and altering his voice, for some deeper christological reason? He doesn't seem to have perpetrated this kind of extended ruse with any of the other disciples—so why now? Could he not have delivered his messianic message just as effectively by identifying himself from the start? It's odd.

I wonder whether Cleopas and Mary didn't recognize him because the very possibility was so far beyond their conceiving, like a Neanderthal encountering a copy of *On the Origin of Species*. As far as they knew, Jesus had been executed and his body had vanished, so when a stranger starts talking to them about the Messiah, in the third person nonetheless, how were they to guess that this was the Messiah himself? Consider this crude analogy: it would be like chatting with someone in line at Starbucks who claims to know what happened to Jimmy Hoffa without revealing the fact that he is in fact Jimmy Hoffa.

All of which sounds as if I'm preparing to challenge the veracity of the Emmaus road account. But that's not the case. In truth, I find the story compelling largely *because* of its improbability, *because* it raises so many questions, *because* it's a mystery. And I love it all the more because our strict theological logicians feel the need to explain away those weird, inconsistent details in the narrative, proposing convoluted theories, as if every puzzle piece must fit before the whole can be trusted. But sometimes—just sometimes—*un*likelihood is the best evidence of truth.

I love narratives that demand that we, as readers, either dismiss them, which I often do, as bizarre fabrications or accept them as inexplicable realities, powerful but oddly illogical circumstances—which, when you think about it, are like many of the circumstances we confront day to day. I've never been able to grasp, for instance, the fact of being *myself*—that I am who I am and no other, that this consciousness is mine alone, and that this *I* who is me once never existed. But here I am. And while scientists can explain the *how* of the sun coming up each morning and going down each night, they have yet to explain the ontological *why*. When viewed as existential phenomena, all experiences are improbable. Sometimes only the improbable makes sense.

The fact that Cleopas and Mary don't recognize Jesus seems oddly normal because it points to an important truth (again in the form of a question): Would *we* recognize Jesus if we met him on the road? To borrow Eliza Doolittle's crisp phrase, "Not bloody likely."[10]

If Cleopas and Mary couldn't recognize Jesus, even after having followed him for months or even years, after having seen his face and heard his voice, then what chance do we have? Cleopas and Mary are all of us, and their story is our own. I suspect that's why Luke's gospel never identifies Cleopas's companion—so that any of us can slip into that anonymous character's dusty robes and worn sandals and be present with the unrecognized Jesus who walks beside us. We're on the road to Emmaus every day.

But notice this: Cleopas and Mary weren't entirely clueless. When Jesus vanishes after breaking the bread, which no doubt reminded them of the final meal in the upper room, Cleopas says, "Were not our hearts burning within us while he talked with us on the road and opened the Scriptures to us?"[11] (See figure 3.2.) Just as Thomas recognized Jesus by the touching of the wounds, Cleopas and Mary knew him not so much by the breaking of the bread, I think, as by the burning of their hearts, even if they hadn't been quite conscious of it at first. That's the nub of why I believe their story. That single detail seems real. How many times have you known something in your heart—no matter how unlikely it seemed—that turned out to be true?

Seventeen centuries later, John Wesley experienced something similar when he heard an Aldersgate preacher describe "the change which God works in the heart." Wesley wrote, "I felt my heart strangely warmed. I felt I did trust in Christ, Christ alone for my salvation."[12] Or as Mahalia Jackson used to sing, "My God is real for I can feel Him in my soul."[13]

That, I think, is the fruit of the Emmaus story: We often don't recognize the Jesus that lives within us, burning in our hearts.

Figure 3.2. Karl Schmidt-Rottluff's companion to *The Road to Emmaus*, called *Emmaus* (1918). This, better than many portrayals I've seen, depicts the utter shock at the moment of recognition.

Whenever we act out of love, we walk beside him whether we recognize him or not. He lives in our concepts of charity and in our acts of kindness and in our moments of self-sacrifice; he lives in the compassion we feel for the poor and the prisoner and the oppressed. At some point or other, everyone finds himself or herself walking beside this unacknowledged Jesus. Some hearts are warmed; some aren't, but one way or another, we're all on that road. As T. S. Eliot wrote in *The Waste Land*, "There is always another one walking beside you / Gliding wrapt in a brown mantle, hooded."[14]

✳ ✳ ✳

In contrast to Luke's account, the other three gospels suggest that someone else was the first to see the resurrected Christ. Although they differ about the specifics, they grant that distinction to someone whose reliability would have been mistrusted in the culture of first-century Palestine. A woman. Mary Magdalene. And she too did not recognize Jesus at first.

At the start, let's dismiss such fanciful misrepresentations of her as that odd, centuries-old portrayal of her as a reformed prostitute. That notion began in the sixth century, when Pope Gregory I mistakenly assumed that she was the same "woman . . . who lived a sinful life" and who anointed Jesus's feet at the Pharisee's dinner.[15] No textual evidence supports this. While the gospel says that Jesus cast "seven demons" out of Mary, it also says that she and a few other women supported Jesus and his disciples "out of their own means," which suggests she was wealthy.[16]

Mary Magdalene is also sometimes imaginatively portrayed as Jesus's wife or lover, as in such modern novels as Dan Brown's *Da Vinci Code* or June Kerr's *Rabboni, My Love*. What little actual evidence exists to support such ideas is found solely in apocryphal books dating from two or three centuries after the time of Jesus, sources that are frankly bizarre and even surreal (as we'll see in chapter 8).

Mary Magdalene is also sometimes confused with Mary of Bethany, the sister of Martha and Lazarus. The name *Mary* was in fact the most common name for women at that time, so the confusion is understandable. The gospel writers provided the convenient qualifiers *Magdalene* (meaning "from the town of Magdala") and *of Bethany* to distinguish between them, and others are mentioned as well, such as *Mary mother of Jesus*, *Mary mother of James*, *Mary of Jacob*, and as we've seen, *Mary of Clopas*.

All four gospels agree that Mary Magdalene was present at the crucifixion, and all but Luke's gospel contend that she, either alone or with other women, was the first to see the resurrected Jesus (figure 3.3). According to John's gospel, she runs back to the tomb accompanied by Peter and another disciple. The men soon leave when they find the tomb empty. But Mary stays behind, sobbing ("with outforth wepynge,"[17] in Wycliffe's lovely phrase). When she turns back to the tomb's interior, she sees two "angels in white, seated where Jesus' body had been, one at the head and the other at the foot."[18] These are certainly

Figure 3.3. *Christ among the Women* (1919) by Karl Schmidt-Rottluff. Mary is traditionally portrayed as the one kneeling.

the men in "shining garments" mentioned in Luke's gospel.[19] Why she is not terrified, as nearly everyone else is in the Bible when encountering angels, is not explained. Her mourning overshadows her fear.

They ask her why she's crying. She says, "They have taken my Lord away . . . and I don't know where they have put him."[20] For some reason, they don't respond. It's eerie to think of these glowing beings just sitting there mute.

She then turns away from the tomb's entrance, sees someone standing nearby, and assumes it's the gardener. He too asks her why she's crying. This time, a bit more forcefully, she states that she doesn't know where Jesus's body has been taken.

The man says, "Mary," and she immediately recognizes him.

Again, we're presented with someone who doesn't recognize Jesus at first. Perhaps his back was turned when she first spoke, or perhaps she couldn't see through the tears in her eyes, or perhaps her head was bowed, or perhaps—as with Cleopas and Mary—she couldn't fathom the thought that he was still alive. She'd seen him unnailed from the cross, dead, and deposited in a hollow rock.

The two men inside the tomb contrast sharply with the one outside. The men inside are "angels in white" and in the other accounts are said to be dressed in "clothes that gleamed like lightning." But this man, the one outside, like the one on the road to Emmaus, is ordinary, someone you might mistake for a gardener. We don't know what Palestinian gardeners looked like at that time, but I'm sure they didn't gleam like lightning.

As soon as Mary recognizes him, she says, "Rabboni" (great teacher). She must have then hugged him or touched his arm or fallen on her knees to clasp his legs (which is how the scene is often portrayed in artworks)—for the next thing he says to her is, "Do not hold on to me, for I have not yet ascended to my father."[21]

Much is made of that line misleadingly translated in the King James Version as "touch me not" (*noli me tangere* in the Vulgate).[22] Older commentaries suggest that Jesus's body was still in some ethereal transitional stage of resurrection (Matthew Henry called it a "state of glory"[23]) and could not be touched, as if he were a clay pot that hadn't yet dried. (Presumably, by the time Thomas is invited to touch Jesus's wounds the following week, the clay had hardened.)

But linguists tell us that the Greek grammar indicates that Mary has already touched Jesus. She's embracing him. Jesus may simply be telling her not to waste time clinging to him because he still has much to do before he returns "to the father." First, he wants her to get word to the disciples, though why he needs her to deliver that message is unclear, for Jesus himself will appear to them in the locked room that same evening. Does he want her to warn them to forestall another episode of *not* being recognized? We don't know.

But the touching, which many commentators focus on, is not what interests me here. In fact, I don't even think that's central to the passage. Rather, the turning point is that single word *Mary*. As soon as he speaks her name, she knows him.

✳ ✳ ✳

Finally, one entire group of people fails to recognize Jesus. At some point after the resurrection, Peter, Thomas, and a few other disciples are fishing on the Sea of Galilee. After catching nothing, they hear a voice. A stranger is shouting to them from the shore, "Throw your net on the right side of the boat." As soon as they do, they are "unable to haul the net in because of the large number of fish."[24] They are dumbfounded, presumably ankle-deep in flopping fish, until someone in the boat says, "It is the Lord." Peter tears off his cloak, dives in, and swims to shore as the others row back. Even though they were within the sound of his voice, the disciples failed at first to recognize the stranger.

* * *

All these stories point to an important truth—that the Jesus we often fail to recognize is the one who lives inside us. When the Pharisees asked Jesus when the kingdom of God would arrive, he answered, "Behold, the kingdom of God is within you."[25] We feel him burning within our hearts, we see him in our own eyes, and we hear him speak our names in our own ears. And like the fishermen, when we hear him calling from a great distance, it is from the depths of our own souls. As Thomas Merton wrote, there is a "little point of nothingness and of *absolute poverty* [that] is the pure glory of God in us. . . . It is like a pure diamond, blazing with the invisible light of heaven. It is in everybody, and if we could see it we would see the billions of points of light coming together in the face and blaze of a sun that would make all the darkness and cruelty of life vanish completely."[26]

4

"ON THE RIGHT HAND OF GOD"

Stephen, Paul, and Ananias

Behold, I see the heavens opened,

and the Son of man standing on the right hand of God.

—Acts 7:56 KJV

After speaking these words to the assembly of the Sanhedrin, Stephen was dragged beyond the city gates of Jerusalem and bludgeoned to death with rocks. As far as we know, he was the first follower of Jesus to be murdered for his faith, which in the volumes of church history has earned him the title of *protomartyr*.

✳ ✳ ✳

In the three or so years after Jesus's crucifixion, Stephen served as a deacon in the newly formed community of Christ followers in Jerusalem, which meant that his job was "to look after orphans and widows in their distress" and to see to it that all physical needs were met whenever "a brother or a sister [was] without clothes and daily food."[1] The writer of Acts describes him as a man "full of faith and of the Holy Spirit . . . a man full of God's grace and power [who] performed great wonders and signs among the people."[2]

He also had a gift for disputation. Adept at engaging the local synagogue leaders in debate, he powerfully defended the mission of those who believed that God had made a new covenant with his people. He was a forceful apologist. So trenchant were Stephen's arguments that some of those leaders plotted against him by inventing accusations and persuading at least two men—the number of accusers needed to charge someone with a crime—to testify that they had "heard Stephen speak blasphemous words against Moses and against God."[3]

Stephen was brought before the Sanhedrin, the highest court in Jerusalem in matters of the Jewish law. When the high priest asked Stephen if the charges were true, Stephen delivered a passionate capsule history of Judaism, starting with Abraham, continuing through Joseph and Jacob and Moses, and culminating with the prophets who, he said, were persecuted and killed for prophesying the coming of "the Righteous One."[4] The implication was clear—and anathema to the judges—that the entire history of the Jewish people had been a foreshadowing of a coming Messiah. Jesus, Stephen claimed, was the fulfillment of the Bible's prophecies.

At the climax of his oration, the courtroom erupted in chaos. The judges "were furious and gnashed their teeth at him,"[5] and just as they were about to drag him from the hall, Stephan, instead of defending himself, gazed upward—and one imagines him with a look of serene detachment on his face. The scene is dramatic, but most stunning is that Stephen's long and closely argued speech, the longest in the Book of Acts, was followed by a single, simple, prophetic declaration that seemed to slice through the point-by-point niceties of the sermon he had just delivered. As he looked up, he said, "Behold, I see the heavens opened, and the Son of man standing on the right hand of God."[6]

✳ ✳ ✳

So what did he see? What does a vision of the Son of man on God's right hand look like? We don't know. While the Book of Acts gives us no further details, we do know that Stephen was echoing the words of Jesus, who had also been brought before the Sanhedrin a few years earlier, perhaps in front of some of the same judges, at which time Jesus declared, "I say to all of you: From now on you will see the Son of Man sitting at the right hand of the Mighty One and coming on the clouds of heaven."[7]

Stephen's use of that phrase—*the Son of man*—must have incensed the Sanhedrin as much as his entire speech. The epithet finds its source in the Hebrew prophets, as when God addresses Ezekiel as "the son of man" as if it were a nickname and as a way of acknowledging Ezekiel's humanness in contrast to God's immense divinity. And in Daniel's vision, "one like a son of man" is led into the presence of the "Ancient of Days,"[8] by which Daniel is suggesting that this mysterious figure looks not odd, divine, or otherworldly but human—not an angel but a man. Early Christian writers were quick to interpret this to mean that Daniel had seen Jesus himself approaching God's throne.

None of those associations would have been lost on the judges of the Sanhedrin—which is what Stephen, the sharp polemicist, most likely intended when speaking that short phrase.

Was Stephen quoting Jesus and the prophets simply to enflame the judges, to exacerbate an already fraught situation? Was he throwing out the phrase just to get under the judges' skin? No, the writer of Acts doesn't seem to give us that option. Just before Stephen delivered his stunning declaration, the narrator emphatically states, "Stephen, full of the Holy Spirit, looked up to heaven and saw the glory of God, and Jesus standing at the right hand of God,"[9] which is then followed by Stephen's own use of similar words. If we are to believe the writer of Luke, this was no rhetorical challenge, no combative summation to the jury. It was an actual vision.

Moments later, just outside the city gates, as he was being stoned, Stephen cried out, "Lord Jesus, receive my spirit. . . . Do not hold this sin against them,"[10] which echoes Jesus's words from the cross: "Father, forgive them, for they do not know what they are doing."[11]

✳ ✳ ✳

As a form of execution, stoning looked much as it's portrayed in the Victorian Bible illustrations many of us grew up with (figure 4.1): a group of men battering someone to death with rocks. But it may not have been that simple. A passage in the Talmud paints a different picture: a person condemned to death is to be thrown from about the height of a second-story building (or twice the height of a man), after which a boulder, large enough to require two men to lift, is to be dropped onto the body from that same height. The average healthy man can dead lift about half his body weight, which means that two men—each weighing, say, 160 pounds—could conceivably lift a rock of 160 pounds between them. That's a rock the size of a large school backpack, which would most likely be lethal from twelve feet depending on what part of the body it

Figure 4.1. *The Stoning of Stephen* by German artist Julius Schnorr von Carolsfeld from *Die Bibel in Bildern* (1852)—a classic nineteenth-century Bible illustration. The man at the far right is Paul, guarding the cloaks.

struck. The two men, by the way, are required to be the condemned person's accusers, and in the unlikely event that the accused survives, then bystanders are asked to finish the job with smaller rocks, though as much out of mercy as justice.

Conceivably—just conceivably—this method could have been used in Stephen's case. The Book of Acts states that he was taken "out of the city"[12] and, according to tradition, to one of the city gates. Perhaps he was thrown from the city wall or guard tower. Acts also states that the men who stoned Stephen removed their outer clothing first, a curious detail. Perhaps they did so to free up their arms, to make throwing easier, or so that they could haul a backpack-sized boulder to the second floor. The fact that they also asked someone to guard their clothes suggests that they were heading to a separate location, out of sight of their personal belongings—as if to the top of a wall or tower. They did not want them stolen. But that's speculation.

Although we don't know exactly what the scene looked like, we do know the identity of the man who was asked to guard the clothing. In fact, we have that person's own account of the event: "When the blood of your martyr Stephen was shed, I stood there giving my approval and guarding the clothes of those who were killing him."[13]

Those are the words of Saul—also known by his Roman name, Paul—who was a Pharisee "descended from Pharisees,"[14] as he described himself, and whose religious credentials were unimpeachable. He was present at Stephen's death. The scene is movingly portrayed in a poem called "St. Paul" by monk and writer Thomas Merton:

When I was Saul, and sat among the cloaks,
My eyes were stones, I saw no sight of heaven,
Open to take the spirit of the twisting Stephen.[15]

Within a few short years, Paul would become one of the most influential evangelists and Christian apologists in history, but only after having his own private vision of Jesus.

✳ ✳ ✳

The story is familiar. Paul is a persecutor of the emergent Jewish sect of those who believe Jesus is the Messiah—and Paul spends much time "breathing out murderous threats against the Lord's disciples," as the Book of Acts states.[16] He seems particularly incensed by the non-Jewish believers who are then becoming more numerous in places farther afield from Jerusalem. So with letters of authorization and an accompanying entourage, Paul rides toward Damascus with the intention of rounding up gentile believers and bringing them back to Jerusalem for trial and execution.

And no small journey this. The two-hundred-mile trek from Jerusalem to Damascus takes at least four or five days. Presumably, they carry their provisions with them, and the entourage is large enough to handle the group of prisoners that is expected on the return journey.

At about noon on the last day, as they near Damascus, something unexpected occurs:

> Suddenly a light from heaven flashed around him. He fell to the ground and heard a voice say to him, "Saul, Saul, why do you persecute me?"
>
> "Who are you, Lord?" Saul asked.
>
> "I am Jesus, whom you are persecuting."[17]

The flash blinds Paul (figure 4.2), incapacitating him so thoroughly that the men accompanying him have to carry him to the city. For three days, he lies stunned and sightless at the house of a man named Judas.

Jesus then appears in a vision to another man in Damascus named Ananias, in which Jesus tells Ananias to find Paul at "the house of Judas on Straight Street."[18] I love the fact that Jesus provides the address, which implies that Ananias is not already

Figure 4.2. Another image from von Carolsfeld's *Die Bibel in Bildern*: *The Conversion of Paul*. Paul's eyes are closed. Only he is aware of Jesus speaking to him from within the blinding burst of light.

acquainted with Judas—a sort of letter of introduction. Jesus informs Ananias that Paul has had a vision of his own and was told to expect Ananias, who is to heal him of his blindness.

Unlike the patriarch Abraham when he was told to sacrifice his son, Ananias does not set out on this errand unquestioningly. Alarmed at the task required of him, he argues that Paul is a brutal persecutor of Christians, to which Jesus replies, "This man is my chosen instrument to proclaim my name to the Gentiles and their kings and to the people of Israel."[19]

So Ananias goes. He places his hands on Paul as an act of healing as well as blessing, after which "something like scales fell from Saul's eyes, and he could see again."[20] Within days, Paul is baptized, and within weeks, he begins preaching "in the synagogues that Jesus is the Son of God."[21] As anyone who has read Acts and Paul's letters knows, Paul never does anything by halves. He goes on to succeed beyond everyone's expectations, except for perhaps Jesus's.

✳ ✳ ✳

These visions—Stephen's, Paul's, and Ananias's—are linked. They form a narrative chain. Paul is likely to have been present when Stephen had his vision of a magnificent, triumphant Christ standing on God's right hand. According to one of Paul's letters, two of Paul's relatives may have already become Jesus followers by that point,[22] so Stephen's sermon before the Sanhedrin may have been particularly galling, enflaming Paul's hatred of this new Jewish sect even more, and it may explain why he was so willing to aid Stephen's executioners.

We picture Paul on that five-day journey to Damascus—perhaps years after Stephen's death—riding in the heat of a midday sun. Was he pondering the events in Jerusalem and reflecting on Stephen's blasphemous speech? We don't know. But the stage was set for an overwhelming spiritual confrontation. Of Paul's vision, we know only that he saw a flash of light, was knocked to the ground, and heard a voice. He spoke with Jesus and Jesus spoke back. It was sudden and unexpected. At least one neurologist attributes Paul's vision to temporal lobe epilepsy,[23] which often induces the sensation of bright lights and voices, but as neurologist Oliver Sacks says of Joan of Arc's possible epilepsy, "The evidence is soft, as it must be for all historical cases."[24]

Paul thought of himself as a latecomer to encountering Jesus. He wrote, "He appeared to James, then to all the apostles, and last of all he appeared to me also, as to one abnormally born."[25] Paul actually wrote those words decades before the Gospels themselves were written, and in fact, his testimony is not only the earliest record of the resurrected Jesus; it is also the only one written in the first person—"He appeared to *me*."

Like Paul, Ananias too has a back-and-forth dialogue with a visionary Jesus, and Jesus lays out a plan for each man to follow. Still, you will find no Bible illustrations of Ananias's vision, which contained none of the dramatic trappings of Stephen's and Paul's. Jesus tells Ananias to do something, and after a short conversation, he complies.

❋ ❋ ❋

Writers on mysticism distinguish between three types of visionary experiences: appearances, apparitions, and visions. *Appearances* are tangible, physical, able to be seen by more than just the visionary. Between the resurrection and the ascension, Jesus had appeared in physical, bodily form to many people—to Thomas and the disciples, to the two on the road to Emmaus, to Peter, to five hundred more, even if they didn't recognize him at first. Witnesses could testify to the authenticity of their shared experience. With *apparitions*, a figure only seems to be located in the physical world but is invisible to everyone but the visionary. The person experiencing a true *vision* is usually aware that the figure is visible only to him or her and that the experience is, as Charles Finney will later call it, "a mental state." In this book, we will refer to apparitions and visions interchangeably because both are internal experiences.

Not only is Stephen the first follower of Jesus to be martyred, he also seems to be the first to experience a private, internalized vision of the ascended Christ, which is a turning point in Christian history. With Stephen's vision, we enter a new era, though it was anticipated by the visions of the Hebrew prophets centuries before. When Stephen exclaims "Behold, I see . . ." in the midst of the Sanhedrin, he is acknowledging his awareness that the Son of man is appearing to him alone at that moment. His is a powerful but also a lonely experience. No one else could see what he saw. Not only was he the *protomartyr*; he was the *protomystic*. From this point on, Jesus will appear almost exclusively to individuals as a solitary, inner vision.

Paul's vision too is an internal one. Those with him see a flash and hear a rumbling but no voice, no person. Later, in Damascus, Paul has one or more additional encounters. He's told to expect Ananias, whose own vision of Jesus is solitary and internal. Concerning his own Christian theological insight, Paul wrote, "I did not receive it from any man, nor was I taught it; rather, I received it by revelation from Jesus Christ."[26]

While Stephen was the first *believer* to have a vision of Jesus, Paul seems to have been the first *nonbeliever*. Stephen experienced his vision in extremis, at a moment of unimaginably heightened stress, a kind of vision that we'll see in such people as Jerome and Julian of Norwich.

Paul's vision led to a radical conversion, and so crucial was his experience to the history of Christianity that it has ever since been called "a road to Damascus experience." We'll see this repeated in the experiences of people like Sojourner Truth and Sundar Singh.

As far as Ananias, he is a believer who simply follows instructions—just as Francis of Assisi and Mother Teresa will do centuries later.

✳ ✳ ✳

Three men and three interlocking visions, and from that time on and for centuries to come, seeing Jesus will be a matter of personal experience . . . one person's word against an often skeptical and disbelieving world.

5

VOOM!
John of Patmos

Recently, I had a small revelation. In a sort of smack-my-palm-on-my-forehead moment, I realized that Dr. Seuss's classic children's book *The Cat in the Hat Comes Back*, published in 1958, is about the anti-Communist frenzy of the 1950s. Seriously.

The book, as you know, tells the story of a brother and sister who have been left to their own devices on a snowy day. Their mother has gone out, and they've been tasked with shoveling the walkways in front of their house.

Enter the cat.

From the previous book, *The Cat in the Hat*, we know that this shifty feline means trouble. Sporting his iconic bowtie, white gloves, and tall striped hat, he previously managed to disrupt just about everything in the children's lives, wrecking the house and bestowing chaos in every direction while still managing to clean up after himself the instant before the mother walked back through the door. And now, in the second book, the cat is back.

The first thing he does is take a bath . . . a seemingly harmless act, but no sooner does the boy drain the tub and order the cat to leave than they discover that a pink bathtub ring has been left behind. The cat says it's easy to clean, but the more he tries, the more it spreads throughout the house. So he summons reinforcements. To clean the ever-spreading pink stain, he calls on another smaller cat called Little Cat A, who lives under his hat, and this cat in turn reveals yet another cat, Little Cat B, under his hat, and so on until before you know it, there is a clowder of Little Cats C, D, E, F, G, and so on running amok, making things worse. The problem soon shifts outdoors, until every inch of snow is a deep, dirty pink.

When the children demand a solution, the cat calls on one final cat, Little Cat Z, who lives, of course, under the hat of Little Cat Y and is so small as to be invisible, and under the hat of the imperceptible Little Cat Z dwells something called *VOOM!* When the Cat in the Hat tells that final cat to doff its hat, a sort of cyclonic explosion occurs—*VOOM!*—and every bit of pink vanishes in a blinding flash. Even the sidewalks have been miraculously shoveled.

As I said, only recently did I realize that Dr. Seuss, who had once been a political cartoonist, wrote this children's book as a satire. The ever-multiplying pink stains, which spread more as you try to eradicate them, represent the "creeping threat of Communism"—pinkos!—and the *VOOM!* under Little Cat Z's hat is the hydrogen bomb. When its walloping energy is unleashed, *VOOM!* makes all the pinkos disappear like a nuclear Mr. Clean. Everything is spic and span once again, the sidewalks are shoveled, and the world is safe for democracy.

That, I think, is what Dr. Seuss's book is *really* about—a spoof of the overzealous anti-Communism of the nuclear era.

✳ ✳ ✳

Now, I sincerely hope that as some of you read that, you said to yourself, "Well, that sort of takes all the fun out of it, doesn't it? Isn't the book *really* just about a brother and sister on a snowy day encountering a crazy cat?"

And the answer is yes. That *is*, in fact, my point.

Whether valid or not, my theory is much less fun than the story itself . . . and frankly not as interesting. And of course, it's *only* a theory. Even if the book is about the Cold War, well . . . so what?

By taking the story at face value, we're freed to enter into its wacky, delectable, imaginative world. We become the little boy and girl ourselves, seeing through their eyes and feeling their frustrations and anxieties and ultimate relief as our own. No theories. No explanations. The real story is the story itself.

And that, in a nutshell, is my approach to the Book of Revelation.

❊ ❊ ❊

Scholars have proposed not just one theory to explain Revelation but hundreds. Experience has taught me to be wary of anyone who claims to know *exactly* what the book means; it tends to bring out the crackpot in even the most devoted Bible readers—perhaps especially the most devoted Bible readers. Modern scholars and self-proclaimed experts have written books to uncover its *real* meaning, ranging from *The Book of Revelation: The Smart Guide* at one extreme to *The Book of Revelation for Dummies* on the other. Judging from the titles listed on Amazon alone, you'll find Revelation *Revealed*, *Decoded*, *Unveiled*, *Made Clear*, *Interpreted*, *Made Easy* and *Made Easier*, *Unlocked*, *Illuminated*, *Observed*, and *Simplified*. I'm confident that no other book in the Bible—or perhaps in history—has aroused so much speculation or caused so much controversy.

First, there are those who assert that Revelation is a symbolic account of the reign of Nero, a creative religiopolitical commentary about Rome's persecution of Christians. They are the *preterists*. Then there are others, the *historicists*, who think the book describes the unfolding history of the church over the centuries. The *futurists* and *millennialists* contend that Revelation, through its veil of symbols, foretells specific future—and present—events, and even among those groups, a debate rages as to the identity of the beast of Revelation, that mysterious figure tagged with the numeral 666. In my lifetime, Henry Kissinger, Mikhail Gorbachev, and Barack Obama have all been proffered as candidates. Several decades ago, some interpreters even argued that Revelation was *really* about the Cold War and the nuclear age—just like *The Cat in the Hat Comes Back*!

A specific controversy smolders over the word *millennium*— the thousand-year period described in chapter 20 of Revelation— with the *amillennialists* insisting that the thousand-year reign of Christ is a spiritual one and is already in process. The *postmillennialists* believe that Christ will return to establish his kingdom only after the thousand years, in contrast to the *premillennialists*, who think Christ will come beforehand. One waggish friend of mine claims to be a *panmillennialist*. As he says, "I believe everything will pan out in the end!"

I am not alone in my impatience with the thousand-and-one interpreters of Revelation. G. K. Chesterton wrote that although John "saw many strange monsters in his vision, he saw no creature so wild as one of his commentators."[1] Famed English preacher Charles Spurgeon wrote of these "interpreters of prophecy," "The whole business is childish and nonsensical. . . . One of them sees in the sublimities of Revelation the form of Louis Napoleon, where two or three hundred years ago half of Christendom saw the Pope, and the other half Martin Luther. The other day one of the seers saw Sebastopol [under siege during the Crimean War] in the prophecies, and now another detects the Suez Canal [under construction at the time]. . . . The fact is, when fancy is their guide men wander in a maze."[2]

In place of those "fancies" that explain, decode, and illuminate Revelation, I propose a simpler approach, a sort of Occam's razor. That is, I take the book at face value. I try to listen to it speak for itself and not to read too far outside the text for its meaning. The Book of Revelation, I'm convinced, carries its own baggage, you might say, giving us everything we need to appreciate it. Bible scholars and professors of religion might say that my approach is anti-intellectual or uneducated, but frankly, the alternative is chaos . . . "wandering in a maze." What's needed is a *VOOM!* to clear away the clutter.

✳ ✳ ✳

The Book of Revelation is just that—a sort of journal of visions, or revelations, that appeared to a man named John, who was apparently exiled on Patmos, an isolated island in the eastern part of the Aegean Sea. One of the first things we notice about his visions is that like Stephen's and Paul's, they are private, visible to him alone, and "sent and signified," as he states at the beginning, "unto his servant John."[3] But unlike Stephen's and Paul's, John's vision of Jesus is astonishingly complex, rich in sensual detail, numerological mysteries, and pyrotechnic metaphors. The language, at least as it's rendered in our familiar King James Version, is elevated, ecstatic, and as lyrically resonant as anything in English literature.

Which leads to my *VOOM!*—the inescapable realization that some commentators mention but few expand on. That is, Revelation is a poem. It's not just poetic; it's a cinematic, epic, prophetic/poetic drama on a cosmic scale, among the greatest pieces of visionary literature ever written. It offers complexly interrelated images, allegorical symbols, scenes of war in heaven, plagues and devastation, thunder and violence, and a breathtaking restoration that emerges with a new heaven and earth. It is magnificent literature. Dante the Catholic, Milton the Puritan, and Blake the political radical all admired it and emulated it in their own poetry.

Since Revelation is a poem, it demands to be read in a certain way—neither as fiction nor as nonfiction but as a vicariously lived experience in itself, an encounter meant fully to involve our senses and emotions, a work of art that elicits from us wonder and horror and a sense of majesty by turns. It requires not exegetical acumen but aesthetic sensitivity, an openness to its beauty, and a fervent honesty. It asks not so much that we interpret it as that we simply pay attention to it.

Like great poetry, Revelation is subversive, another fact often skipped over by commentators. Jesus's messages to the twelve churches make this clear; his letters contain critiques and encouragements, but in the end, he implies that those churches are, at best, frail institutions. The status quo is dead. The new heaven and earth, however we interpret them, will replace the old, and this newly established order will wipe away not just the worldly kingdoms of rulers and potentates (and presidents and prime ministers) but also the churches and their self-appointed hierarchies. In the final vision, God is on the throne—not denominations, not doctrines, not priests or pastors or popes, but God alone.

✳ ✳ ✳

The entire poem is, as John says, a "Revelation of Jesus Christ,"[4] and while Christ appears again and again in various guises throughout, we'll focus here on his first appearance, if for no other reason than it is John's own first glimpse of this towering figure.

"Behold, he cometh with clouds," writes John, which suggests the inner mists of vision more than atmospheric condensation.[5] While "in the Spirit on the Lord's day," John hears a loud voice behind him, sounding like a trumpet.[6] The voice, whose source is at first unknown, tells him to write a book describing the wonders he's about to experience, and the voice directs him to send this book to seven specific churches, in some cases to serve as a word of consolation and in others a message of admonition.

This visionary poem, in other words, is intended for a narrow readership, for specific, real people in need of comfort and guidance, people without political power, who were despised and oppressed by persecution, temptation, and defeat, who needed the hope that this vision could offer. As William Blake wrote in *The Four Zoas*, "John Saw these things Reveal'd in Heaven / On Patmos Isle & heard the souls cry out to be deliver'd."[7] To read the poem properly, we need either to be such people ourselves or to have extraordinary empathy for them. It is a vision meant to offer hope to the hopeless.

Then John turns toward that voice. But better yet, read his own description. Here, I've broken the King James Version into lines and stanzas to highlight its poetry.

I turned to see the voice that spake with me.
And being turned, I saw seven golden candlesticks;

And in the midst of the seven candlesticks
    one like unto the Son of man,
clothed with a garment down to the foot,
and girt about the paps with a golden girdle.

His head and his hairs were white like wool,
    as white as snow;
and his eyes were as a flame of fire;

And his feet like unto fine brass,
    as if they burned in a furnace;
and his voice as the sound of many waters.

And he had in his right hand seven stars:
and out of his mouth went a sharp two edged sword:
and his countenance was as the sun shineth in his strength.

And when I saw him, I fell at his feet as dead.
And he laid his right hand upon me,
saying unto me, Fear not; I am the first and the last:
I am he that liveth, and was dead;
and, behold, I am alive for evermore, Amen;
and have the keys of hell and of death.[8]

Now reread that passage . . . aloud. John himself says that "blessed is the one who reads aloud the words of this prophecy."[9] Hardly a line doesn't ring like a dark cathedral bell—so sonorous does it sound when spoken. Notice the magnificent torrent of conjunctions—thirteen of the twenty-one lines begin with the word *and*—which gives the whole passage a headlong, breathless kind of inevitability. The stately cadences of the King James, its phrasing and imagery and pacing, are all so sublime, and the loftiness of its tone anticipates by sixty years the high religious rhetoric of Milton's *Paradise Lost* (such lines of Milton's as "God from the Mount of Sinai, whose gray top / Shall tremble, he descending, will himself / In Thunder Lightning and loud Trumpets sound"[10] owe not a little to John of Patmos).

The King James Version often falls into regular iambic, as in the opening line "I *turned* to *see* the *voice* that *spake* with *me*," but then it throws in multiple accented syllables for special emphasis: "a *sharp two edged sword*" and "laid his *right hand* upon me."[11] Alliterative language is used throughout: "golden girdle," "flame of fire," "seven stars," "his head and his hairs were white like wool," and "alive for evermore."[12] One of the most complexly musical lines in Revelation is "his countenance was as the sun shineth in his strength."[13] So powerful.

Upon seeing this (see figure 5.1), John falls at the feet of Jesus "as dead."[14] We can't imagine anyone reacting any other way. After describing the intense visual and aural experience of seeing a blazing Jesus and hearing the roaring ocean of his voice, something unexpected and even more shocking occurs. This fantastic, astral Jesus places his hand on John's shoulder. It's an astonishing moment because now the vast empyrean vision becomes localized . . . personalized for both John and us, the readers, with that touch. It's heart-stopping.

Figure 5.1. Albrecht Dürer's *Saint John's Vision of the Seven Candlesticks* (1498). Note the fidelity to each detail. Even the flickering candle on the left represents the Laodicean Church, for which Jesus had the sternest admonishment.

"Fear not," says Jesus (two words of comfort that are spoken more than a hundred times in various contexts throughout the Bible).[15] It's an admonition not just for John but for his original readers in the twelve churches and for the modern reader as well. No matter how violent the unfolding terror and disorder in the rest of "the Revelation of Jesus Christ" become, we will carry the imprint of that hand on our shoulders and the words *fear not* in our ears.[16] Why should we *not* fear? Because, as Jesus explains in a series of paradoxes, he is "the first and the last," and he "liveth, and was dead."[17] And then he ends with that stunning line that introduces the rest of John's vision: "I am alive for evermore, Amen; and have the keys of hell and of death."[18] That line alone is enough to make one shiver.

✳ ✳ ✳

As in all great poetry, John evokes the senses, every one of them, heightened to an almost excruciating degree. He notices colors: the golden girdle, the white hair, the brass of the feet. He implies reds and oranges and yellows in the images of the flaming eyes, the feet burning as if in a furnace, the stars in Jesus's hand, and his face shining like the sun. Then, in the midst of these fires, comes a voice like "the sound of many waters"[19]—like a cooling ocean surf to temper the conflagration. We have that tactile touch on the shoulder, and later (in chapter 10), John will eat the little book that the angel gives him (figure 5.3), and it will at first taste as "sweet as honey" before turning bitter in his stomach.[20]

Throughout Revelation, John continues to engage the senses fully and intensely. In chapter 18, for instance, he sees a vision of the fall of Babylon and how their venal merchants are now without customers. Notice the luxurious sensuality of this list:

> And the merchants of the earth
>   shall weep and mourn over her;
> for no man buyeth their merchandise any more:
>
> The merchandise of gold, and silver,
>   and precious stones, and of pearls,
> and fine linen, and purple, and silk,
>   and scarlet, and all thyine wood,
> and all manner vessels of ivory,
>   and all manner vessels of most precious wood,
> and of brass, and iron, and marble,
>
> And cinnamon, and odours, and ointments,
>   and frankincense, and wine, and oil,
> and fine flour, and wheat, and beasts, and sheep,
>   and horses, and chariots, and slaves,
> and souls of men.[21]

Again, that final line is devastating.

✳ ✳ ✳

Even if no commentary had ever been written, even if we knew nothing of its history and provenance, Revelation would stand as a magnificent, prophetic poem full of sensual imagery and conveying a message of comfort to oppressed people in terrorizing times. Of all the supposed prophecies for the future in the

Book of Revelation, the most important, in my opinion, is this: God *will* overcome; everything *will* pan out in the end. God *will* create a *VOOM!* to destroy all suffering, pain, and death. And of all hopeful messages, few are as hopeful as this from one of the book's final scenes . . . in which John sees Jesus on the throne of heaven (figure 5.2):

> And I saw a new heaven and a new earth:
> for the first heaven and the first earth were passed away;
>> and there was no more sea.
> And I John saw the holy city, new Jerusalem,
>> coming down from God out of heaven,
>> prepared as a bride adorned for her husband.

> And I heard a great voice out of heaven saying,
> Behold, the tabernacle of God is with men,
>> and he will dwell with them,
>>> and they shall be his people,
>> and God himself shall be with them,
>> and be their God.

> And God shall wipe away all tears from their eyes;
> and there shall be no more death, neither sorrow, nor crying,
>> neither shall there be any more pain:
>> for the former things are passed away.

> And he that sat upon the throne said,
>> Behold, I make all things new.
> And he said unto me,
>> Write: for these words are true and faithful.
> And he said unto me,

Figure 5.2. John repeatedly sees Jesus as the Lamb of God. Here Dürer's *Hymn in Adoration of the Lamb* (1498) combines elements from chapters 7 and 14 of Revelation. John is kneeling in the foreground, speaking with one of the elders.

It is done. I am Alpha and Omega,
   the beginning and the end.
I will give unto him that is athirst
   of the fountain of the water of life freely.[22]

* * *

I trust the intense reality of John's vision the way I trust
the reality of a violently stormy sky . . . and the majesty of the
brilliantly shining sun and rainbow afterward. I'm awed by
them without understanding them, without feeling the need
to interpret them. Virginia Woolf once wrote, "There is an
ambiguity which is the mark of the highest poetry; we cannot
know exactly what it means. . . . The meaning is just on the
far side of language. It is the meaning which in moments of
astonishing excitement and stress we perceive in our minds
without words."[23]

   And that is how I read Revelation. I take it at face value and
am awed. Whether it's literal or symbolic, allegorical or historical, I don't pretend to know, and I don't particularly care,
but I don't doubt its inner truth. Not only is the richness of its
sensual detail convincing, but so too is its psychological consis-
tency (John, like any of us, falls down "as dead" but then is told
not to fear). This is the function of prophetic poetry—to shock,
to enliven, to comfort, and to speak truth to our deepest selves.

   We must also examine what we mean by the word *prophetic*
because I think we tend to view it from the wrong angle. Here's
a metaphor that helps me understand this. Imagine that a man
is watching his young daughter play on her soccer team. As he
stands there, he realizes that she's more than just a player—she's
an encourager, a promoter of team spirit, a lively center of

activity, and someone who brings out the best in everyone. After the match, this man, amazed by this new information, says to her, "I didn't realize it, but *you* are a *leader*!" While that truth is spoken in the present, it hints at what this girl will become. It is prophetic.

Prophetic poetry, like Revelation, works in just that way. John speaks a present truth that doesn't predict future events so much as it illuminates them. It shapes more than it foretells.

✳ ✳ ✳

With John, visions of Jesus enter the realm of the creative imagination—that is, the *literary* imagination. Without Revelation, Dante Alighieri and Milton would never have written the way they did. Modern poets like W. B. Yeats, David Jones, T. S. Eliot, and Czesław Miłosz drew liberally from John's apocalyptic vocabulary. In emulating John's apocalyptic tone (think of Yeats's "The blood-dimmed tide is loosed"[24] or Eliot's "hooded hordes swarming / Over endless plains, stumbling in cracked earth"[25]), they inherit his prophetic authority.

William Blake, who perhaps emulated John more than any poet short of Dante, even illustrated scenes from Revelation (figure 5.3) and wrote his own prophetic books—epic poems so dense as to be incomprehensible (which doesn't stop scholars from trying to comprehend them). But the poems are beautiful in themselves. Consider these lines from Blake's *Milton*:

Glorious as the midday Sun in Satan's bosom glowing,
A Female hidden in a Male, Religion hidden in War,
Nam'd Moral Virtue, cruel two-fold Monster shining bright,
A Dragon red & hidden harlot, which John in Patmos saw.[26]

Figure 5.3. Blake's illustration of the angel in book 10 of Revelation: "And he had in his hand a little book open: and he set his right foot upon the sea, and his left foot on the earth."[27]

PART TWO
ASCETICS

6

DEMONS AND A DREAM
Anthony of Egypt and Martin of Tours

In Roman times, as in ours, actors, athletes, writers, and artists were popular public figures, widely admired, wildly gossiped about, and often earning ridiculously huge sums of money. One third-century Roman actress, Bassilla, was so beloved for her dancing, singing, and acting (especially her intense death scenes) that she was dubbed "the Tenth Muse." Second-century charioteer Gaius Appuleius Diocles, who managed to finish first or second in three-quarters of the more than four thousand chariot races he competed in, is thought to have been the highest-earning sports figure in world history. And who can forget the poet Ovid, author of *The Metamorphoses* and the scandalous *Art of Love*? He was banished by Emperor Augustus to the distant shores of the Black Sea for some unnamed indiscretion, which, according to Ovid's own cryptic report, amounted to "a poem and a mistake."[1]

Celebrities then were much like celebrities now, though with one intriguing difference. Beginning in the fourth century, an odd new kind of celebrity began to capture the public's imagination: desert hermits, anchorites, stylites, and assorted religious hyperascetics. "There is, perhaps, no phase in the moral history of mankind," wrote one historian, "of a deeper or more painful interest than this ascetic epidemic."[2]

After the Edict of Milan put an official end to the persecution of Christians in 313, these odd but alluring religious figures began to pop up, often on the margins of society, in such desert wastes as those of Syria, Egypt, and Palestine. Somehow they managed to become the superstars of the early Christian era, tapping into a universal need for spiritual heroes, for people through whom the faithful could vicariously achieve a stratospheric level of moral perfection.

Due to their popularity, ascetics often wielded tremendous influence. They advised emperors and popes and weighed in on the critical theological debates of the time. One stylite (that is, a person who lives full-time atop a pillar, exposed to the elements, praying and meditating) was so revered for his austerities that when he threatened to interrupt them and descend from his pillar to admonish the emperor in Constantinople over some policy issue, the ruler backed down, fearful of the public's recrimination.

Among the notables of that time, the most beloved was Anthony (or Antony) of Egypt, also referred to as Anthony the Great.

✳ ✳ ✳

He was born in Egypt to a wealthy Christian family in 251. When he was about twenty, he heard a church lector read from Matthew 19, the passage in which Jesus tells the rich young man, "If thou wilt be perfect, go sell all that thou hast, and give it to the poor; and come, follow me and thou shalt have treasure in Heaven."[3] Feeling "as though the reading had been directed especially at him,"[4] Anthony gave away his entire inheritance and embraced poverty.

For the next eighty-five years, he lived as a monk, a desert hermit, an antiheresy zealot, and a much-sought-after spiritual guide. Emperor Constantine and his sons once wrote to Anthony to solicit his blessing. Although the hermit was far too humbled at first to respond—they were the rulers of the known world, after all—he eventually sent them a humbling message of his own, suggesting that they "not to think highly of the things of this world, but rather to bear in mind the judgment to come" and that "Christ alone is the true and eternal king."[5]

But such pieties are sure to draw the devil's wrath. Anthony found himself besieged by temptations—demons—that distracted him from his rigorous fasting and long hours of prayer. These devils prodded, beat, and berated him as he prayed (figure 6.1).

When Anthony was about thirty-five, he experienced a particularly vicious series of demonic attacks, one of which left him nearly dead. Some companions, after caring for his wounds, settled him back into the empty tomb in which he lived, at which point his biographer and friend Athanasius picks up the narrative: As the hermit sat praying in his tomb, "it was as though demons were breaking through the four walls of the little chamber . . . phantoms of lions, bears, leopards, bulls, and of serpents, asps, and scorpions, and of wolves . . . and the fury shown was fierce." Though racked with pain, Anthony resisted, invoking the name of Christ and taunting them, saying, "It is a sign of your helplessness that you ape the forms of brutes," in response to which "they gnashed their teeth against him."[6]

But Athanasius assures his readers that Anthony was not alone:

Figure 6.1. Martin Schongauer's fantastic image *The Temptation of Saint Anthony* (ca. 1470). This engraving, admired for its swirling energy and grotesque figures, was copied by both Michelangelo and Brueghel the Elder.

The Lord was not forgetful of Antony's struggle, but came to help him. For he looked up and saw as it were the roof opening and a beam of light coming down to him. The demons suddenly were gone and the pain in his body ceased at once and the building was restored to its former condition. . . . And he asked the vision: "Where were you? Why did you not appear at the beginning to stop my pains?"

And a voice came to him: "Antony, I was right here, but I waited to see you in action. And now, because you held out and did not surrender, I will ever be your helper and I will make you renowned everywhere."

Hearing this, he arose and prayed.

Despite Jesus's dramatic intervention (figure 6.2), Anthony continued to experience demonic assaults throughout his life, though whenever he invoked Jesus's name, the tempters would flee. Once, for instance, while weaving one of the baskets he would trade for food and water, he noticed that a strand kept mysteriously unraveling itself. He realized that someone—or something—was playing a trick on him. He turned and saw a stranger at the door behind him, though this was no ordinary stranger—human above the waist but with the legs and feet of a donkey. Anthony calmly said, "I am Christ's servant. If you are on a mission against me, here I am." Immediately, writes Athanasius, "the monster . . . fled so fast that its speed caused it to fall and die."[7]

While such anecdotes may seem odd or even quaint to us today, fourth-century believers found them profoundly moving. Anthony was one of the most admired and influential Christians of the time. Augustine later credited Anthony's example as being instrumental in his own conversion, and Jerome (whom we'll

Figure 6.2. Amid Anthony's temptations, Jesus appears. An aquatint from *El Arte en España* (1864), based on a painting in the Museo Nacional.

meet in the next chapter) admired him deeply. More importantly, by mentoring the small group of disciples who gathered around him, Anthony founded what became the world's first monastic community, so today, he's considered the father of Western monasticism.

✳ ✳ ✳

While the Bible contains several clear precedents for visionary encounters with Jesus—Stephen's, Paul's, John's—nowhere does it describe the kind of physical demonic assaults that Anthony experienced. The Hebrew Bible almost never refers to demons or devils. While demon *possession* was accepted as a fact by the time of Jesus, demon *appearances* do not occur in the Gospels. Like microscopic parasites, they invade their host unseen. Even the demons named Legion, whom Jesus expelled from the two Gadarene men, simply relocated invisibly into the swine, who then threw themselves into the sea. We have no idea what they looked like.

Only once do demons adopt an animal shape in the Bible. In Revelation 16, John, in the throes of his vision, saw "unclean spirits like frogs" coming "out of the mouth of the dragon, and out of the mouth of the beast, and out of the mouth of the false prophet." These "spirits of devils" were assigned to go to the "kings of the earth . . . to gather them to the battle of that great day of God Almighty"—that is, the battle of Armageddon, the final war with God.[8]

In the Gospels, the primary target of an embodied demon is Jesus himself, who, after fasting in the wilderness for forty days and nights, sparred with "the tempter," the devil, though even then the passage doesn't make clear what form the tempter took.[9] The fact that the devil transports Jesus to an "exceeding high mountain" to show him "all the kingdoms of the world, and the glory of them," suggests that this could have been an internal, visionary encounter, since no literal mountain offers such a view.[10]

Still, encounters with demons were commonly reported among the ascetics of Anthony's time. Any distraction from prayer and devotion was thought of as a demonic attack by actual physical beings. One can imagine that in the harsh conditions of the desert—where fasting was practiced, water was scarce, shelter was meager, illness was prevalent, and let's face it, sexual impulses were unavoidable and persistent—demons would seem to be everywhere. In addition, the rigorous, self-imposed sensory deprivation often practiced by ascetics surely contributed to their visual anomalies. Neurologist Oliver Sacks writes, "Whether darkness and solitude is sought out by holy men in caves or forced upon prisoners in lightless dungeons, the deprivation of normal visual input can stimulate the inner eye instead, producing dreams, vivid imaginings, or hallucinations."[11] The line between vision and hallucination is thin.

Athanasius's *Life of Saint Anthony*, beloved throughout the Middle Ages, popularized the notion that devils, whether internal or external, commonly attack humans, a notion, by the way, that is still assumed in such practices as exorcism, prayers of deliverance, and the laying on of hands. In March 2020, one prominent Christian preacher, invoking the name of Jesus, publicly and energetically "cast out" the demon of the COVID-19 virus—to take effect immediately. Sadly, he had less success than Jesus and Anthony.

✳ ✳ ✳

Martin of Tours, another fourth-century monk, also experienced a well-known vision of Jesus. Although he was Anthony's junior by sixty-five years, they were still roughly contemporary, since Anthony lived to be 105, dying when Martin was forty years old. One of Martin's disciples, Sulpitius Severus, wrote *The Life of Saint Martin*, a hagiography that tells us most of what we know about Martin, and like Athanasius's *Life of Saint Anthony*, the book was fabulously popular throughout the Middle Ages.

Martin was born in the northern Roman province of Pannonia. He became a Christian at the age of ten, much against his parents' wishes. Since his father served as a tribune in the Roman army, Martin too was expected to serve, and as a cavalryman, he journeyed as far west as Gaul. Soon, though, at the age of twenty-two, he renounced the army, declaring, "I am a soldier of Christ; it is not lawful for me to fight,"[12] and since the Roman authorities viewed this as an act of cowardice, he was jailed. Today, he is the patron saint of conscientious objectors.

Upon his release, he became a disciple of Bishop Hilary of Poitiers, one of the most renowned theologians of the time. Martin lived as a monk and an ascetic, battling demons much as Anthony did, and in one legend, he went so far as to preach repentance to the devil himself. He traveled widely, returning home to Pannonia long enough to convert his mother. He battled the major heresies of his time, destroyed pagan temples, healed the sick, and cast out demons.

One of his most famous miracles occurred after he persuaded a group of Druid-like priests in Gaul to cut down an enormous pine tree that was sacred to their local cult. Knowing that Rome had already declared their religion illegal, they reluctantly agreed, but only if Martin himself would lie, bound hand

and foot, beneath the spot where the tree was to fall—as proof of his Christian God's protection. Martin agreed. When the tree was cut through, it toppled directly toward him, but at the last second, writes Severus, it swung around "after the manner of a spinning-top" and nearly fell on the pagan priests instead. Severus continues, "The well-known result is that on that day salvation came to that region. For there was hardly one of that immense multitude of heathens who did not . . . [make] a profession of faith in the Lord Jesus Christ."[13]

According to legend, when the people of Tours called on Martin to become their bishop, he hid in a barn, thinking himself unworthy. His whereabouts were discovered, though, when some geese cackled and gave away his hiding place, and to this day, roast goose is the traditional meal eaten every year on Saint Martin's feast day, November 11.

While he was famous for many things, his vision of Jesus is the most fabled and beloved incident in the life of this fabled and beloved saint.

✳ ✳ ✳

On one abnormally cold winter day, when Martin was twenty years old, he was riding with his cavalry regiment toward the city of Amiens. At the city gates, he spied a beggar, half naked, freezing, and crying out for help. No one but Martin took any notice of the man. Martin stopped and dismounted. Although he'd already given away most of his winter clothing to other needy souls and now had but a single cloak to protect himself from the cold, Martin drew his sword, sliced his cloak neatly in two, and gave half to the beggar (figure 6.3). Some of Martin's fellow cavalrymen laughed at the absurd gesture.

Figure 6.3. Schongauer's *Saint Martin* (late fifteenth century). Compare this to Schongauer's *The Temptation of Saint Anthony* (figure 6.1).

The next night, as Martin slept, Jesus appeared in a dream—dressed in the same cloak that Martin had given the beggar. Jesus turned to the angels surrounding him and said, "Martin, who is still but a catechumen, clothed me with his robe," echoing the words of Matthew's gospel: "Whatever you did for one of the least of these brothers and sisters of mine, you did for me."[14] Since Martin was indeed still a "catechumen"—that is, a Christian who has yet to be confirmed—he took this as a sign that he should be immediately baptized.

The symbolism of the cloak is significant. It brings to mind the soldiers at the foot of the cross who agreed not to divide Jesus's cloak but to gamble for it in order to keep it whole. Now, three centuries later, another Roman soldier, wearing the red cloak of a Roman cavalryman and also symbolic of Christ's blood, is willing to tear his own cloak in half so that he might share it with Christ himself. On the cross, in other words, Jesus himself gave his own cloak to the world, a symbol of warmth and comfort. Martin hadn't shared his own cloak at all but was returning part of what was Jesus's in the first place.

* * *

Two monks. Two radically different visions.

Anthony's vision is inner directed. Jesus relieves Anthony's distress in the midst of his battle to maintain his fidelity, purity, and devotion. Martin's vision, by contrast, is outer directed, originating in an act of charity. As a soldier and man of action, Martin is acutely aware of the needs around him, less absorbed by his own inner struggles. He acts decisively.

Both Anthony and Martin lived as ascetics, but their austerities took different forms. Anthony's involved isolation, both psychological and geographic; extreme self-abnegation; and a renunciation of the world. By contrast, Martin's asceticism was more communal. He became a beloved bishop, traveled widely, preached, and established two of the oldest monastic communities in Europe.

Ascetics—at least the most austere—are a puzzle. Like Anthony, they seem to indulge in the very thing they claim to renounce; that is, they find pleasure in their avoidance of pleasure. They refuse the sensual gratifications that God created for people to enjoy: the smell of spring blossoms, the taste of spices, the sound of musical instruments. One Victorian writer characterized the average desert hermit as someone "passing his life in a long routine of useless and atrocious self-torture, and quailing before the ghastly phantoms of his delirious brain."[15] Even Athanasius says of Anthony, "He was ever fasting, and he had a garment of hair on the inside. . . . And he neither bathed his body with water to free himself from filth, nor did he ever wash his feet." Anthony even hated the dawn and would pray, "Oh sun! why do you rise already and turn me from contemplating the splendor of the true light?"[16]

Such abandonment of the created world borders on Manicheanism, the belief that the physical world is evil and the spiritual world alone is good. Augustine, of course, put the final nail in the coffin of that heresy with his famous pronouncement: "While the higher things are indeed better than the lower things, the sum of all creation is better than the higher things alone."[17] Or, in the words of the Jewish Kabbalah, "at the judgment seat, God will ask you to account for all the allowable pleasures that you did not indulge in."[18]

While Anthony rigorously struggled to conquer his impulses and desires, Martin surrendered them to God. There is a vast difference between the two. Anthony's vision of Jesus was a refuge from his demons; Martin's was a reward for his charity.

The great British historian Arnold Toynbee summed it up neatly: "Mankind's right spiritual guides are not the Christian ascetics but the Buddha, Jesus, and Francis of Assisi, each of whom scandalized his ascetic-minded contemporaries by the discovery, through personal experience, that love, not asceticism, is the true end of man."[19]

7

GOD'S GROUCH

Jerome

Spend an afternoon at any major art museum in any major city, and you're likely to encounter Saint Jerome. Although you might not recognize him at first, this late fourth- and early fifth-century theologian, scholar, and controversialist—one of the four acknowledged Doctors of the Western Church—was a phenomenally popular subject among Renaissance artists. This was due to the immense influence of his Latin translation of the Bible, the Vulgate, which virtually shaped Christianity. It was *the* Bible for more than a thousand years.[1]

The times Jerome lived through were tumultuous. He was born in about 347 on the eastern coast of the Adriatic Sea in the town of Stridon, the precise location of which is lost to history because it vanished after being sacked by Goth invaders when Jerome was in his thirties. His parents were probably killed during that invasion. A decade later, the Roman Empire split into East and West, never to reunite, and later, when Jerome was in his sixties, the Visigoths ransacked Rome itself, the cultural center of the empire and the city where Jerome had been educated. Upon hearing the news, he wrote to a friend, "My voice sticks in my throat; and, as I dictate, sobs choke my utterance. The City which had taken the whole world was itself taken."[2] Within a decade after Jerome's death in 420, the Vandals swept into North Africa, besieging the city of Hippo, where Jerome's great contemporary, Augustine, served as bishop.

As a young man, Jerome had studied philosophy, rhetoric, and grammar, both Greek and Latin, and was a passionate devotee of classical literature. After his conversion to Christianity, he, like Anthony, got caught up in the ascetic movement, eventually living as a hermit in the Syrian and Palestinian deserts, though the term *hermit* in his case is misleading, since he kept a substantial library, traveled widely, lived in communities with genial fellow ascetics, and wrote letters to a wide circle of correspondents—especially a group of women to whom he was a mentor. As a Bible translator, his great innovation was in translating the Hebrew Bible directly from the original language rather than depending on the Greek of the Septuagint, which meant that his Vulgate (from *Vulgata editio*, "the ordinary people's version") was more accurate, authoritative, and accessible than any other version then available.

Aside from translating the Bible, Jerome was on the front lines of the theological controversies of the day. Harsh in his critiques and dogmatic in his beliefs, he wrote persuasively and forcefully—so much so, for instance, that when he condemned one popular heresy, adherents of that sect mounted an attack on his monastery and forced him to flee. Theology was a matter of life and death. His well-known irascibility, both in person and in his writing, prompted Thomas Merton to dub him "God's grouch."[3]

Jerome penned some of the most consequential documents of the early church, including commentaries, saints' lives, treatises,

church histories, and letters. Augustine was one of his correspondents as well as an occasional intellectual sparring partner,
and among the writers of that generation, Jerome was second
only to Augustine in his range and productivity.

Yet for all of Jerome's vast influence, such Renaissance artists as Botticelli, Bosch, da Vinci, Dürer, Michelangelo, Titian,
Brueghel, El Greco, Caravaggio, and Rembrandt—all of whom
depicted the saint, and some of them repeatedly—had another
reason for finding him irresistible. He was visually spectacular. Among the iconographic symbols associated with him—all
those visual motifs suggested by the many biographies and
legends—are a lion, a rocky cave, tree stumps, books and papers,
spectacles, a quill pen, tweezers, a skull, a candle, an hourglass,
and a red cloak. Often portrayed half naked with a rock in his
fist, Jerome was an eyeful—colorful, ardent, theatrical.

The lion appears in many of the paintings because, according to legend, when a lion lumbered into Jerome's desert community one day, everyone but the saint fled. Realizing that
the animal was wounded, Jerome patiently removed a thorn
from its paw, after which the beast, in gratitude, stood guard
at the entrance to Jerome's dwelling and followed "the doctor
about like a dog."[4] In the paintings, that dwelling is sometimes
depicted as a few sheltering trees, sometimes a scholar's formal
study, and sometimes, as in Jan Sadeler's engraving (figure 7.1),
a cave-like jumble of rocks.

Beyond that legend (which may have originated in the earlier folktale "Androcles and the Lion"), Jerome's own leonine
personality contributed to his identification with the animal.
Not only was he rough in appearance, but he was a fierce and
tenacious polemicist when it came to defending his faith. As
poet Marianne Moore put it,

Figure 7.1. Flemish engraver Jan Sadeler's version of Mostaert's painting *Saint Jerome* (late sixteenth century). With a crucifix in one hand, Jerome prepares to strike his breast with a rock. A skull and lion lie nearby. A statue of Mary and the Christ child has displaced a shattered sculpture of Venus, symbolizing Jerome's renunciation of pagan classical culture.[5]

> The vindicated beast and
> saint somehow became twinned;
> and now, since they behaved and also looked alike,
> their lionship seems officialized.[6]

As the patron saint of translators, scholars, and librarians, Jerome is often shown amid a scattering of books and papers (figure 7.2), sometimes with a pair of eyeglasses nearby—an anachronism, since glasses wouldn't be invented for another nine hundred years. Jerome's red clothing, which is sometimes a mere strip of cloth wound around his waist and at other times a full cardinal's regalia, complete with a broad-brimmed hat known as a *galero*, indicates that he was considered one of the first cardinals of the Roman Catholic Church—another anachronism because the church didn't officially designate cardinals until three centuries later. A human skull, usually present, is a symbol of mortality—a memento mori—as were the hourglass and candle.

The central theme of those old paintings is penance. Often shown kneeling before a crucifix, Jerome holds a rock in his hand or is sometimes in the act of thumping it against his bare chest—indicating his self-abnegation and repentance—and his body sometimes displays wounds or scars.

But hidden within these symbols, unstated but unmistakable, is the reason we are discussing him here: he had a well-documented visionary encounter with Jesus.

❊ ❊ ❊

In about 373, when Jerome was in his twenties, he set out from Italy for Antioch (now in modern Turkey) with a group of

Figure 7.2. Albrecht Dürer portrays Jerome (1514) as neither a penitent nor a cave dweller but a Renaissance scholar. Still present are the crucifix, the lion, the skull, the *galero* on the wall, but Dürer adds a pet dog sleeping on the floor.

friends—fellow scholars and ascetics. Their goal was to reach Jerusalem. With him, he brought the books he'd amassed as a student, his favorites being the great Roman writers—Horace, Virgil, Plautus, and above all, Cicero, whose elegant rhetorical stylings captivated him. So enamored was he with his collection that it became an obsession, a guilty pleasure, a distraction to his faith. After extended periods of prayer and fasting, he would reward himself by reading his favorite Latin authors in lieu of more edifying devotional works. The classics seemed far more alluring than even the Bible; as he later wrote to a friend, "When at times I returned to my right mind, and began to read the prophets, their style seemed rude and repellent."[7]

During Lent in Antioch that year, Jerome contracted a serious illness, one that had already claimed the lives of two of his companions. As his condition worsened, he began losing weight until, as he said, "my flesh could scarcely cling to my bones."[8] At the height of his fever, he lost consciousness, and his friends, expecting him to die any minute, began planning his funeral. Jerome himself recounts what happened next: "Suddenly I was caught up in the spirit and dragged before the tribunal of the Judge. Here there was so much light and such a glare from the brightness of those standing around that I cast myself on the ground and dared not look up. Upon being asked my status, I replied that I was a Christian. And He who sat upon the judgment seat said: 'Thou liest. Thou art a Ciceronian, not a Christian. *Where thy treasure is, there is thy heart also.*' I was struck dumb on the spot."[9]

The Judge is unnamed, but the context is clear. As Jerome himself would later translate from John's gospel, "Neque enim Pater judicate quemquam: sed omne judicium dedit Filio" (For neither does the Father judge any man: but hath given all judgment to the Son[10]). Jesus was the Judge.

After accusing Jerome of being a follower of Cicero rather than Christ, the Judge ordered those standing by, radiant angels, to thrash Jerome with whips, which Jerome says was not as painful as his own pangs of conscience. He cried out, "Have mercy on me, O Lord; have mercy upon me," so piteously that even those who were scourging him dropped their lashes and pleaded with the Judge to relent. At this point in his fevered dream, Jerome vowed to forsake the pagan writers, and he promised to dedicate the rest of his life to reading only the Bible and edifying spiritual works: "O Lord, if ever I possess or read secular writings, I have denied thee."[11]

With that vow in his mind, his fever broke and his health was restored. Upon waking, he told his friends what he'd experienced, feebly insisting that it "had not been mere sleep nor meaningless dreams,"[12] and he showed them the bruises on his back, though they were more likely due to illness than to an angelic thrashing.

Such is the story behind those old paintings—what we might call Jerome's *back*story. The saint's bare shoulders symbolize the beating he received, and the rock that he pounds on his chest shows the sincerity of his repentance. Sometimes books are scattered on the ground in the paintings, but not those that he wrote; they are the classics he cast aside. The stacks of papers are the pages of the Bible that would later become the Vulgate, and the crucifix, which is usually either in his hand or hanging on a wall or tree nearby, represents the Judge himself.

✳ ✳ ✳

Jerome's account prompts a number of questions: What do we make of dreams? How do we distinguish between "meaningless dreams" and meaningful visions? How do we know such things aren't just symptoms of a runaway imagination or a guilty conscience?

The biblical writers take for granted the idea that God communicates with us in our sleep, that dreams are a form of divine revelation. Of the twenty-one dreams recorded in Scripture (as opposed to waking visions), fifteen are found in the Hebrew Bible, as when Jacob dreams of angels ascending and descending the ladder to heaven[13] or when Daniel dreams of the four beasts and one "like the son of man" coming "with the clouds of heaven."[14]

Only six dreams are reported in the Gospels, all of them in Matthew.[15] All but one involve angelic messengers, and all concern Jesus. In the first chapter, God's messenger appears to Joseph, Mary's betrothed, instructing him not to "put her away privately" but to marry her because her child is the long-awaited "Emmanuel . . . God with us."[16] In the second chapter, the Magi are warned in a dream "that they should not return to Herod," and also in that chapter, Joseph has three more dreams, in which an angel directs his journey to Egypt to keep the child Jesus safe.[17]

In the final dream in Matthew, Pontius Pilate's wife tells him that she has "suffered many things this day in a dream because of [Jesus]," and she warns her husband to have nothing to do with "that just man."[18] Curiously, Pilate's wife, whose name is unknown (though Jerome believed it to be Procula), is the only female dreamer mentioned in the entire Bible. A later unreliable legend claimed she was secretly a Christian.

These instances suggest that both the Hebrew and the Christian Testaments endorse dreams as communications from God, provided as guidance for the present and warnings about the future.

But the Bible also includes admonitions *against* dreams and dreamers. For instance, among the many sins against God's laws committed by Judah's King Manasseh is that of observing dreams,[19] and Jeremiah warns the exiles in Babylon, "Hearken not to your prophets, and diviners, and dreamers, and soothsayers, and sorcerers."[20] The Book of Sirach in the Apocrypha warns, "Dreams lift up fools. The man that giveth heed to lying visions, is like to him that catcheth at a shadow, and followeth after the wind. . . . For dreams have deceived many, and they have failed that put their trust in them."[21] The author of Ecclesiastes too dismisses dreams: "Where there are many dreams, there are many vanities."[22] (Of course, the author of Ecclesiastes believes that *everything* is vanity, not just dreams.)

Many theologians side with the negative view, arguing that people are too easily misled by dreams and that confusion would result if everyone were able to receive private visionary messages from God. If disputes arise, for instance, whose dream revelation has greater authority, and how do we separate the bona fide from the bogus?

The negative view seems to have been endorsed by Jerome himself, though in a curiously roundabout way. According to some scholars, Jerome, years after his own vision of the Judge, seems to have deliberately mistranslated two passages in the Vulgate in a possible attempt to tip the scale against dreams and visions.[23] He rendered Deuteronomy 18:10 as this: "Neither let there be found among you any one . . . that consulteth soothsayers, or observeth dreams and omens, neither let there be any wizard" (DRB). Likewise, he renders Leviticus 19:26 this way: "You shall not divine nor observe dreams" (DRB).

The Latin phrases Jerome uses here are, respectively, *observet somnia* and *observabitis somnia*. The word *somnia* does indeed mean "dreams," but what is odd here is that the word in the original Hebrew Bible is *anan*, which means "witchcraft" or "fortune-telling" rather than "dreams." Throughout his writings, Jerome proves himself to be a meticulous scholar, so his mistranslation here is puzzling. And perhaps deliberate. He knew the literal definition of *anan* because he translated it correctly elsewhere in the Bible—seven times, in fact. But in those two instances, he spins it in the direction of condemning dreams.

So why would someone whose entire life changed course because of a dream slant his translation that way?

We can't know for sure, but one intriguing possibility is that his own dream actually *didn't* change the course of his life as much as he wanted people to believe. What if Jerome—like all of us who backslide on our New Year's resolutions to eat less and exercise more—simply couldn't keep his vow? Perhaps he felt compelled to diminish the value of dreams because he was ultimately unable to resist the lure of the pagan authors he had once vowed to forsake. We know that for the rest of his life, he continued to season his writings with zippy, accurate quotations from the Greeks and Romans. He either had a remarkable memory or kept those books on hand.

Nor did this fact go unnoticed at the time. During an exchange of dueling treatises between Jerome and one of his former friends, a man named Rufinus, things got out of hand. When Jerome accused Rufinus of willfully misinterpreting something Jerome had written, Rufinus responded by accusing Jerome of hypocrisy, noting that ever since Jerome had famously vowed to renounce the classics, he continued to quote them—and to quote them extensively, even in the course of the written barbs they were currently exchanging. In Rufinus's own harsh words, "Tell me whether there is a single page . . . in which [Jerome] does not declare himself a Ciceronian, or in which he does not speak of 'our Tully,' 'our Flaccus,' 'our Maro,' . . . he scatters their names around him like a vapour or halo, so as to impress his readers with a sense of his learning and literary attainments."[24] Jerome responded that "he had not promised to forget what he already knew,"[25] and elsewhere, he defended himself by saying, "Dye your wool once purple, and what water will cleanse it of that stain?"[26]

In contrast to Rufinus, fourteenth-century English priest and librarian Richard de Bury had a gentler perspective. He recognized that if Jerome had *not* thoroughly and passionately immersed himself in the classic writers, the Christian faith—and all of Western culture—would have been poorer for it. Without Jerome's intense study of the Greeks and Romans, we would have neither the Vulgate nor Jerome's other writings. De Bury, a lover of the classics himself, wrote, "Those things are not to be considered trifles without which great things cannot come to pass. It follows therefore that through ignorance of [classical] poetry we do not understand Jerome . . . and very many others, a catalogue of whom would more than fill a long chapter."[27]

In other words, if Jerome had not been a Ciceronian as well as a Christian, he would not have been equipped to create a Bible that Latin readers throughout the empire would find not just readable but authoritative. Without a familiarity with the elegancies of Virgil and the rhetorical clarity of Cicero, he could never have approached the literary precision of the Vulgate. Even in our own time, such familiar Latin phrases as *de profundis* (out of the depths), *fiat lux* (let there be light), and *ecce homo* (behold the man)[28] might never have found their way into our culture, and we might lack such common terms as *salvation*, *sanctification*, *justification*, *angel*, and *apostle*—all of which are drawn from the Latin of Jerome.

✻ ✻ ✻

So am I skeptical about the veracity of his vision (a skepticism that Jerome himself seems to have shared)? Yes and no. His astonishing dream in extremis, clearly the result of a dire illness, could have been divinely inspired as well, though perhaps in a circuitous way.

Similar to Paul's vision on the road to Damascus, Jerome's dream is an example of what might be called a "vision of conscience"—that is, the product of a mind dealing with its own troubling dissonances, its deepest insecurities and guilts. As religious people all over the world believe, God is the source of each person's moral conscience. God put it there.

One approach to dreams is to view them as a sort of free-wheeling, internal guerrilla theater, reenacting the anxieties and conflicting desires we've felt throughout the day. If my father appears in a dream, for instance, and is angry with me for something, it is not really my father in the dream—but everything he represents in my unconscious mind. It is the universal father within me, portrayed in my dream by an inner actor who only wears a fatherlike costume. His disappointment in me is not my dad's but my own lurking disappointment in myself. He is me, or at least a part of me.

Likewise, if Jesus appears in my dream, is it the *real* Jesus or just an inner actor in a Jesus costume, enacting the Jesus part of my thoughts? In a sense, it doesn't matter because, like the father in me, the Jesus part of my inner life is synonymous with my conscience, my sense of right and wrong—which I do believe was given to me directly by God.

Jerome's dream, I think, was of this kind. Did he see the real Jesus—the real Judge—or was he confronting that "Judge part of himself"? Was his dream the result of his own guilty feelings about enjoying Cicero far more than the prophets? If we believe that our conscience is built into our psyches—put there by God—then Jerome's dream was indeed God-given.

Or put it this way: Is there really any difference between Jesus and the Jesus part of our souls? Didn't Jesus himself say, "Before long, the world will not see me anymore, but you will see me. Because I live, you also will live. On that day you will realize that I am in my Father, and you are in me, and I am in you."[29]

＊ ＊ ＊

As far as Jerome's vow, I think God intended it to be broken. God takes the pieces of our broken vows and reassembles them in unexpected ways, and in breaking his vow to the Judge, Jerome expanded the Judge's influence across the world.

How do we make sense of visions like Jerome's? For me, the question is this: If our dreams are like theater, is God the director and playwright—the manipulator of the action? Or does God simply provide us with the inner stage and enough internal actors, including occasional appearances by an inner Jesus, to help us work things out for ourselves?

8

APOCRYPHAL VISIONS
The Gnostics

If Jesus were to appear suddenly and miraculously to you and your friends, I'm sure that the first words out of your mouth would *not* be, "Lord, we would like to know the deficiency of the aeons and their pleroma."[1] And yet that, according to the Letter of Peter to Philip, is precisely what Peter and the other disciples are purported to have asked Jesus when he made a surprise postresurrection appearance on the Mount of Olives.

Welcome to the curious world of the Christian apocryphal writings—those early documents written to resemble books of the Bible . . . but aren't. And the visions of Jesus they contain are quite unlike the others we'll encounter.

✳ ✳ ✳

The four centuries after the time of Christ were contentious. Rival sects, offshoots, and heresies vied for attention and dominance, with issues of basic doctrine at the forefront, to say nothing of the establishment of a biblical canon. Adding to the turmoil was the fact that no universally recognized central church yet existed, so each sectarian voice had to speak loudly to make itself heard.

Often proffered as arguments for the various theological points of view were documents purporting to have been written by the disciples or others known to have been associated with Jesus. What better way to prop up your own pet doctrines than by proof texting them with some freshly minted words from Paul or Peter or Mary Magdalene or Jesus himself? All of them and more were invoked, at least in the creative imaginations of some, to propose alternate visions of what faith should look like. In a sense, these writings were early Christianity's equivalent of deepfake videos—propaganda made to look like the genuine article. A favorite technique of these writers was to report a previously unknown story about Jesus and, better yet, to claim to have experienced a mystical visitation from him.

* * *

As far as the Bible, the canonical sheep were largely separated from the noncanonical goats at the Synod of Hippo in 393, a conclave that Augustine may have attended, and at a series of later councils. But a dizzying array of documents competed for inclusion or, at the very least, influence. Among the rejected gospels were those purported to have been written by James, Judas, Peter, Mary, Nicodemus, and others, all of which scholars now date as being from the middle of the second century to the end of the third, well past the lifetimes of the original disciples or even those disciples' disciples—too late to claim authenticity. Also rejected were a variety of epistles, acts of the apostles, and apocalypses.

Many of the books seem alien, disorienting, and even ludicrous to us. Consider the inadvertent humor in the supposed exchange of letters between King Agbarus of Edessa and the newly resurrected Jesus. King Agbarus asks him to come and heal him of some unspecified disease, and in a crisp, courteous reply, Jesus thanks him but regrets that he's currently busy, saying, "As to that part of your letter, which relates to my giving you a visit, I must inform you, that I must fulfill all the ends of my mission." Courteous as always, Jesus adds, "After my ascension, I will send one of my disciples."[2] You almost expect him to end with a perfunctory "Sincerely, Jesus."

A number of so-called infancy gospels exist, purporting to reveal the lost years of Jesus's childhood, most of which present an astonishing combination of whimsy and grotesquerie. The Infancy Gospel of Thomas, for example, offers a fantastic story about the child Jesus making clay birds—sparrows, twelve of them, significantly—on the Sabbath. When his father, Joseph, hears about this, he scolds his son, but in response, "Jesus clapped his hands, ordering the birds with a shout in front of all, and said, 'Go, take flight like living beings!' And the sparrows, taking flight, went away squawking."[3] (See figure 8.1.)

Less charming is the story that immediately follows the clay-birds incident. It tells of a child who, while playing, bumps into young Jesus; no sooner does Jesus curse him than the child drops dead (figure 8.2). When the boy's parents complain, Jesus strikes them blind, though Joseph, ever the disciplinarian, "took his [Jesus's] ear and pulled hard."[4]

Another infancy gospel, which scholars refer to as the Gospel of Pseudo-Matthew, contains stories of miracles performed by Jesus as a boy, as when he tamed a fierce lioness that was known

Figure 8.1. Jesus, at right, brings the clay sparrows to life. From the illuminated manuscript *Klosterneuburger Evangelienwerk* (ca. 1340), containing a German translation of the Gospels along with apocryphal material.

Figure 8.2. Jesus and the dead child. Joseph, at left, admonishes his son. From *Klosterneuburger Evangelienwerk*.

to attack passersby. When Jesus enters her cave, the lioness and her cubs kneel before him in worship, after which he leads them in procession across the Jordan River, which parts before them à la Moses and the Israelites.

* * *

Unlike the Canonical Gospels, the apocryphal ones occasionally offer descriptions of Jesus's appearance, though they tend toward the oddly self-contradictory. In the Acts of John, the supposed apostle of that name recalls the day he and his brother, James, first met Jesus. John's impression is that Jesus was "rather bald, but the beard thick and flowing," though John is mystified by the fact that his brother perceived of Jesus "as a youth whose beard was newly come." John continues, "Oft-times he would appear to me as a small man and uncomely, and then again as one reaching unto heaven." One trait noted by this John—a trait I find unusually creepy—is that Jesus never blinked his eyes.[5]

Similarly, a book called the Gospel of Peter reinforces this theme of contradictory perceptions. When Peter prays for the healing of a group of blind women, Jesus miraculously appears and heals them, but he looks different to each one: "We saw an old man of such comeliness as we are not able to declare to thee; but others said: We saw a young man; and others: We saw a boy touching our eyes delicately, and so were our eyes opened."[6]

Such opposing perceptions say more about the perceiver than the perceived. Jesus assumes the shape of each person's expectation or even the person's own appearance—old to the old, young to the young. I would not be at all surprised to find that whoever wrote the apocryphal account in the Acts of John was bald with a thick beard. As the Greek philosopher Xenophanes once wrote, "If oxen or horses or lions had hands, horses would draw the gods shaped like horses, and lions like lions."[7]

This same principle holds true for the doctrines advanced by these texts. The polemicists of those early centuries readily conformed Jesus to their own views—a tendency that persists into our own time. The Gnostic writers of the second and third centuries were adept at this kind of theological appropriation, creating a Jesus in their own image.

In the Gnostic documents, Jesus makes many dubious appearances in which he propounds, not surprisingly, doctrines dear to the ascetic Gnostics themselves, about the relationship of the soul to the body, the afterlife, and the hidden nature of truth. The Apocryphon of James, for instance, details one of Jesus's postresurrection appearances to James and Peter in which Jesus explains a rather complicated theological concept (the parentheses and angle brackets indicate assumed words and the clarifications provided by modern scholars):

> If the soul is saved (when it is) without evil, and if the spirit also is saved, (then) the body becomes sinless. For it is the spirit which <animates> the soul, but it is the body which kills it—that is, it is it (i.e., the soul) which kills itself. Truly I say to you (pl.), he (i.e., the Father) will not forgive the sin of the soul at all, nor the guilt of the flesh. For none of those who have worn the flesh will be saved. For do you imagine that many have found the Kingdom of Heaven? Blessed is the one who has seen himself as a fourth one in Heaven.[8]

In another book, called "The Dialogue of the Savior," Jesus somewhat confusedly teaches Mary and the disciples about the nature of reality and the pursuit of hidden knowledge: "That which supports the earth is that which supports the heaven. When a Word comes forth from the Greatness, it will come on what supports the heaven and the earth. For the earth does not move. Were it to move, it would fall. But it neither moves nor falls, in order that the First Word might not fail. For it was that which established the cosmos and inhabited it, and inhaled fragrance from it. . . . And to someone who will not know the root of all things, they remain hidden."[9]

The boldest of all the Gnostic documents is the Gospel of Judas, in which Jesus takes Judas aside to explain to him "the [mysteries that no] human [will] see, because there exists a great and boundless realm whose horizons no angelic generation has seen, [in] which is a [great] invisible Spirit, which no [angelic] eye has ever seen, no heart has ever comprehended, and it's never been called by any name."[10] (Again, editorial insertions are in brackets.) Jesus gives to Judas alone the secret of his message, and it is for this reason, according to Jesus, that Judas will be forever outcast and misunderstood. Judas alone, in this account, is able to grasp the Truth.

✳ ✳ ✳

Which brings us back to the Letter of Peter to Philip. This Gnostic document is a philosophical dialogue that starts with a conventional greeting from Peter but then shifts oddly to the third person. Sometime between the resurrection and the ascension, according to this epistle, Peter has gathered the disciples on the Mount of Olives in the hope that Jesus will appear to them once again. This might seem to be the stage setting for an overwhelming, dramatic revelation, the imparting of some profound otherworldly wisdom. Instead, here are the questions they ask:

- Lord, we would like to know the deficiency of the aeons and their pleroma.
- How are we detained in this dwelling place?
- How did we come to this place?
- In what manner shall we depart?
- How do we have the authority of boldness?
- Why do the powers fight against us?[11]

These questions would have been of far more interest to a third-century Gnostic than to any of the original disciples. *Aeons* are the "emanations" of God and the source of being—while *pleroma* are the regions of light, the lowest of which is the physical world itself. So when they ask about their "dwelling place," they are talking not about Jerusalem but about our existence in this world itself. The Gnostics, in essence, are asking Jesus to explain the meaning of life. In a rough sense, they've transformed Jesus into an Eastern guru, a hermit-saint dispensing wisdom from a literal mountaintop—in this case, the Mount of Olives.

Even if it would occur to us to ask Jesus about the meaning of life, I think most of us would be disappointed by his answers in the Letter of Peter to Philip. They involve a complex and arcane cosmology without any apparent application to daily life. For example, in answer to the question about the "deficiency," Jesus responds, "This is the deficiency, when the disobedience and the foolishness of the mother appeared without the commandment of the majesty of the Father. She wanted to raise up aeons. And when she spoke, the Arrogant One followed. And when she left behind a part, the Arrogant One laid hold of it, and it became a deficiency. This is the deficiency of the aeons. Now when the Arrogant One had taken a part, he sowed it. And he placed powers over it and authorities. And he enclosed it in the aeons which are dead."[12] In short, the Gnostic fabricator of the Letter of Peter to Philip has co-opted the historical Jesus to talk philosophy (blaming Eve for the "deficiency"), to espouse a specific view.

Portraying a fictional Jesus is not necessarily a bad thing. It is the basis for countless biblical novels and dramas, whether classics like Lew Wallace's *Ben-Hur*, modern novels like Nikos Kazantzakis's *The Last Temptation of Christ*, or hilarious send-ups like Christopher Moore's *Lamb: The Gospel According to Biff, Christ's Childhood Pal*. Our Christmas and Easter pageants are, in a sense, fictionalized portrayals of Jesus in largely unbiblical ways for a specific purpose.

Co-opting Jesus occurs in nonfiction as well. Thomas à Kempis does this in his *Imitation of Christ*, the last two sections of which are a complex dialogue between Jesus and a disciple. But even Thomas makes it clear that he is not reporting an actual conversation: "Truth," he writes, "speaks inwardly without the sound of words."[13] And in a sense, every painting of Jesus does the same—imagining Jesus as a way to make a moral or aesthetic statement.

The problem is not the co-option but the implication that the co-opted Jesus is factual and divinely inspired, legitimating the writers' viewpoints and granting them a higher authority to impose those views on others. As if to convince us of the reality of this supposed appearance of Jesus, the writer of the Letter of

Peter to Philip ends his book with a sort of supernatural exclamation point: "Then there came lightning and thunder from heaven, and what appeared to them in that place was taken up to heaven."[14]

❋ ❋ ❋

Although I dismiss the visions of Jesus found in the Christian apocryphal books as partisan fabrications, I confess to enjoying many of those books, especially those that read like speculative fiction, contain relevant spiritual wisdom, or lend insight into those early cultures.

When it comes to Jesus, these books teach a valuable lesson: we need not accept every reported vision of Jesus as true, nor do we need to feel shy about calling any of them out as fakes and frauds. Our litmus test still applies: If the vision's fruit has done great good in the world, then we might look twice at its value. But when such appearances are propounded for sectarian theological or political reasons—because, it is supposed, you can't argue with Jesus—then we can do no better than to ignore them or even laugh them out of all legitimacy. Or perhaps, metaphorically, we can, like Joseph, pull their ears . . . hard.

PART THREE

MYSTICS

9

THE SHADOW OF LIVING LIGHT

Hildegard of Bingen

Who doesn't love that moment in *The Wizard of Oz* when, just after the tornado, Dorothy emerges from her lopsided farmhouse to discover that the black-and-white world of Kansas has been supplanted by the Technicolor Land of Oz?

We experience something similar when we step from the fourth century of Jerome and Martin of Tours into the twelfth and thirteenth centuries of Hildegard of Bingen and Francis of Assisi. The rocky huts of the desert fathers have been superseded by the magnificent Gothic cathedrals of Europe and grand abbeys of the new monastic orders. Never since Jerome himself has there been such a widespread and intense scholarly interest in the Roman classics, and with its revived passion for theology and philosophy, the twelfth century witnesses the founding of the great universities. The church itself is not just a cultural force but the dominant economic and political one as well. Writers refer to this era as the Christian Renaissance.

Visionary experiences are transformed as well. The brief, monochromatic glimpses of Jesus seen by Anthony, Martin, and Jerome have been displaced, and a new kind of Jesus appears—colorful, tactile, voluble, brimming with an over-the-rainbow kind of mystique. We now find ourselves in the ecstatic, sensuous world of the medieval mystics who, in the words of John Ruskin, were possessed by a "beautiful madness."[1] We're not in Kansas anymore.

Not that mystics were unheard of in those centuries between the early and late Middle Ages, but they were few and far between. The great minds of Christendom were otherwise engaged. Missionaries, zealous to convert pagans to the faith, pushed westward into Spain and Gaul and northward into the Celtic lands of the British Isles. The basic teachings of the faith were hammered out by earnest priests and practical monks—monks who were themselves trying to hammer out the basic contours of monasticism. Those were the centuries of Eastern iconoclasm and the great schism between Eastern and Western Christianity, when vehement, even violent, debates raged over creeds and doctrines and forms of worship. It was a time when mystical visions seemed largely extraneous to faith . . . quirky at best and heretical at worst.

Still, for a number of Celtic saints, like Columba of Iona (sixth century) and Cuthbert of Lindisfarne (seventh century), visions of angels and heaven were as natural as breathing. In the East, the Byzantine monk Symeon the New Theologian (tenth century) experienced repeated, overpowering visitations of a dazzling light that he believed to be the emanation of the Trinity. In his own beautiful words, "It shines on us without evening, without change, without alteration, without form. It speaks, works, lives, gives life, and changes into light those whom it illuminates."[2]

By the eleventh century, Christian thought comes to a fork in the road, and due to its own brand of spiritual genius, it manages to travel both at once, though not always comfortably. In one direction, the so-called Scholastic school of theology emerges, based on the conviction that Christian belief can be organized into a rational system of thought as unassailable as that of the Greek and Roman philosophers. Plato and Aristotle are regarded as "pre-Christian" thinkers, even prophets in their own way.

The other direction—intuitive, contemplative, and ecstatic— is that of the mystics. While never relinquishing a rational, doctrinal Christianity, they manage vastly to enlarge the circle of what orthodox faith contains. For them, an inner aliveness to spiritual reality has for too long been ignored by the theologians—a visceral, personal, day-to-day perception of God as both an indwelling and an all-encompassing presence has been lost. Visionary experiences become more common, and new to this fresh approach is the vigorous participation of women, whose voices until then were absent from theological conversations.

Some Scholastics like Hugh of Saint Victor and his student Richard (twelfth century), in their own systematic way, begin to formulate a theology that encompasses mystical experience, positing the notion that God and Christ can appear to the inner eye as a presence as well as to the mind as a concept. Anselm of Canterbury, one of the founders of Scholasticism, is said to have experienced his own remarkable vision as a child, when it occurred to him that the most direct path to the "Court of Heaven" might be found by scaling a nearby mountain. So he began to climb one day. To his surprise, he did indeed find himself in God's presence—"The Invisible, in fashion as a king, throned in majesty, sat before him."[3] The Invisible asked him polite questions about himself and then ordered that bread be brought to the boy. Anselm, after eating it, fell asleep, only to awaken the next morning in his own bed at home.

So these two roads, the Scholastic and mystic, converge, and Christianity tentatively becomes a religion that speaks to the heart as well as the mind. Sadly, the mystic and Scholastic paths are in contrast to another less-attractive direction. In our *Wizard of Oz* analogy, that direction is comparable to the Wicked Witch of the West—the way of violence, torture, and murder, for the twelfth century witnesses the Crusades, anti-Jewish and anti-Muslim fervor, and the birth of the Inquisition.

✳ ✳ ✳

One surprising feature of late-medieval mystic visions of Jesus is their superabundance. For many, especially women, visionary experiences began in childhood and recurred throughout their lives. As a small child, for instance, English anchoress and visionary Christina of Markyate "used to talk to [Jesus] at night and on her bed as if he were a man whom she could see."[4] Mechthilde of Magdeburg had her first vision at the age of twelve. At ten, Bridget of Sweden conversed with a visionary Jesus on the cross. Christina von Stommeln had her first vision of Jesus at the age of five, and Catherine of Siena at six. As an adult, Catherine even experienced what she believed was her mystical marriage to Christ, with Jesus's foreskin as the wedding ring.

Each of these women deserves an entire chapter to themselves, but one woman, brilliant and highly accomplished, will serve to represent these spiritual riches: Hildegard of Bingen.

✳ ✳ ✳

She was born into a noble and devout German family in 1098, the youngest of ten children. Since two of her brothers had studied to be priests and one of her sisters was in a convent, Hildegard seemed destined for the church. At the age of eight, she was sent to live with a devout recluse named Jutta von Sponheim, an anchoress attached to the Benedictine monastery at Disibodenberg. Jutta took responsibility for the young girl's upbringing, teaching her to read and write and effectively becoming her parent, mentor, and spiritual director.[5]

Most importantly, under Jutta's tutelage, Hildegard was able to confide a secret she had kept hidden since childhood; namely, she had regularly experienced startling, overpowering visions. They took the form of a bright flashing of lights, sometimes forming jagged geometric shapes that overwhelmed her, emotionally and physically. But these were not just "dreams nor . . . delirium," Hildegard insisted. "I received them when I was awake and looking around with a clear mind, with the inner eyes and ears, in open places according to the will of God."[6]

A community of women soon grew up around Jutta, so much so that the single room in which Hildegard and Jutta lived was expanded into several rooms to accommodate the newcomers. In time, the group grew large enough to be recognized by the monastery's abbot as a convent in its own right, with Jutta as abbess. During that time, one of the Benedictine monks taught Hildegard how to play the psaltery and how to write musical notation, and soon she was composing hymns and singing them in worship with the women of the community.

When Jutta died, Hildegard, who was thirty-eight, replaced her as abbess. For the next four decades, she became one of the most brilliant thinkers and writers of her era, composing three books of visionary theology, two medical treatises, Bible commentaries, saints' lives, more than seventy hymns (some of which are still sung today), poetry, and letters to the religious and political leaders of the day.

Even more remarkably, when she was in her seventies, she abandoned her cloistered life to become a traveling preacher, despite the apostle Paul's biblical admonition "Do not permit a woman to teach . . . ; she must be quiet."[7] We think of women leaders in our day as breaking "glass ceilings," but Hildegard, in her own firm but persuasive way, took a sledgehammer to the whole glass house. She opened the door for other women and mystics who came later. Never one to refuse a divine urging, she challenged both the religious and the political authorities—that is, the men—of her time. This preaching tour was a formidable challenge not only because of her age but also because of her ongoing, lifelong illnesses.

✳ ✳ ✳

But earlier, at the age of "forty-two and seven months,"[8] as she wrote, a voice—the voice of God—spoke to her, instructing her not only to share the content of her visions in a book but to interpret them as well. The idea terrified her. In her mind, it smacked of pride, an exercise in spiritual exhibitionism, making her vulnerable, exposing her most secret thoughts to the world. Before then, she'd told only Jutta and one or two others about her visions.

She wrote to Bernard of Clairvaux, the most influential religious figure of the era, for his advice. Should she obey the voice? In response, he said yes, obey the command, and further-more, he assured her that he had consulted Pope Eugenius III on her behalf, and the pope concurred. So began the creation of Hildegard's first visionary treatise, *Scivias* (which means "knowledge of the ways"), which she dictated to two friends who acted as her secretaries, a monk named Volmar and a nun in her own community named Richardis of Stade.

One of the most remarkable passages occurs at the beginning of the second book, in which she describes an ecstatic vision of the Trinity—with Christ at its center: "And then I saw a bright light, and in this light the figure of a man the color of sapphire, which was all blazing with a gentle glowing fire. And that bright light bathed the whole of the glowing fire, and the glowing fire bathed the bright light; and the bright light and the glowing fire poured over the whole human figure, so that the three were one light in one power of potential." And then she interprets her vision this way:

> Therefore you see a bright light, which without any flaw of illusion, deficiency or deception designates the Father; and in this light the figure of a man the color of sapphire, which without any flaw of obstinacy, envy or iniquity designates the Son, Who was begotten of the Father in Divinity before time began, and then within time was incarnate in the world in Humanity; which is all blazing with a gentle glowing fire, which fire without any flaw of aridity, mortality or darkness designates the Holy Spirit, by Whom the Only-begotten of God was conceived in the flesh and born of the Virgin within time and poured the true light into the world . . . so that the three are one light in one power of potential.[9]

The concept is subtle—and so beautiful. Christian writers had long struggled for metaphors to explain how God could be three persons but one at the same time, a concept that seemed irrational to the polytheists and pagans who were the targets of evangelization. Early on, the image of the triangle, called the Shield of the Trinity, was used—three points, one triangle. Patrick of Ireland, according to legend, compared the Trinity to the three leaves of the shamrock.

But Hildegard takes the concept in a different direction, neither geometric nor botanical—but multisensual. For her, the Trinity embodies three qualities of light: First is the fire itself, or the source, which is God the Father. That fire then emanates a radiant warmth, which is the Holy Spirit. And the light of that fire allows us to see things, especially the miracle of color all around us, represented by the sapphire blue of Jesus in the center. Three persons, one light. Fire, warmth, and vision/color. While the pure fire of God is untouchable, the Holy Spirit warms us and Jesus appears to our own eyes. Jesus himself said, "I am the light of the world."[10]

Hildegard provided an illustration (figure 9.1) of what she saw, though we don't know whether she or her assistant actually painted it. The image is shocking and beautiful, rich in symbolism. The outer circles represent the flames, encompassing everything. The inner circles are the glowing warmth. Notice the small aperture above Jesus's head, like an opening in a maze, which connects Jesus directly to the fire's source, and that source flows all around him, embracing his entire form. Jesus's raised hands face outward, as though giving a blessing to the entire world or, more intimately, inviting us to place our own hands against his, to share the warmth of the radiant energy within those scintillating circles. Notice too how the outer circle pushes against the frame that surrounds the picture, symbolizing the fact that God's presence knows no boundaries, impinging on everything. It's everywhere.

Figure 9.1. Hildegard's depiction of her vision of the Trinity with Jesus at the center, from *Scivias* (1141–51)

Hildegard, though, called her visions only the Shadow of Living Light, or in Latin, *umbra viventis lucis*, for in this world, the divine Living Light itself (the *lux vivens*) is too brilliant for us to bear, as it was for Moses when God told him, "For there shall no man see me, and live."[11] We do not see the full Light in this world, only its shadow.

✳ ✳ ✳

Lovers of mystical literature are not alone in their fascination for Hildegard and her visions. Modern medical researchers find her interesting as well.[12] Her accounts of vibrant visions and flashing lights may be the earliest recorded instances of a severe headache condition known as migraine aura. The telltale signs of this disturbance, according to the Mayo Clinic's reference guide, are "blind spots (scotomas), which are sometimes outlined by simple geometric designs. Zigzag lines that gradually float across your field of vision. Shimmering spots or stars. Changes in vision or vision loss. Flashes of light. . . . Numbness. . . . Speech or language difficulty. Muscle weakness."[13] Oliver Sacks cites studies that "have collected many reports of complex hallucinations in migraine from the world literature. People may see human figures, animals, faces, objects, or landscapes—often multiplied."[14] Research finds that this type of migraine headache occurs more often in women than men.

Here is Hildegard's own description of the *umbra viventis lucis*, the visions she'd experienced since early childhood: "A fiery light, flashing intensely, came from the open vault of heaven and poured through my whole brain. Like a flame that is hot without burning it kindled all my heart and all my breast, just as the sun warms anything on which its rays fall." She adds that after experiencing these visions, she seemed to understand the Psalms and the Gospels intuitively even though "I could not interpret the words of the text; nor could I divide up the syllables, nor did I have any notion of the cases or tenses."[15] Although she was a tirelessly energetic woman, she was in poor health for much of her life, and her visions often seemed to result in physical weakness.

One of her paintings, which serves as the frontispiece to *Scivias*, may well be a vivid portrayal of such a headache (figure 9.2). The filaments of flashing light envelop not just her eyes but the sides of her head and her forehead as well.

So are we to dismiss Hildegard's visions as symptoms of illness? I don't think so. If God can use Jerome's uneasy conscience to teach him about his personal obsessions, God can use Hildegard's headaches as well. The fruits of her revelations, whether they resulted from headaches or divine agency or both, managed to shape the way mystics for centuries would intuit God in their lives. Remember that even Paul's vision of Jesus on the road to Damascus was a vision of overpowering light—as were Anthony's and Jerome's and Symeon's.

Evelyn Underhill, one of the leading scholars of mysticism, says of Hildegard's visions, "Before dismissing these stories as absurdities we should remember that her career proves her a woman of genius; and that such spiritual psychical precocity undoubtedly exists, and is the raw material from which a certain sort of mysticism may develop. . . . We are far from understanding the conditions underlying human greatness."[16]

Figure 9.2. The frontispiece to *Scivias*, showing the abbess in the midst of receiving the flames of a vision and dictating to one of her scribes

10

"REPAIR MY HOUSE"

Francis of Assisi

In the year 1200, the map of Europe looked nothing like it does today. England and a large portion of France were uncomfortably conjoined. Germany, Austria, Switzerland, Holland, Italy, and many adjacent countries constituted what was known as the Holy Roman Empire, which was holy only insofar as it shared a single religion and Roman only in its ambition to emulate the expansiveness of ancient Rome, though lacking Rome's administrative cohesion. While ruled by a Holy Roman emperor, the empire itself was a hodgepodge of bickering, often warring states, which were themselves made up of smaller duchies and fiefdoms.

Innocent III was pope. In his eighteen years on the papal throne, he managed to have an outsized influence on the empire by asserting the church's absolute spiritual authority over the kings of Europe and by involving himself in international relations and matters of royal succession. In 1202, he launched the ill-fated Fourth Crusade, the purpose of which was to recapture Jerusalem from its Muslim rulers, but instead, the Crusaders besieged and ultimately sacked Constantinople, the seat of Eastern Christianity and the capital of the Byzantine Empire. While at first grieved by this tragedy, Innocent consoled himself by claiming that the city's humiliation was God's plan to reunite Eastern and Western Christianity. At the Fourth Lateran Council in 1215, Innocent ordered a harsh crackdown on heretics, wide-ranging reforms of ecclesiastical law, and the imposition of draconian restrictions on Jews and Muslims.

Innocent dominated Europe . . . which makes one small incident that took place in 1210 notable.

While pacing the high terrace atop Rome's Basilica of Saint John Lateran, the official papal cathedral, Pope Innocent was startled by a ragged stranger kneeling before him. At first, he thought the man might be a shepherd. After a brief conversation, Innocent asked his retainers to escort the man from his presence.

That would have been the end of the story had it not been for a vision. That night, Innocent dreamed that the towering pillared facade of the cathedral began to tilt crazily as if it were about to topple over like a gigantic chest of drawers. At the last second, a mysterious figure appeared and wedged his back beneath the tipsy edifice to keep it from falling. This figure was the ragged stranger from earlier that day.

Feeling he'd received a sign from God, Innocent summoned the stranger.

* * *

Or so the legend goes.

The reality was more prosaic. The stranger was in fact a pious, energetic twenty-eight-year-old from central Italy named Giovanni di Pietro di Bernardone. Having drawn up a set of monastic-style rules for himself and his thriving band of like-minded followers, Giovanni and eleven of his friends had gone to Rome to ask Innocent to bless their effort. So quickly had Giovanni's community grown that it ran the risk of being regarded as heretical. The pope's approval would allow them to continue to do what they were doing, which was to live as mendicant monks with no possessions or prestige, to preach repentance, to attend the sick, and to care for the poor and dispossessed.

Innocent and his cardinals listened to Giovanni but were unable to reach a decision. Some thought it counterproductive to encourage an order of homeless, uneducated monks with no means of support other than begging, and such a lifestyle was far too stringent to attract followers. So, undecided, the pope asked Giovanni and his friends to pray for wisdom.

While not yet granting them the status of an official order, the pope eventually permitted them to continue their preaching under the supervision of a bishop. Expediency rather than a prophetic dream was the deciding factor. The pope reasoned that a group of charitably minded, wandering street preachers might be helpful in encouraging faith among the poor, perhaps even creating a spiritual revival. One irony is this: the most long-lasting and far-reaching decision of Pope Innocent's entire career was not the edicts he issued nor the crusades he launched but rather his decision to sanction this ragtag group of would-be monks.

Giovanni, of course, is known to history as Francis of Assisi, the most remarkable of the many remarkable saints of the Roman Catholic Church. Countless legends grew up around him, making it difficult now to separate fiction from fact, and while I don't know what to make of these legends, some of which strain credulity, I do wish to focus on one curious aspect of his biography: his short but astonishingly influential life was rounded on either end by extraordinary visions of Jesus.

✳ ✳ ✳

As the pampered son of an affluent fabric merchant, Francis spent his adolescence in what old books call "riotous living"— drinking heavily, chumming around with undesirable friends, and getting into scrapes. Still, convinced that he was destined for great things, he joined the militia in search of glory, though after fighting a few battles, being taken a prisoner, and surviving a serious illness, he left the military in his early twenties, emotionally adrift. His escapades had left a mark. He'd become aware of the suffering around him, the pervasiveness of poverty, and the persistence of disease—all of which plunged him into despair. He became, in the words of one poet, "blinded with weeping for the sad and poor."[1]

For example, while riding his horse down the road one day, a leper crossed his path. Despite Francis's deep revulsion of the disease, he felt he must do something to help. So, reaching into his pouch, he gave the poor man all the money he had. Still, a few coins seemed a paltry gift, so Francis dismounted and kissed the man, fully embracing him. Forever after, Frances felt a special affinity for lepers and years later founded a leprosarium.

While he was still in the midst of his early spiritual depression, Francis had his first visionary encounter with Jesus.

✳ ✳ ✳

Just a short hike from the village of Assisi is the Church of San Damiano, which stands on a low rise, surrounded by pines and cypresses, beyond which stretches a fine view of the surrounding Umbrian hills and countryside. Francis loved to walk there because the path was lined with olive trees, rosemary, and lavender. The facade of this little-used, wayside church was crumbling, and the priest who cared for it was poor, nearly starving. The small, usually vacant sanctuary was in sharp contrast to the Gothic splendor of the great vaulted cathedrals that were being built across Europe at the time. The altar was fashioned from disintegrating bricks and mortar, and above the altar hung a bold, Byzantine-style crucifix.

While kneeling at the altar, alone and overcome with doubts (figure 10.1), Francis gazed at the painted face of Jesus on the crucifix. Then he heard a voice . . . the voice of Jesus: "Francis," it said, "go and repair my house, which, as you see, is falling utterly into ruin."[2]

This was no grand mystical vision like Paul's. Rather, like Ananias twelve centuries earlier, Francis received a command, a commissioning directive, and it energized him.

Francis swung into action. First, he stole a shipment of his father's fabric, sold it, and gave the money to the church's priest. His father, incensed, had him arrested for theft, though when brought before the judge, Francis freely confessed and promised to return the money. But then the proceedings took a bizarre turn. After formally renouncing his father, his patrimony, and all his possessions, Francis stripped himself naked and left the court wrapped only in a robe hastily given to him by a local bishop. Thus began his life of poverty, homelessness, preaching, and ministering to the poor—all because Jesus had spoken from a painted cross.

French theologian Paul Sabatier says that the actual crucifix at San Damiano (figure 10.2) is unusual in one respect. The

Figure 10.1. *Francis Kneeling before the Crucifix of San Damiano*—sketch attributed to eighteenth-century Italian artist Marco Benefial. The cross here is smaller than the actual San Damiano crucifix.

eyes of Jesus are wide open. Unlike most European crucifixes of the era, which emphasized Jesus's agony, "the Crucified One" of San Damiano, writes Sabatier, "has an expression of inexpressible calm and gentleness; instead of closing the eyelids in eternal surrender to the weight of suffering, it looks down in

Figure 10.2. *The San Damiano Cross* (ca. 1100), which spoke to Francis. It now hangs in the Basilica of Saint Clare in Assisi, Italy.

self-forgetfulness, and its pure, clear gaze says not '*I suffer*,' but '*come unto me*.'"[3] The San Damiano Jesus looks inward, into each individual soul, but also outward, toward the needs of the world.

By begging for stones and coins in the months that followed, Francis did, in fact, manage to rebuild San Damiano, as well as other local churches, and in this quixotic quest, he attracted followers. They eventually called themselves the Order of the Friars Minor—that is, the Order of Younger Brothers, which was significant in an age of primogeniture, when only oldest sons could inherit a family's wealth. While ascetics and monastics of earlier centuries had sought simply to avoid riches and possessions as a spiritual discipline, Francis's attitude was revolutionary. For him, poverty was not a command but a comfort, not a sacrifice but a privilege. Rather than being an arduous virtue, poverty was a fathomless joy to be embraced because it brought him closer to becoming like Jesus.

Each brother, like Francis himself, was expected to adopt a lifestyle as close as possible to Jesus's own. Since Jesus had said, "To be perfect, go, sell your possessions and give to the poor,"[4] that is what these brothers did. Since Jesus had told his disciples, "Do not get any gold or silver or copper to take with you in your belts—no bag for the journey or extra shirt or sandals or a staff,"[5] Francis's followers took those instructions to heart. They possessed nothing but the robes on their backs, and for belts, they used plain lengths of rope.

At the heart of Francis's Damiano experience, though, was a curious misunderstanding. He believed Jesus was directing him to refurbish the Church of San Damiano itself, which prompted Francis to beg for bricks from door to door. In time, those words came to have a meaning deeper than even the pope and his cardinals could have foreseen, for Francis had actually set about repairing the institution of the church as a whole, investing it with fresh energy and a renewed focus on following Jesus and caring for the poor. It revitalized Christianity.

In time, with the help of a younger woman named Clare, Francis founded the Order of the Poor Clares for women who likewise wished to embrace poverty. Since Francis realized that not everyone could live a life of sacrifice and denial—after all, some were needed to harvest the fields, shear the sheep, weave the cloth—he founded what was called the Third Order, made up of ordinary people, called tertiaries, who wanted to emulate Jesus in their daily lives of work and marriage.

✳ ✳ ✳

After the botched Fourth Crusade, Pope Innocent launched yet another. And Francis joined. In 1219, having long wished to preach the gospel outside of Italy, Francis traveled to Egypt, where the armies of Europe were besieging the Muslim city of Damietta, near the mouth of the Nile. Boldly, Francis walked across the no-man's-land between the Crusaders and the walled city and managed to be admitted to the presence of Sultan al-Kamil, the Muslim leader. Francis's intention was to broker a truce by converting the sultan to Christianity, but should that fail, Francis was fully satisfied with the prospect of martyrdom. No one knows exactly what happened in that historic encounter. All that is known is that Francis returned safely to the Crusaders' lines and eventually returned to Italy.

✳ ✳ ✳

In 1224, two years before his death, Francis experienced another and far more dramatic encounter with Jesus on the cross—not a command this time but a gift. During Lent, he was alone and in failing health on Mount Alverna at a retreat provided for him by a wealthy admirer. While praying in a "seraphic glow of longing," in the words of his biographer, Bonaventure,

> he beheld a Seraph having six wings, flaming and resplendent, coming down from the heights of heaven. . . . There appeared betwixt the wings the Figure of a Man crucified, having his hands and feet stretched forth in the shape of a Cross, and fastened to a Cross. Two wings were raised above His head, twain were spread forth to fly, while twain hid His whole body. . . . He rejoiced at the gracious aspect wherewith he saw Christ, under the guise of the Seraph, regard him, but His crucifixion pierced his soul with a sword of pitying grief. . . . At length he understood . . . that he was to be wholly transformed into the likeness of Christ Crucified, not by martyrdom of body, but by enkindling of heart. Accordingly, as the vision disappeared, it left in his heart a wondrous glow, but on his flesh also it imprinted a no less wondrous likeness of its tokens. For forthwith there began to appear in his hands and feet the marks of the nails, even as he had just beheld them in that Figure of the Crucified. . . . The right side, moreover, was—as if it had been pierced by a lance—seamed with a ruddy scar, where from ofttimes welled the sacred blood, staining his habit and breeches.[6]

This was the first instance of a follower of Jesus receiving the wounds of Christ as a special spiritual blessing, as a tangible sign. The stigmata.

* * *

Francis's stigmata has been a subject of debate. Roman Catholics accept it as an article of faith, while skeptics point out that only one of Francis's followers seems to have seen the actual wounds, and many doubt that person's testimony. Bonaventure states that Francis preferred to keep the wounds—and the excruciating pain he experienced daily—hidden.

But to debate the validity of Francis's experience is futile. G. K. Chesterton, in his small book about Francis, has no patience for writers like Matthew Arnold and John Ruskin who admire Francis but dismiss his visions and miracles, especially his stigmata. With his usual cheery contrarianism, Chesterton argues that "it's as rational for a theist to believe in miracles as for an atheist to disbelieve in them. . . . The world is in a welter of the possible and impossible."[7]

For myself, I don't pretend to know. It would be presumptuous of anyone to claim certainty. But the fruits of Francis's visions are astonishing, and their influence persists in the form of the Franciscan order, which has even extended to the Lutheran and Anglican communities. Hospitals—and entire cities, like San Francisco—bear his name. Christian environmentalists credit him with inspiring a God-centered, creation-based theology because he viewed himself not as above or apart from the natural world but as a fellow creature. In his most famous prayer, "The Canticle of the Sun," he praises God for creating "Brother Sun . . . Sister Moon . . . Brother Wind . . . Sister Water . . . Brother Fire . . . and Mother Earth."[8]

Still, I wonder whether the true fruits of Francis's visions are as yet unresolved—unripened, you might say. Despite all the charitable work and vital scholarship done in Francis's name, Jesus's mandate to "repair my house" is not only an unfinished project; it is one that has hardly even begun. While Francis preached a poverty of spirit, he also preached a poverty of possessions, of privilege, of clout. Though obedient to those in authority—the bishops and cardinals and the pope—he exemplified with his own life the notion that not just humility but a certain human powerlessness, not just in attitude but in everyday life, was central to faith. Jesus never ran for office or became the chairman of a board. His plan was never to start a new religion. The closest he came to wielding earthly power was to be a teacher for twelve idiosyncratic, often baffled followers.

What if, when Jesus told Peter that he was the rock on which he would build his church, he meant for that church to look not like a magnificent cathedral or even a white-frame chapel in the country but simply like Jesus and his disciples and like Francis and his brothers—that is, each individual ministering to the needs around him or her, building loving personal relationships, not accumulating wealth or power or status, not presuming to have political authority over anyone nor building a theological pecking order. Perhaps the followers of Jesus were meant to be members, as comedian Flip Wilson used to say, of "the church of what's happenin' now"—a committed lifestyle more than a social club or a political party.

History tells us that the organized church has done great good in the world—incalculably positive. But history also suggests that when the organized church attains too much power, too much prestige and privilege—and it often doesn't take much—things go terribly, terribly wrong. Philip Yancey wrote, "C. S. Lewis observed that almost all crimes of Christian history have come about when religion is confused with politics.

Politics, which always runs by the rules of ungrace, allures us to trade away grace for power, a temptation the church has often been unable to resist."[9]

Perhaps Jesus meant that the work of repairing the church should involve clearing the ground first. Perhaps by *my house* Jesus meant neither San Damiano nor the church establishment but each individual soul. Perhaps by *repair* he meant for each of us to start from the ground up, learning day by day "to act justly and to love mercy and to walk humbly with your God."[10] Jesuit philosopher Pierre Teilhard de Chardin once wrote that there is "a deep satisfaction in working in obscurity—like leaven, or a microbe. In some way, it seems to me you become more intimately a part of the world."[11] Person by person is how the church gets rebuilt.

So like Chesterton, I offer a contrarian spin of my own: I think we find it easier to venerate Francis as a saint than to grapple with his example, and I think we find it easier to worship Jesus in a beautiful church than to follow in his steps each day.

Repairing the house begins within.

11

"ALL SHALL BE WELL"

Julian of Norwich

"As far as I'm concerned, God's got a *lot* of explaining to do."

I suspect we all know people like that. We may even be like that ourselves. Something deep within us wants to know why an all-powerful, all-loving Creator would allow such things to exist as pandemics and plagues, natural disasters, poverty and disease, human trafficking, starvation, racism, wars, genocide . . . How could a good God let suffering, pain, and violence flourish unabated while decency, kindness, and compassion are in such short supply?

God has a lot to answer for, it would seem.

Sometimes that concern takes a more pious, less contentious tone: "I can hardly wait until I get to heaven so that all my questions will be answered"—or in the words of the old hymn, "We'll understand it better bye and bye."[1] Till then, the questions persist.

According to C. S. Lewis, the impulse to cross-examine the Almighty is symptomatic of a cultural shift in human history. "The ancient man," he wrote, "approached God (or even the gods) as the accused person approaches his judge. For the modern man the roles are reversed. He is the judge; God is in the dock."[2] The reason, Lewis believed, was that we no longer have as profound a sense of personal sin, an awareness that our species is to a large extent responsible for the fix it finds itself in, so in order to assign blame for all those things that go so terribly wrong, we look elsewhere, outside ourselves, toward a Creator and in creation itself.

Still, this urge to examine God's motives, to understand just what's going on, has precursors well before our own time. In the seventeenth century, Milton stated in the opening lines of *Paradise Lost* that his poem's "great Argument" is to "assert Eternal Providence, / And justifie the wayes of God to men."[3] Milton, sensing the extent to which God was indeed in the dock, appointed himself as counsel for the defense, and his defense consisted of explaining the origins of the fall: Satan's rebellion and Adam and Eve's first yielding to temptation and sin.

But even three centuries before Milton penned his great epic, a woman living in the eastern part of England experienced a series of mystical revelations containing God's own stunning personal defense. And this woman was not only unafraid to ask God hard questions; she also received some unexpected answers.

She is known as Julian of Norwich.

* * *

One of the curious things about Julian is that the unknowns vastly outnumber the knowns. We're not even sure, for instance, that her name was Julian. While one writer at that time referred to her as "Dame Julian,"[4] she may have only acquired that name by virtue of living in a recluse's hut attached to the wall of St. Julian's Church in Norwich, which was named for a saint that had lived centuries before. That writer, Margery Kempe, whom we'll read about in the next chapter, came to know Julian shortly before Julian's death, at which point the moniker may have already stuck, a contraction for "the lady (or dame) of Saint Julian's Church."

While the place-name *Norwich* is customarily bracketed with *Julian*, no evidence exists that she was a native of that thriving commercial city in Norfolk. Scholars suggest that the Middle English dialect found in her two extant narratives is more characteristic of Yorkshire or Lincolnshire than Norfolk.[5] Then again, she may have simply dictated her book to a scribe from one of those more northerly counties. This uncertainty also throws into doubt the location of her visionary experience, which may well have taken place somewhere other than Norwich. All we know about her death is that it occurred sometime after 1413.

Although it would have been unusual for her not to be married in that society at the time, no records exist to indicate that she was. She may have been widowed during the Black Death. Whether she had children, we don't know, though it is possible, since she wrote so feelingly about the motherliness of Jesus, a fact that particularly endears her to feminist theologians. Some historians have theorized that she had been educated by Benedictine nuns, but again, they have no documentary evidence. While she dictated her writings to others, humbly referring to herself as "a simple creature that cowde [knew] no letter,"[6] still, her flair for vivid language and her familiarity with the Vulgate as well as classic Christian writers suggest someone who possessed a wide learning. She's an enigma.

Despite the uncertainties, we are sure of a few things.

She was born in late 1342. Sometime before her fiftieth year, she came to live in Norwich as an anchoress—that is, a woman who lives apart from the world to focus on devotion and prayer. She dwelt in a small one-room cell, called an anchorhold, a sort of flint-and-mortar lean-to attached to the southern wall of St. Julian's Church (figure 11.1).

We also know that at some point in her teens or twenties, she prayed that God would give her three "graces," or gifts: First, a deeper understanding of Christ's sufferings, which she called "the mind of his passion." Second, to help her achieve this understanding, she prayed that a life-threatening illness, "a bodily sickness," would strike her at the age of thirty, the age

Figure 11.1. St. Julian's Church, Norwich, from the northeast. Julian's shelter was on the opposite side, with a warmer southern exposure. This Anglo-Norman church was largely destroyed in a bombing during World War II but later rebuilt. (Lithograph by James Sillett, 1828.)[8]

at which Jesus began his ministry. Third, she prayed to receive the "three wounds" of "contrition . . . kind compassion . . . and willful longing for God."[7]

While such devotion may seem extreme, her zeal is understandable in that she lived through one of the most devastating plagues in history, the Great Pestilence, or as historians later dubbed it, the Black Death. Becoming an anchoress was, in part, a fourteenth-century form of social distancing in response to a global pandemic.

The bubonic plague arrived in southern England in mid-1348, when Julian was six years old. By the time she was eight, it had spread to every corner of the country and killed, according to some estimates, between 40 and 60 percent of the population. When Julian was twenty years old, a second wave reached England, killing another one out of every four people. So it is reasonable that an exceptionally sensitive young woman, living in the midst of that pandemic, would dwell on issues of mortality and eternity and that at a time when many people viewed disease and premature death as nearly inevitable, Julian would pray that her own life and death might be as spiritually profitable as possible.

❊ ❊ ❊

On the eighth day of May 1373, when she was, in her words, "thirty winters old and a half," her prayer was answered. She fell seriously ill. Attended by her mother, Julian lay in bed for three days, coming in and out of consciousness and slowly losing all feeling below her chest. On the fourth day, a priest administered last rites. She clung tenuously to life for the next three days. Sensing that death was imminent, she asked her mother to help her sit up in bed so that she might "have more freedom at heart to do God's will," at which point the local curate arrived. To give her comfort, he held a crucifix before her eyes, saying, "Daughter, I've brought you the image of your Savior. Look at it and find comfort in it, in reverence to him who died for you and me."[9]

Then everything grew dark except for the crucifix alone, which seemed illuminated mysteriously as if from within. Her pain vanished, which she took to mean that she had been "delivered from this world" by death. Then when she recalled her youthful prayer to have a deeper understanding of Christ's passion, something happened. The face of Jesus on the crucifix began to stream blood, flowing from beneath the crown of thorns encircling his head—blood that was "all hot, fresh, plentiful, and alive, just as it had been when the garland of thorns was thrust on his blessed head."[10]

And so began the first of the fifteen revelations that came to her over the next five hours, with a sixteenth occurring on the following day.

❋ ❋ ❋

Julian wrote two accounts of the experience, which together are the earliest known writings by any woman in English. The first account, which scholars call the Short Text, was written soon after she received her sixteen revelations, or "shewings," as she called them. In the Middle English edition on my shelf, it runs to thirty-two pages. But for the next twenty years, those showings became a major focus of her meditations, prompting her to expand her initial account into a book nearly five times the length of the original. To place it in historical perspective,

Julian wrote it around the same time Chaucer was writing his *Canterbury Tales*.

To this day, Julian's Long Text, titled *The Revelations of Divine Love*, is cherished by millions as a major work of mystical theology, a masterpiece of devotional literature. In 1911, the great historian of mysticism Evelyn Underhill called Julian's *Revelations* "the most beautiful of all English mystical works." Julian, she wrote, had "'a genius for the infinite' of a peculiarly beautiful and individual type. She was a seer, a lover, and a poet." In 1962, Thomas Merton wrote to a friend, "Whereas in the old days I used to be crazy about St. John of the Cross, I would not exchange him now for Julian if you gave me the world and the Indies and all of the Spanish mystics rolled up in one bundle. . . . It was necessary that I bear witness to my love for the Lady Julian."[11]

To convey the beauty and depth of *Revelations* is beyond the scope of this chapter, but we will examine what happened immediately after Julian first saw the face of Jesus.

* * *

Some visions of Jesus, like those of John of Patmos and Hildegard, are grand, bigger than life. While Julian's too was expansive, elaborate even, it was astonishingly intimate. At the beginning, Jesus shows her "a ghostly sight of his humble love," and one thought immediately occurs to her: "He is our clothing, for love wraps us and enfolds us, holds us and guides us, clings to us for tender love, so that he may never leave us. . . . He is everything that is good."[12] Julian's Jesus does not have a sword coming from his mouth, nor is he surrounded by the blazing,

Living Light of God. He is, instead, as close to us as our own skin, embodying warmth and protection and presence.

After seeing the blood stream down the face of Jesus on the crucifix, a series of interactions takes place. First, Jesus shows her something—a small, round object, "a little thing, the size of a hazel nut," she writes, and he places it in the palm of her hand. "What is this?" she wonders, and Jesus, knowing her thoughts, answers, "It is all that is made."[13]

Looking at it, Julian is fearful, alarmed that something so small and fragile could be easily dropped and lost. Sensing her anxiety, Jesus says, "It lasts, and ever shall, because God loves it. And so, all things have their being in the love of God." Julian then writes that she understood this to mean three things: "God made it . . . God loves it . . . God keeps it."[14]

After a time, the face on the crucifix becomes so drenched in blood that it seems to disappear, and in the darkness, Julian sees "God in a point, that is to say, in my understanding, by which sight I saw that he is in all things." But the thought occurs to her, "What is sin?" Now that God is contained within a point in her mind, where does sin fit in . . . "for in all this was sin not shown"?[15] This question is much larger than it seems. For Julian, the word *sin* implied everything wrong in the world. For her, natural disasters, disease, pain, death, evil—all were the result of Adam and Eve's sin in the garden of Eden, all the consequences of the fall. In asking this question, Julian is asking about what philosophers call the problem of pain and suffering.

The answer comes: "See, I am God; see, I am in all things; see, I do all things; see, I never removed my hands from my works, nor never shall, without end; see, I lead all things to the end I ordained for them from the beginning, by the same might, wisdom, and love with which I made them. How should anything be amiss?"[16]

This seems to satisfy her, but later in her vision, she seems to realize that Jesus's answer doesn't really explain things. Though he asserted that nothing is amiss, why, she wonders, does she herself still experience sin and pain? It's one thing to see things from an eternal perspective, but that still doesn't make day-to-day living any easier.

Jesus responds by explaining to her the meaning of his own suffering on the cross, his death and resurrection, and at this point, he reassures her with what has become the most quoted sentence from Julian's magnificent book: "All shall be well, and all shall be well, and all manner of thing shall be well."[17]

As comforting as that phrase is, another passage deals with Julian's question even more powerfully. After Julian has contemplated the sufferings of Christ, she concludes, "No tongue can tell, no heart can comprehend the pains that our Lord suffered for us. . . . But the love that made him suffer all this passes so far above his pains as heaven is above the earth."

Then a change in mood takes place. The agonized Jesus on the crucifix, on whose face she has focused her meditations, is suddenly filled with "blissful cheer." Says Julian, "The changing of his mood changed mine and I was as glad and merry as it was possible to be."

Jesus then has a question for her: "Are you well paid that I suffered for you?"

She replies, "Yes, good Lord. . . . Thank you, good Lord, blessed are you."

"If you are paid," Jesus says, "then I am paid. It is a joy and a bliss and an endless pleasure to me that ever I suffered for you, and if I might have suffered more, I would have."[18]

✳ ✳ ✳

No, Julian never received a definitive answer to the age-old problem of suffering, sin, and evil, despite having the great presence of mind to ask those questions in the midst of her illness. She was a mystic, after all, and the answers she received are far better than any philosophy book could provide—that is, Jesus's assurance that she is loved and that he can be trusted.

Her trust in the Jesus who appeared to her was not like the naive faith of those who refuse to believe that evil exists or that our world is somehow "the best of all possible worlds" that God could have created. Julian knew the terrifying realities of her own time all too well. She had survived wave after wave of the Black Death, lived during the devastation of the Hundred Years' War, and understood that religious people had been persecuted and even burned at the stake for their faith. She was not averting her gaze and refusing to see the pain. Rather, she lived with the unanswered questions because she trusted in the one who had said to her, "All shall be well."

At one point, God gives her this further assurance: "You shall not be overcome." She qualifies this by adding, "He did not say, 'You shall not be tempted; you shall not face trials; you shall not suffer from disease.' Rather he said, 'You shall not be overcome.'" And then, she concludes, "soon after, all grew dark, and I saw no more."[19]

Julian's vision took place in extremis, like Stephen's and Jerome's, which is not to say that it was an aberration. She remembered it clearly and in detail as one remembers a complex dream—and, as modern psychoanalysts suggest, dreams are full of significance. Only the dreamer can truly interpret a dream, said Freud, and that is what Julian did for much of the rest of her life, though her vision had a deep and powerful meaning not only for her but for the world at large.

*** *** ***

These few scenes from Julian's remarkable book only hint at its riches. It is a six-hundred-year-old document that speaks to our time even more powerfully than it did to Julian's. Apart from her local reputation as a spiritual counselor, she was relatively unknown in her time. Her book didn't find its way into print until 1670 (figure 11.2), two and a half centuries after her death, and even then, it attracted little attention. The first modern-English edition didn't appear until 1877,[20] and she only began to attain general notice in religious circles when Evelyn Underhill included Julian in her seminal 1911 study *Mysticism: A Study in the Nature and Development of Man's Spiritual Consciousness*. Underhill calls Julian "the most attractive, if not the greatest of the English mystics."[21]

Although neither the Roman Catholic nor Anglican Churches have officially declared her a saint . . . and although no major biographies were written about her . . . and although no church statuary or stained glass windows were erected in her honor before the twentieth century—still, one honor sets her above all others. She has been beloved by poets. More than anyone, she is the songbirds' saint.

W. B. Yeats carried a copy of *Revelations* in his pocket, and he wrote that Julian was the embodiment of "that life where passion and thought are one."[22] After reading Evelyn Underhill's books, T. S. Eliot fell in love with Julian's writings and quoted her in the final lines of "Little Gidding."[23] W. H. Auden references her in "Memorial for the City."[24] Thomas Merton

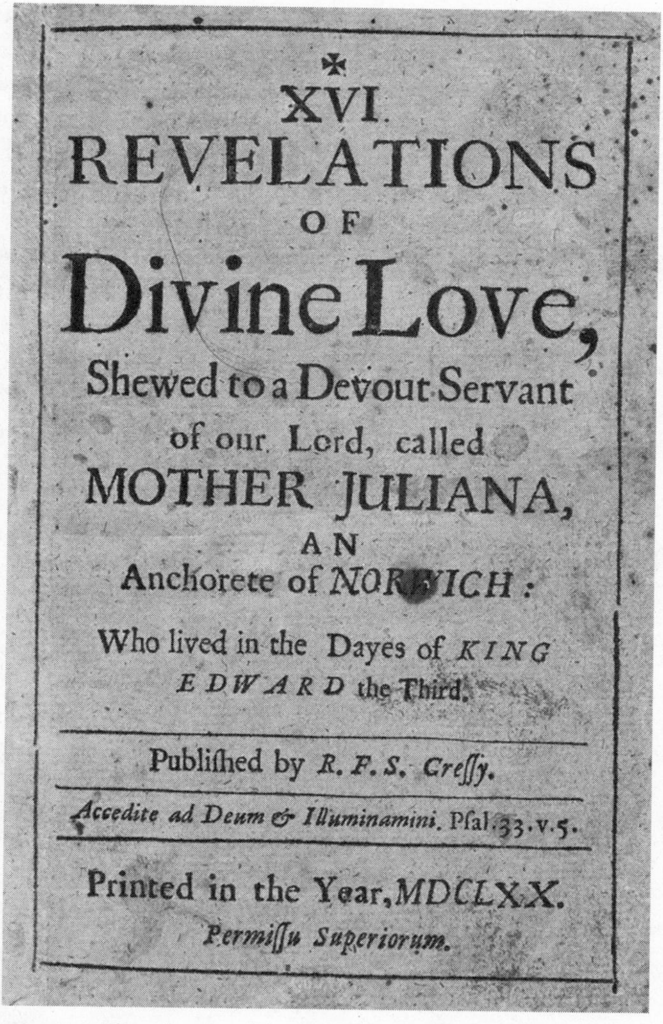

✠

XVI
REVELATIONS
OF
Divine Love,
Shewed to a Devout Servant
of our Lord, called
MOTHER JULIANA,
AN
Anchorete of *NORWICH*:

Who lived in the Dayes of *KING EDWARD* the Third.

Publiſhed by *R. F. S. Creſſy.*

Accedite ad Deum & Illuminamini. Pſal. 33. v. 5.

Printed in the Year, *MDCLXX.*

Permiſſu Superiorum.

Figure 11.2. The title page of the first edition of Julian's *Revelations of Divine Love*, published in 1670 wrote, "Julian is without a doubt one of the most wonderful of all Christian voices,"[25] and he alludes to her in his prose poem "Hagia Sophia."[26] Denise Levertov wrote two poems about her;[27] Malcolm Guite wrote a sonnet for her;[28] and songwriter Sydney Carter, famous for penning the words to "Lord of the Dance," set some of Julian's words to music: "Ring out, bells of Norwich . . . / All shall be well again, I know."[29]

But she was also the songbirds' saint in a more literal sense. At one point in the Long Text of *Revelations*, Julian hears an abrasive noise that sounds like a blacksmith's bellows. Jesus, in her vision, then fine-tunes the sound so she can hear it more clearly. First, it sounds like the cooing of a dove, then like the song of a robin redbreast. Thereafter and throughout her life, whenever she heard the sounds of birds, no matter how oppressed she felt by the weight of pain and suffering in the world, she would reflect on what Jesus told her about the meaning of the songs of birds: "By these tokens may you know well that I love you."[30]

12

"IT IS FULL MERRY IN HEAVEN"

Margery Kempe

Julian's anchorhold was a one-room cell just large enough to eat, sleep, and pray in. Her cell shared one wall with the exterior of St. Julian's Church; the other three were made of mortared flint, a kind of rough quartz that was plentiful around Norwich.

Although Julian lived there by herself, she was not alone. On most days, she could hear the clamor of the farmers and river merchants—and smell the livestock—at the docks on the River Ware, just a few hundred feet from where she lived. Wagons and barrows rumbled past throughout the day. Norwich was a dominant player in Europe's wool trade and about as bustling a commercial city at the time as can be imagined.[1]

Cut into the wall she shared with the church was a small aperture that looked into the interior of the main chapel, and through this beveled window, she could hear the shuffling of the congregants' feet and observe Mass while remaining largely unseen. Below the opening stood a low chair with a high back, called a prie-dieu, on which Julian could kneel in prayer and also receive the Eucharist from the priest inside the church.

The cell had one door and most likely a southeast-facing window to catch the warmth of the morning sun, though a thick, dark curtain usually hung across the window, especially when she spoke with those who came for spiritual guidance. Her reputation as a counselor attracted many visitors, especially women.

One of these was Margery Kempe.

* * *

Margery Kempe was born around 1373, within months of the day on which Julian experienced her sixteen revelations. Margery's father, John Brunham, was a moderately well-to-do merchant who became the mayor of their hometown of Bishop's Lynn, Norfolk, as well as a member of Parliament.

Little is known of her childhood, though she was most likely high-strung, mischievous, and like most girls of her era, illiterate. This last detail is notable because she would grow up to write what is now considered the first autobiography in the English language—though the word *write* is not quite apt. She dictated *The Book of Margery Kempe* first to a local man, possibly one of her sons, and later to a priest. Referring to herself throughout in the third person, often as "this creature," she told story after story of her visions, travails, and pilgrimages—not in chronological order "but just as the matter came to this creature's mind."[2]

The great London printer Wynkyn de Worde published extracts from her book in a compilation in 1501, and in 1521, printer Henry Pepwell added to those earlier portions in a volume called *Dyvers Doctrynes* (figure 12.1). Still, it was not until the 1930s that the complete manuscript of Margery's book was discovered and subsequently issued.

From her writing, we know Margery loved being read to, especially from the works of Richard Rolle and Walter Hilton,

Figure 12.1. Jesus in torment, from printer Henry Pepwell's *Dyvers Doctrynes* (1521). The poem reads, "O man unkind / Bear in thy mind / My pains' smart / And ye shall find / Me true and kind / Lo here my heart."[3]

two of the most revered mystical writers of fourteenth-century England. Also among her favorites was Bridget of Sweden's *Revelations*, made up almost entirely of Bridget's detailed and complex visionary dialogues with God, Jesus, and Mary— conversations that began when Bridget was ten years old. The book had a profound effect on Margery.

The most transformative period in Margery's life took place in the early 1390s, when she was about twenty-one. A year or so after marrying a local man named John Kempe, she gave birth to their first child. The experience shattered her. Emotionally drained and confused, she experienced almost continuous demonic attacks, spending more than six months being besieged by "devils opening their mouths all alight with burning flames of fire, as if they would have swallowed her in, sometimes pawing at her, sometimes threatening her, sometimes pulling her and hauling her about."[4] They taunted her for her spiritual weakness and urged her to desert her faith. As she daily grew more spiteful toward her family, she began to harm herself physically, biting her own hands and arms and ripping her skin with her fingernails. Her family, thinking her mad, tied her up and locked her in a room for her own protection. While she lay bound and isolated, something happened. She described it this way:

> Our merciful Lord Christ Jesus . . . appeared to his creature who had forsaken him, in the likeness of a man, the most seemly, most beauteous, and the most amiable that ever might be seen with man's eye, clad in a mantle of purple silk, sitting upon her bedside, looking upon her with so blessed a countenance that she was strengthened in all her spirits, and he said to her these

words: "Daughter, why have you forsaken me, and I never forsook you?"

And as soon as he had said these words, she saw truly how the air opened as bright as any lightning, and he ascended up into the air, not hastily and quickly, but beautifully and gradually, so that she could clearly behold him in the air until it closed up again.[5]

She soon convinced her husband and family that she was cured, and she begged for their forgiveness. Although the devils ceased to bother her, two new temptations assailed her, vanity and pride. She began dressing in costly clothes and coveting her neighbors' possessions. Feeling ashamed that her husband was not nearly as prosperous as her own father, she went into business for herself. She tried brewing ale at first, which was not unusual at that time, since after the plague, many women worked at traditionally male trades. But the venture failed. She then built a horse mill to grind grain, but the horses refused to cooperate, so that business too collapsed.

Suspecting that these failures were a divine punishment, she vowed to practice the most severe austerities, in effect punishing herself. She discarded her fine clothing, fasted, prayed day and night, went to confession two or three times daily, and wore haircloth garments under her clothes. Although she begged her husband to cease having sex with her, their family continued to grow. (They eventually had fourteen children.) By weeping openly in public, falling prostrate on the ground, loudly pleading for God to forgive her, she acquired a reputation as a religious fanatic, even alienating her closest friends, who thought she was making a hypocritical show of piety. On top of all this, she was resisting the temptation to have an affair with a man who attended her church.

Then, a few days before Christmas, as Margery was praying at the altar of a church in Bishop's Lynn, Jesus appeared to her again. First, he reassured her that "when you pass out of this world, within the twinkling of an eye, you shall have the bliss of heaven. . . . I am your love and shall be your love without end." (Margery later had that last phrase engraved on a ring as a token of her spiritual marriage to Christ.)

Then he addressed her austerities. They'd gone too far, he told her. She should moderate them, since they too exhibit a kind of pride. "You have a hair-shirt on your back," he said. "I want you to leave off wearing it, and I shall give you a hair-shirt in your heart which shall please me much more than all the hair-shirts in the world." He advised her to limit her meals so that she might take Communion more often. He then asked her to cease her "praying of many beads" by six o'clock each night so that she might simply lie in bed and "think such thoughts as I shall put into your mind."[6] Don't pray rote prayers, he was telling her, but simply think about him instead. Again, Jesus had kept her from harming herself.

* * *

Years later, in 1413, at the age of forty and just as she was about to set out on a pilgrimage to Rome, Margery came to Norwich to sit at the window of Julian's tiny cell. "Dame Jelyan"[7] (as Margery's scribe spelled the name) was seventy years old.

Margery wanted advice. Unlike Julian, whose visions were limited to a two-day period during a severe illness—in extremis—

Margery's persisted for twenty years, accompanied by wildly ecstatic episodes and interspersed with uncontrollable weeping. Margery wanted to know if this was normal in a life devoted to Christ or "if she had been deceived by any delusions."[8]

She'd stopped first at the cell of a Carmelite monk in Norwich named William Southfield. After listening patiently, he assured her that her visions were signs of "the Holy Ghost plentifully working his grace in your soul."[9]

Comforted but hoping for more confirmation, Margery sought out Norwich's famous anchoress. Sitting outside Julian's thick-curtained window, she described her visions and her emotional outbursts and asked "if there was any deception in them, for the anchoress," wrote Margery, "was expert is such things and could give good advice."[10]

Julian advised her to "be obedient to the will of our Lord and fulfill with all her might whatever he put into her soul, if it were not against the worship of God and the profit of her fellow Christians." Furthermore, Julian affirmed, "when God visits a creature with tears of contrition, devotion, or compassion, he may and ought to believe that the Holy Ghost lives in his soul . . . for St. Jerome says that tears torment the devil more than do the pains of hell."[11]

That was exactly what Margery Kempe had hoped to hear. She wrote, "Great was the holy conversation that the anchoress and this creature had through the talking of the love of our Lord Jesus Christ."[12] The visit lasted several days. With that confidence, Margery continued her trip to Rome, though by the time she returned a year or so later, Julian had most likely died.

✳ ✳ ✳

So here's a "what-if."

What if the woman inside Julian's cell had not been a brilliant Christian mystic but a modern psychotherapist transported six centuries back in time? What would the diagnosis have been? Intrigued by this question, I actually presented the facts of Margery's case to a trained counselor, and the answers were alarming.[13]

One of the first questions a therapist asks is, "Do you hear voices?" and if the answer is yes, then the next question is often, "Do the voices tell you what to do?"

You don't have to read more than a dozen pages of *The Book of Margery Kempe* to know how she would have answered. Yes, of course, God and Jesus spoke to her audibly and constantly, and she had committed herself to doing exactly what those voices told her to do.

Although we know nothing of her early life, it is likely that after the birth of her first child, Margery suffered from what is called *puerperal psychosis*, a rarer condition than ordinary postpartum depression. According to the medical literature, the symptoms of puerperal psychosis, if not treated early, can result in lifelong complications, including hallucinations, delusions, paranoia, rapid bipolar mood swings, loss of inhibitions, irritability, self-harm, and suicidal thoughts. At one point or other, Margery experienced all of these.

One online diagnostic site says of women suffering from these hallucinations, "The delusions and beliefs make sense to her; they feel very real to her and are often religious."[14] Studies show that about half of all women who experience this form of mental illness after the birth of their first child will experience it with subsequent births.[15] Keep in mind that Margery gave birth to at least thirteen more children.

So were Margery's visions psychosomatic, figments of a diseased imagination?

First, we need to acknowledge how much suffering has been caused by truly disturbed individuals—the unbalanced, the self-deluded, the leaders of cults—who believe God has spoken to them and ordered them to impose their wills on others. Delusions of that kind destroy lives, the person's own and the lives of those around them.

But then I remind myself that if God can reach people through their own inborn conscience, as in Jerome's case, then it is possible that God can reach some people through their mental disturbances, even the most severe. God and psychosis are not necessarily always mutually exclusive. The fruits of Margery's many visions were largely positive. Although she occasionally used her assumed divine authority to criticize others, to point out their sins and shortcomings, her visions were nearly always healing . . . both for herself and for others.

✳ ✳ ✳

Like Anthony of Egypt and Martin of Tours, Julian and Margery make a striking contrast. While Julian had a singular series of grand visions that took place over two days, Margery had countless visions throughout her life, often about simple day-to-day things—for instance, about her attitudes toward specific people, about her sex life, or even about not getting seasick while on a ship.

Julian spent her life in solitude, in contemplation, meditating on the meaning of her visions, while Margery seems to have accepted each one of hers in the moment and moved on. And she "moved on" quite literally. She traveled widely, went on pilgrimages to Rome, the Holy Land, Spain, and Germany, interacting with people, actively engaging, evangelizing, and like Hildegard, preaching, which was still illegal for women at the time. Arrested and jailed for heresy on several occasions, Margery was always able to convince her accusers that she was innocent.

Julian's visions, like Martin's, were outer directed, intended to help fellow Christians understand the grand and mysterious ways of God. Her sixteen mystical revelations, which began with the bloodied face of Jesus, grew into one of the most expansive and beautiful statements of devotional theology ever written. Her vision, whether you believe it was divinely inspired or simply an amazing dream in extremis, has had a profound impact on lovers of medieval literature, on Christian thinkers both Catholic and Protestant. Thomas Merton once wrote, "Julian of Norwich is, with Newman, the greatest English theologian."[16] Her vision was large and orchestral, like one of Bach's Passions.

Margery's visions, by contrast, were more parochial, more inner directed. They were targeted at her own immediate spiritual challenges, beginning with the birth of her first child—not that her experiences aren't an encouragement to her readers, but they are more diffuse, less intended to make grand generalizations about the nature of the divine. Her visions were localized, homey, like a collection of folk tunes rather than a symphony.

Whether we view her visions as revelations or symptoms of psychosis, we can't help but sense a spark of divine fire in Margery. As irritating as her constant public weeping and aggressively overt piety were, we have to admire her plucky, indomitable (if erratic) character and her fearlessness in asserting her rights as a woman living in a culture that was averse to granting women any such rights—the right to start her own business, the right to control her body sexually, the right to travel where and when she saw fit, the right to preach, even the right to tell male religious leaders to their faces that they were hypocrites. Margery may be one of the best examples of William Blake's proverb "The road of excess leads to the palace of wisdom."[17] Margery was a one-woman spiritual whirlwind. Eccentric. Confrontational. Devout. Passionate. Human.

My favorite scene from *The Book of Margery Kempe* is a cozily domestic one from chapter 3, a scene reminiscent of Julian's auditory hallucination of the birds: "One night, as this creature lay in bed with her husband, she heard a melodious sound so sweet and delectable that she thought she had been in paradise. And immediately she jumped out of bed and said, 'Alas that I ever sinned! It is full merry in heaven!'"[18]

I can picture her exuberance . . . and her husband's exasperation, since he'd probably been asleep. But forever after, according to Margery, whenever she felt defeated or oppressed, she would simply recall that dream of divine music and repeat to herself that hopeful, healing phrase like a mantra: "It is full merry in heaven!"

PART FOUR
TRAILBLAZERS

13

QUAKERS, SHAKERS, AND GROUNDBREAKERS

George Fox, Jacob Boehme, Public Universal Friend, Mother Ann Lee, Emanuel Swedenborg, and the Spanish Mystics

"Here the Lord opened unto me, and let me see a great people in white raiment by a river side, *coming to the Lord*." These words of George Fox (figure 13.1), the founder of the Religious Society of Friends—the Quakers—describe a life-changing experience he had in the spring of 1652. While traveling through rural Lancashire, England, he was, as he said, "moved of the Lord to go up to the top" of a large bluff called Pendle Hill, though only "with difficulty, it was so very steep and high." There it was "opened unto" him that God was laying before him "in what places he had a great people to be gathered . . . people in white raiment . . . *coming to the Lord*."[1]

He was twenty-seven at the time. Having been tormented by spiritual doubts throughout his youth—and finding few answers from the Anglican priests and Puritan ministers (one of whom advised him to "take tobacco and sing psalms"[2])—he came, little by little, to formulate his own personal brand of

Figure 13.1. A portrait of George Fox (seventeenth century), possibly by Dutch portraitist Peter Lely

QUAKERS, SHAKERS, AND GROUNDBREAKERS | 173

Christian belief. Among its tenets are the following: that the church is not a building or a set of doctrines but a people; that creeds, rituals, and sacraments are largely irrelevant to faith; that preachers are raised up by God rather than churches or schools; and most importantly, that Jesus dwells within each believer's heart as "an inward light"—a light that is crucial to interpreting Scripture and making day-to-day ethical decisions.

The Pendle Hill vision fired his passion to broaden his ministry, and within decades, Quakerism flourished throughout England and spread to the American colonies and across the world. But Pendle Hill was symptomatic of something well beyond the Quakers. The rumblings of a new spiritual torrent were being felt across Europe, as if the heavens had opened, and those who were neither Catholics nor monastics, and without the intervention of priests or ministers or religious training, were now freed to experience a new kind of intimacy with God, which included visions of angels, heaven, and Jesus. While Fox was by no means alone in having such visions, nor was he the first, he represented a fresh approach to faith, a uniquely Protestant form of mysticism that emerged in the centuries immediately after the Reformation.

While many religious communities, like the Bohemian Brethren and the Moravians, had broken with the Roman Catholic Church in the 1400s, historians conventionally date the beginning of the Protestant Reformation as 1517, when Martin Luther issued his Ninety-Five Theses. Four years later, in 1521, the Holy Roman emperor Charles V issued the Edict of Worms, which officially declared Martin Luther and his followers as heretics, though by then, the tide of dissent had turned, and others followed in Luther's wake. In 1534, with the English Parliament's passage of the Act of Supremacy, Henry VIII officially declared himself the head of the Church of England, displacing the pope. In 1536, John Calvin published his *Institutes of the Christian Religion*, which espoused doctrines that veered sharply from Catholic orthodoxy, and in 1560, John Knox led the reform movement in Scotland by issuing the *First Book of Discipline*, which led to the formation of the Presbyterian Church.

While the early Protestant Reformers largely discounted mystical experiences, that dismissal was short-lived. Protestantism would likely not have survived without those who experienced such visions. Writer Evelyn Underhill referred to this period of renewal as "the awakening of the self . . . the shifting of the field of consciousness from lower to higher levels,"[3] or to borrow Lawrence Ferlinghetti's phrase, "a new rebirth of wonder."[4]

Here, then, are a few quick sketches of some of these new Protestant mystics, all of whom had visionary encounters with Jesus.

* * *

Among the earliest was German shoemaker-turned-philosopher Jacob Boehme, who, in the late 1500s and early 1600s, began to outline a complex mystical theology that was at once rooted in Lutheran doctrine but also unorthodox enough to create controversy. Since childhood, Boehme had experienced visions; like Hildegard, he often had the feeling of being enwrapped within a bright Divine Light—enraptured. His first book, *Aurora*, was in part an attempt to theologize his visions of God and Jesus. In his quirky, enigmatic style, he wrote, "When the light, which is the Son of God, shineth into the sea of nature, then it getteth its *yellowish* or whitish colour, which I cannot compare to anything; you must be content to stay or tarry with this aspect or vision, till you *come into* the other life."[5] Boehme sensed this divine presence as "a most lovely, pleasant, soft, gentle, mild, meek warmth, an effluence or going forth of light, which expandeth itself, rising up *from* the light, wherein the source or fountain of love springeth up."[6] This echoes what the psalmist once wrote: "In your light we see light."[7]

Boehme's book, which opens with an extended metaphor of the spiritual life as a tree, is thought to be the first example of what we now call automatic writing—that is, when the writer acts as an involuntary scribe, a mere note taker, for external spiritual forces. Boehme explained, "Art has not wrote this . . . but all was ordered according to the direction of the Spirit. . . . That fire comes and goes as a sudden shower."[8] *Aurora*, with its swirl of layered symbols, is dauntingly complex, even hermetic in places, though its influence was enormous. Among the later thinkers who found inspiration in his work were Isaac Newton and Georg Wilhelm Friedrich Hegel and poets John Milton, William Blake, and W. B. Yeats. John Wesley, though, was not as impressed, for after reading Boehme's commentary on the Book of Genesis, Wesley wrote, "It is most sublime nonsense; inimitable bombast; fustian not to be paralleled."[9]

* * *

Boehme's books, which were available in English translation while George Fox was beginning his ministry, attracted many of the early Quakers. They found inspiration, as one scholar said, in his emphasis on the "universality of the gift of the Spirit, and of the constant inner light, and motion, and teaching of the Spirit in the soul of each individual believer."[10] Or as Boehme himself phrased it, "The spirit of man is descended not only from the stars and elements, but there is hidden therein a spark of the light and power of God."[11] Like Boehme, the Quakers believed that every person, indwelt by that Holy spark, could find intimacy with God, each believer being a channel of divine communication . . . a mysticism for the masses.

This belief was central to Quaker worship. Fox encouraged his followers to "receive and go with a message . . . to have a word from the Lord as the prophets and apostles had."[12] In their gatherings, Quakers would sit silently until some person or other felt a "quaking" in their soul, the urge to speak a message that God intended the group to hear. As American Quaker John Woolman described it in his journal, he attended meetings so he could wait on "the language of the pure spirit which inwardly moves upon the heart . . . and to wait in silence sometimes many weeks together until I felt that rise which prepares the creature to stand like a trumpet, through which the Lord speaks to his flock."[13]

With the Quakers, the floodgates seemed to open. Ordinary believers now had permission to invite God to speak not only to them but through them, to represent Christ in person. Unsurprisingly, Quakers were reviled by many, persecuted by some, and even martyred.

✳ ✳ ✳

In the century after the founding of the Religious Society of Friends, some Quakers received such startling visions that they were moved to form their own separate communities to explore still more radical "inward lights." One of these pioneers, whom we would now refer to as a nonbinary individual, became one of the most popular preachers in Revolutionary-era America.

This person bore the name Public Universal Friend, or just the Friend.

The Friend was born Jemima Wilkinson in Rhode Island in 1752 and grew up attending the local Quaker meeting. At twenty-three, she came under the influence of a group called the New Light Baptists, or Separates, who believed in living radically holy lives, actively expressing their faith in public, and valuing highly emotional conversion experiences. She was devout, strong-willed, and eager to serve God.

In her midtwenties, she suffered a near-fatal illness, most likely typhus, which is known to cause delirium if left untreated. In Jemima's case, the delirium provoked a life-changing vision, which she described this way (speaking of herself in the third person): "The heavens were open'd and She saw two Archangels descending from the east, with golden crowns upon there [sic] heads, clothed in long white Robes, down to the feet; Bringing a sealed Pardon from the living God; and putting their trumpets to their mouth, proclaimed, saying, Room, Room, Room, in the many Mansions of eternal glory for Thee and everyone. . . . For everyone that will come, may come, and partake of the waters of life freely, which is offered to Sinners without money, and without price."[14] While at first it seems as if Jesus does not appear in this vision, he was present nonetheless. Jemima believed herself to be Jesus. As she wrote, "The Spirit of Life from God . . . was waiting to assume the Body which God had prepared for the Spirit to dwell in. . . . And then taking her leave of the family between nine & ten in the morning dropt the dying flesh and yielded up the Ghost. And according to the declaration of the Angels,—the Spirit took full possession of the Body it now animates."[15] She thought she had died and, like Lazarus, had been brought back to life, though in her case, it was so that Jesus might take possession of the revived body and minister directly to the world a second time.

Upon recovering, she declared to her friends and family that Jemima Wilkinson was dead and that the person who now stood before them was to be called Public Universal Friend (figure 13.2). The Friend, who now dressed in plain, androgynous clothing and was declaring to be neither male nor female, claimed not to recognize any family or friends. The following Sunday, the Friend went to a local meeting house to preach, and so powerful was the message that an ardent circle of devotees soon formed.

The Friend preached throughout New England, and eventually, the followers adopted the name of the Society of Universal Friends. Apart from the Friend's claim to be Jesus reincarnate, the preaching was broadly in accord with traditional Quakerism, the most hopeful message being that no one—absolutely no one—was excluded from God's kingdom, or in the phrase most often associated with the Friend, "there is Room Enough."[16] Such hopeful tidings had far-reaching appeal in the socially unsettled years around the American Revolution.

The sect was often vilified, and even the Friend's most sympathetic modern biographer, Herbert Wisbey, considers the case to be one of "messianic megalomania."[17] The group vanished within a few decades after its founder's death in 1819.

∗ ∗ ∗

Another Quaker woman, an older contemporary of the Friend's, was also believed to be Jesus in the flesh, though this person had a much wider and more lasting impact. Ann Lee was born in

Figure 13.2. Public Universal Friend, from David Hudson's unflattering biography *History of Jemima Wilkinson: A Preacheress of the Eighteenth Century* (1821)

1736 in Manchester, England, and was raised a Quaker. In her midtwenties, her father arranged her marriage, much against her will, to a man named Abraham Stanley. The couple was unhappy, and although they had four children, all died in infancy, tragedies that would profoundly affect Ann's view not only of sexual relations but of faith itself.

In the midst of her distress, she found comfort in an offshoot Quaker sect called the Bolton Society, led by a couple named Jane and James Wardley. Jane in particular was subject to intense visions and came to believe that the second coming of Jesus was imminent. Since according to Genesis, "God created man in his own image . . . ; male and female created he them,"[18] Jane Wardley reasoned that Christ would next return as a woman.

Worship at the Wardleys' involved "mighty trembling . . . singing, shouting, leaping for joy . . . with great agitation of body and limbs, shaking, running, and walking the floor . . . like clouds agitated with a mighty wind."[19] Although the group adopted the name the United Society of Believers in Christ's Second Coming, their energetic style of worship earned them the moniker Shaking Quakers, or simply Shakers. In time, Ann herself would become one of the group's leading members.

While the Shakers advocated hard work, abstinence, honesty, charitable service, and nonviolence, much as the Quakers did, some of their additional tenets caused controversy. They believed in the unqualified equality of the sexes, a communal sharing of all work and property, an openness to ecstatic visions and spiritual gifts, and most controversial of all, strict celibacy. This last tenet, they felt, was essential to holiness. As a result of such beliefs, the Shakers were repeatedly persecuted and attacked, and Ann Lee was even jailed for a time.

In 1770, shortly after her release from jail, she received a "special manifestation of Divine Light," a vision in which she was told that she would henceforth be known as Mother Ann and that she would be the Shakers' chief spiritual guide. "I saw in vision the Lord Jesus in his kingdom and glory," she wrote. "I felt the power of God flow into my soul like a fountain of living water. From that day I have been able to take up a full cross against all the doleful works of the flesh."[20] Although Mother Ann never declared herself to be Jesus incarnate, her followers assumed her to be his female manifestation on earth—the promised second coming.

Four years later, Mother Ann was directed by another vision to sail to America with a few adherents and to establish the Shaker way of faith in the New World. The final ten years of her life were spent preaching and establishing fresh colonies throughout New England, and even after her death in 1784, her followers continued to plant communities as far west as Ohio and Kentucky.

Shaker influence on American culture has been enormous. The group accepted Blacks as equal members and readily adopted orphans. During the Civil War, they cared for the wounded of both armies and were known for their ingenuity, commercial savvy, and technical skill. They traded seeds, furniture, wooden boxes, and household goods. Shaker inventors—including women—devised such now common items as the flat broom, cut nails, adjustable door transoms, round barns, paper packaging for seeds, pegboards, and much more. One of these inventors, a woman named Sister Tabitha Babbitt, came up with the idea of the circular saw after having a dream about a revolving wheel that could cut wood. And of course, the Shakers were famous for their simple, exquisite furniture. The group lasted well into the twentieth century, though in swiftly diminishing numbers, and to this day, there are still reports of isolated Shakers living in New England.

✳ ✳ ✳

No account of Protestant mystics can ignore eighteenth-century Swedish scientist and theologian Emanuel Swedenborg (figure 13.3). Born in 1688, he was, like Jacob Boehme, raised in

Figure 13.3. Emanuel Swedenborg (1766), portrait attributed to Swedish artist Per Krafft the Elder

a Lutheran family, but unlike the German shoemaker Boehme, Swedenborg was highly educated, graduating from Uppsala University in 1709. As a writer and scholar, he proved to be a brilliant polymath, delving into physics, engineering, mathematics, geology, philosophy, biology, and other subjects, taking a special interest in human anatomy, though largely because he was intent on proving the existence of the soul. While he dabbled in theology as a young man, he didn't fully turn his attention to religion and metaphysics until he was fifty-seven . . . when he had an extraordinary, life-altering visionary encounter with God.

In 1744, he began to experience disturbing dreams, which he carefully recorded in a notebook. Jesus appeared in some of them, while others were highly sexual in nature. The dreams continued until one evening in April 1745, when, while dining at an inn in London, the dreams came to life. As he related to a friend, "Towards the end of the meal I noticed a kind of blurring in my vision, it grew dark and I saw the floor covered with the nastiest crawling animals, like snakes, frogs, and creatures of that kind. . . . After a while, the prevailing darkness was quickly dispelled, and I saw a man sitting in a corner of the room. Since I was alone, I was quite frightened when he spoke and said, 'Don't eat so much.' Again it grew dark before my eyes, but just as quickly then became clear. And I found myself alone in the room."

Swedenborg returned to his lodgings, terrified, only to find the strange man there: "I was not frightened then. He said that he was *the Lord God*, the creator and redeemer of the world, and that he had chosen me to explain the spiritual content of the Scriptures for mankind, and that he himself would explain to me what I should write on this subject. That same night, the spiritual world of heaven and hell was opened to me, where I recognized many acquaintances of all estates."[21]

Swedenborg spent the rest of his life chronicling his spiritual adventures as he journeyed through heaven and hell, speaking, for instance, with the apostle Paul and listening to debates between Descartes and Aristotle, neither of whom he felt had a true grasp of Truth. He wrote complex, ecstatic, speculative commentaries on the Bible and theology with titles like *Heaven and Hell*, *The Last Judgment*, *Apocalypse Revealed*, *Doctrine of Sacred Scripture*, and *True Christian Religion*. His goal was to alter the trajectory, if not the entire underlying structure, of Christianity.

As outlandish as his writings seem, they had a powerful influence on later thinkers as diverse as Johnny Appleseed, William Blake (who wrote, "Swedenborg is the Angel sitting at the tomb; his writings are the linen clothes folded up"[22]), Ralph Waldo Emerson (who called Swedenborg "a colossal soul"[23]), Helen Keller (who credits him with giving her "a precious sense of the divine presence in the world"[24]), W. B. Yeats, Carl Jung, Jorge Luis Borges (who wrote that Swedenborg "knew that Glory and Hell too / Are in your soul"[25]), and Robert Frost (who said his own mother was a Swedenborgian[26]), to name only a few.

✳ ✳ ✳

Of course, the Reformation inspired a Counter-Reformation, in which Roman Catholic mystics played an important role. Especially influential were the Spanish mystics of the sixteenth century, people like Ignatius of Loyola, who wrote the influential

Spiritual Exercises. As a young man filled with dreams of chivalry and warfare, he had a powerful conversion experience during a devastating illness. Shortly afterward, he had a vision of the Virgin Mary holding the infant Jesus, which led Ignatius to lay his dagger and sword on the altar of Christ and give up his chivalric ambitions. He went on to establish the Society of Jesus, better known as the Jesuits.

Another Spanish mystic, Teresa of Ávila, helped reorganize the Carmelite order and became one of Christendom's most beloved mystical writers. After experiencing repeated ecstasies that she believed were prompted by Christ's presence, she authored such devotional classics as *The Interior Castle* and *The Way of Perfection.* Describing one of her many visions, she wrote, "It pleased our Lord, one day that I was in prayer, to show me His Hands, and His Hands only. The beauty of them was so great that no language can describe it. . . . A few days later, I saw His Divine Face, and I was utterly entranced."[27]

John of the Cross, yet another Spaniard of that time, was a Carmelite priest and close friend of Teresa's. He wrote commentaries as well as devotional poetry that leaned heavily on erotic imagery. He is most remembered for his profoundly moving work *The Dark Night of the Soul,* which was composed as a commentary on one of his own poems. Like Teresa, he was effective—and highly controversial—in his efforts to reform the Carmelite order. He was even imprisoned for a time by his religious adversaries.

Although he generally discouraged the pursuit of visionary experiences, he too once had a startling and unexpected vision of Christ on the cross. In his vision, he believed he was viewing the crucifixion from above. He then drew a remarkable sketch of what he saw (figure 13.4), and five centuries later, that sketch

Figure 13.4. The vision of Christ crucified, drawn by John of the Cross (late 1570s)

became the inspiration for a well-known painting of the crucifixion by Salvador Dalí.

* * *

How do we make sense of this explosion of visionary experience
in the sixteenth, seventeenth, and eighteenth centuries? How
could there be so many dissimilar visions of Jesus during the
Reformation and Counter-Reformation?

Clearly, the experiences were varied, but one common thread
that runs through these stories is the quest for authority. That is,
each vision seemed to give the person experiencing it the authority to shift the Christian faith in a new direction. It's an intriguing pattern, as though each person felt that Jesus was granting
him or her permission to try something new. They were tacitly
claiming that God had given them not only new wine but new
wineskins to put it in.

The Reformation saw the birth of the modern world—with
all its pluralism, commercialism, rationalism, pragmatism—an
era that began with the Renaissance, with ocean exploration
and expanded mercantilism, an era that culminated in the Scientific Revolution, the Enlightenment, and the Industrial Revolution. Gone were the days of a centralized European faith.
Vast disruptive social changes were taking place, and in many
countries, that even looked like total social disintegration—
the dissolution of age-old verities. If faith were to survive,
new approaches—new visions—were needed. The mystics, non-
Catholic and Catholic alike, were formulating a revised faith for
a revolutionized world.

People like the Quakers, Boehme, Mother Ann, Swedenborg,
and the Spanish mystics were attempting to rescue religion from

the looming rationalism of the Enlightenment, from those who would dismiss the possibility that ordinary people can sense the Divine. And only with Jesus's own imprimatur could these fresh interpretations of the old faith be made acceptable to the world at large—or justified to the mystics themselves. The dissonance in their souls was overwhelming. The visions were a psychological necessity.

✳ ✳ ✳

This impulse to make sense of the New World of exploration and the new world of faith also found expression in poetry and fiction, as visions of Jesus became literary rather than literal. It was a Reformation in the arts. For instance, Jesus became the prevailing hero of Milton's 1667 Puritan epic *Paradise Lost*:

> The Father . . . unfoulding bright
> Toward the right hand his Glorie, on the Son
> Blaz'd forth unclouded Deitie; he full
> Resplendent all his Father manifest
> Express'd.[28]

A decade later, in 1678, Puritan John Bunyan took the bold step of envisioning Jesus in his novel *The Pilgrim's Progress* not as a man but allegorically as the "wicket gate," an allusion to Jesus's words "Strait is the gate, and narrow is the way, which leadeth unto life."[29] In Bunyan's allegory, the protagonist, named Christian, appeals to a man called Evangelist to help him with the heavy load that Christian is carrying so that "I might escape the wrath to come."[30]

In the centuries to come, writers as diverse as Lew Wallace, Fyodor Dostoyevsky, and C. S. Lewis were freed to envision a Jesus of the imagination, though few can compare with William Blake, for whom the veil between vision and imagination was rent from top to bottom.

14

TO IMAGINE IS TO SEE
William Blake

If you've been to London, then you know that Westminster Abbey is, more than anywhere in the world, a place of unearthly *presences* . . . strangely palpable and pervasive. "What august Shades at midnight here convene," said one poet of that famous landmark.[1]

Seventeen English monarchs lie buried there, including Edward the Confessor, Richard II, and Henry V. In 1603, Queen Elizabeth I's body was interred in the abbey, though three years later, her coffin was shifted to the nearby tomb occupied by her half sister and nemesis Queen Mary I, and as if to settle the long-standing rivalry between them—or perhaps to conserve space—Elizabeth's coffin was laid directly on top of Mary's.

A half century later, in 1658, the body of the Puritan "Lord Protector of the Commonwealth," Oliver Cromwell, was ceremoniously laid to rest in the abbey, though within three years, upon the restoration of the monarchy that he had violently helped overthrow, Cromwell was unceremoniously exhumed and posthumously hanged as a traitor. His severed head then adorned a tall spike on the roof of nearby Westminster Hall, where it remained on public display for more than twenty years.

Among the many bards whose bones molder in the famous Poets' Corner in the abbey's south transept are Geoffrey Chaucer, Edmund Spenser, Robert Browning, Alfred Lord Tennyson, Thomas Hardy, and Rudyard Kipling. In 1870, Queen Victoria, ignoring Charles Dickens's express wish to be buried near his home at Gad's Hill, ordered that his body be carted more than thirty miles and interred in Poets' Corner beside the other literary greats.

Among the hundreds of graves contained within the abbey are those of scientists Isaac Newton, Charles Darwin, and Stephen Hawking; statesmen William Wilberforce and William Pitt; composer George Frideric Handel; actor Laurence Olivier . . . it is a realm, as I said, of presences.

Still, when I last visited Westminster Abbey, the presence I felt most keenly was that of someone who is not even buried there, whose grave site was unknown until recently: visionary poet and artist William Blake. In my imagination, his spirit is the one that most conspicuously lurks within the grand Purbeck marble walls of London's famous abbey, as if darting in and out among the pillars and tombs like an evanescent Puck.

Why? First, on my previous visits, I'd somehow missed the larger-than-life-size commemorative bronze bust of Blake by twentieth-century sculptor Jacob Epstein, even though it has perched in Poet's Corner like a presiding spirit since 1957. It is unforgettable. What most draws your attention are the intense, visionary eyes that Epstein has given the poet, as if vast, extravagant cosmologies are whirling behind Blake's overbroad forehead. His gaze is tilted slightly upward, and his eyes are ever so faintly misaligned, so it appears as if he's not focused on anything at all but gazing straight through everything, through the "faint shadow" of "this Vegetable Universe," as he said, to heaven itself.[2] It's an uncanny technical effect.

But more than that, I sensed Blake's presence because Westminster Abbey is where he, as a teenager—well before writing some of the most visionary poetry in English and creating some of the most astonishing artwork the world has known—spent many enraptured hours, wandering, sketching, brooding, and even clambering onto the monuments and effigies themselves to get a better view of their antique grandeur.

The abbey in his time was a relatively unpopulated space, more of an oversized reliquary, a mausoleum of English history, of interest primarily to antiquarians. Tourists had to pay a substantial fee to explore its interior, so few came. Only three private religious services were conducted there each week, as well as an occasional funeral. Otherwise, the cavernous and echoing vaults, subchapels, and hallways were often deserted—except for the spellbound Blake.

But he was not just poking around out of curiosity as teenagers do; he was there on assignment. The master engraver to whom Blake was apprenticed, James Basire, had sent him to study the funerary monuments and draw preliminary sketches for engravings to be included in a book called *Sepulchral Monuments in Great Britain*. Blake sketched the effigies of Edward the Confessor; Edward III and his wife, Philippa of Hainault; Richard II; and others. He was even present on May 2, 1774, when the Society of Antiquaries opened the tomb of King Edward I, who had died in 1307. Although the lid of the sarcophagus was removed for only an hour, Blake managed to sketch the tall, elaborately bedecked corpse of the king, whose six-foot-two frame earned him the nickname Longshanks (figure 14.1). "The face," as one of the antiquaries present said of the five-hundred-year-old king, "retained its exact form."[3]

The assignment proved formative. The abbey became Blake's de facto art studio—his first face-to-face contact with some of the finest sculpture, stonework, wood carving, and metalsmithing to be found in England. It left him with an almost furious reverence for Gothic art and religious iconography, passions that would shape the rest of his life. "Grecian is Mathematic Form," he later wrote; "Gothic is Living Form. . . . Living Form is Eternal Existence."[4]

But as aware as we are of Blake's historical presence in Westminster Abbey, it can't compare with what Blake himself must have felt within those walls, for it was there that he experienced

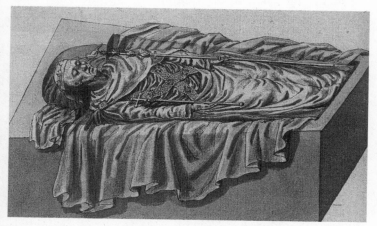

Figure 14.1. Sixteen-year-old William Blake's drawing of the elaborately bedecked body of King Edward I when it was briefly inspected in Westminster Abbey in May 1774

his own formative, overpowering "vision of Christ and the Apostles."[5]

* * *

Since childhood, Blake had been beset by visions. Late in life, when he was asked when these experiences began, his wife reminded him, "You know, dear, the first time you saw God was when you were four years old, and He put His head to the window, and set you a-screaming." When he was about nine, Blake was nearly whipped by his father for claiming he'd seen a tree full of angels on his morning walk, and he once declared that as he watched a group of haymakers at work, he could see "angelic figures" moving among them.[6]

Throughout his life as a poet and artist, such visions were the soul of his work. In his exquisite hand-printed and hand-colored volumes, which came to be called his Prophetic Books, he delineated in word and figure his visions of heavenly beings, his conversations with biblical characters, his visitations from angels and devils, and his vast mythic cosmology. To create these books, Blake used a new method of printing that had itself been revealed to him in a dream—by his deceased brother Robert. In the last decade of his life, Blake sketched a series of "visionary heads" in response to a friend's requests: portraits of, among others, King Solomon; Job; Socrates and Socrates's wife, Xanthippe; Muhammad; the man who built the pyramids; and the man who taught Blake to paint in his dreams. In the Tate Britain museum in London, you can still see Blake's fanciful painting *The Ghost of a Flea*.

So the fact that Blake should have a vision of Christ and the apostles as a teenager is hardly surprising. Although he left no record of his vision, apart from telling a few friends, it seems to have occurred at one of the most formative times in his life, and the abbey itself was the kindling that set this vision alight.

✳ ✳ ✳

For Blake, *imagining* was indistinguishable from *seeing*. To the intensely visually oriented mind of Blake, the imagined world was not only more vibrant but also more real than "this Vegetable Universe" of daily experience. As an older man, he explained this in describing one of his own paintings: "A Spirit and a Vision are not, as the modern philosophy supposes, a cloudy vapor, or a nothing: they are organized and minutely articulated beyond all that the mortal and perishing nature can produce. . . . The painter of this work [Blake himself] asserts that all his imaginations appear to him infinitely more perfect and more minutely organized than any thing seen by his mortal eye. Spirits are organized men"[7]—which explains much of his visionary experience. To imagine is to see.

For him, the statuary in Westminster was alive. Not only was he privileged to see the actual face and body of Edward I—which because of the cool, airtight conditions of the stone tomb had been strangely preserved—but Blake looked upon his own sketches of the funerary monuments not as representations of crumbling stone effigies but as living portraits.

In the abbey, he encountered numerous images of Jesus and the apostles—statues, ornaments, carved panels, stained glass. Upon approaching the building, the first thing Blake would have noticed above the grand double doors of the north entrance were the statues of the twelve apostles, which were a fairly recent addition in his time.[8] Fifty years earlier, famed architect

Christopher Wren had refurbished the exterior, and a sculptor had been commissioned to replace the disintegrating medieval stonework.

Towering above those freshly carved figures was a magnificent rose window, seemingly held aloft by the graceful flying buttresses on either side. The window, also a recent enhancement, was designed by English baroque artist Sir James Thornhill, and the circular kaleidoscope of stained glass panels depicted Jesus and the apostles. Inside, Blake would have encountered Jesuses in nearly every corner and niche, some in stone, others in bronze.

One bust must have made a particularly strong impression. Portraying the head and shoulders of Jesus in white marble and surrounded by a circular frame of gilded stone, the bust was located in an ill-lit hallway near the tomb of a long-dead abbot of Westminster.[9] The piece was sculpted in about 1515 by Florentine artist Pietro Torrigiano, who had been commissioned by a nineteen-year-old King Henry VIII to create a monumental effigy of Henry's father, Henry VII. In the process, Torrigiano created several other works there as well.

Torrigiano portrays Jesus with a number of distinctive features: long hair, parted precisely in the middle, falling in neat, parallel waves to the shoulder with tight pin curls at the ends. The face is impassive, gentle, almost feminine, and the nose long. The beard, like the hair, has a well-defined part in the middle. While these specific features were not uncommon in Florentine depictions of Christ, Blake would have had few other opportunities to study such representations up close.

Modern scholar Mary Ellen Reisner argues that Blake appropriated many visual motifs from the statuary in Westminster Abbey for his later artwork, such as the medieval details in his grand depiction of Chaucer's Canterbury pilgrims.[10] The same process took place in Blake's later depictions of Christ. The facial features that appear in Torrigiano's Christ pop up in nearly all of Blake's images of Jesus, as can be seen in his depiction of *Christ Descending into the Grave*, which appeared in the 1808 edition of Robert Blair's *The Grave: A Poem* (figure 14.2).[11]

But Westminster Abbey did more than fire Blake's imagination; it was where he first seemed to have made a connection between Jesus, as the image of God, and the imagination itself—it was where he developed what would eventually become a rich and complex theology of the imagination. For Blake, Jesus himself is born within the human imagination, living within each person—to such an extent that God's kingdom can only be built by creative people. Christ is the true incarnation of this holy imagination.

Blake articulated this idea many times. In his late forties, for instance, he had a vision of Christ seated in judgment, a vision, as he said, that "appear'd to . . . my Imaginative Eye."[12] He made several attempts to commit that vision to paper and canvas, each version becoming a bit more complex than the one before, culminating in an immense painting, seven feet tall by five feet wide, which he called *A Vision of the Last Judgment*. His intention was to unveil it in 1810 at an exhibition of his work. But because his exhibition of the previous year had been a financial and critical failure, he was forced to cancel this new one. Tragically, his painting, one of the largest he would ever create, was lost and most likely destroyed.

But Blake left a detailed description of the painting, intended for the exhibition catalog, and in that description, we get a sense for not only his approach to the imagination but how he links it specifically to the person of Jesus: "The world of

Figure 14.2. Blake's image of Jesus descending into hell to release the captives. The engraving was made by Italian artist Luigi Schiavonetti for Robert Blair's poem *The Grave: A Poem* (1808).

Imagination is the world of Eternity. . . . All Things are comprehended in their Eternal Forms in the divine body of the Saviour, the True Vine of Eternity, The Human Imagination, who appear'd to Me as Coming to Judgment among his Saints & throwing off the Temporal that the Eternal might be Establish'd."[13]

That comes closest to explaining his vision of Christ and the apostles in Westminster Abbey—an image of Jesus fused with his own artistic imagination, the divine incarnation of his own creative impulses. With this in mind, it is easy to picture the young William Blake excitedly exploring the wonders of that Gothic edifice, thrilled with what he saw both outside of himself and within.

This kind of visionary imagination makes sense to me—the idea that human creativity is a continuation, or extension, of God's creation, what some theologians call "secondary creation." As Samuel Taylor Coleridge wrote, "The IMAGINATION then I consider . . . to be the living Power and prime Agent of all human Perception, and as a repetition in the finite mind of the eternal act of creation in the infinite I AM."[14]

Even when we were children, we were born to create worlds—with blocks or dolls or in the books we read—constructing villages in sandboxes, making tents from blankets, and giving form to things and life to imaginary friends. The most imaginative of us grew up to be artists and novelists and film directors and poets and architects—people cunningly adept at turning the images in their heads into things the rest of us can actually see. Their "Eternal Forms" are embodied—incarnated—in the world.

And so, as with all great artists, this is Blake's most enduring legacy: he was able to incarnate his own visions in poetry and painting so that they might become our visions as well.

15

"I KNOW YOU, AND I DON'T KNOW YOU"

Sojourner Truth

Today, I did something out of the ordinary. On this twenty-first day of September 2020, seven months since the beginning of the COVID-19 pandemic, I made a pilgrimage. My wife, Shelley, and I drove one hour south to the Oak Hill Cemetery in Battle Creek, Michigan. Our destination? The grave of one of the most revered abolitionists, suffragists, and equal rights pioneers of the nineteenth century: Sojourner Truth. The experience was far more emotional than I'd expected.

The afternoon was sunlit, and the air was mild on this last official day of summer. Black squirrels sprinted across the grass and into the trees, and in the distance, a quiet, seemingly slow-motion funeral was in progress, a solemn African American church procession. Emily Dickinson's poem came to mind: "And Mourners to and fro / Kept treading – treading."[1]

A few feet from Truth's grave, Shelley and I sat on the low, tree-shaded wall surrounding the grand mausoleum of C. W. Post (1854–1914), founder of the well-known cereal company. We ate the sandwiches we'd brought. We took photos of Truth's gravestone (figure 15.1), read the historical marker nearby, and watched as the distant mourners eventually dispersed.

Coins lined the base of Truth's monument—apparently a tradition, an acknowledgment that one has made this pilgrimage, as we had, and wishes to impart a blessing of some kind. We left some coins of our own.

The marker said that she died on November 26, 1883, "aged about 105 years," though even more astonishing was her cryptic epitaph: "Is God dead." Despite the lack of punctuation, the syntax suggests a question. A surprising story lurks within those three small words, but to tell it, we need to look at Truth's own journey—which was shaped as much by fable as by fact and which was revolutionized by her own encounter with Jesus.

✳ ✳ ✳

She was born into slavery in upstate New York in about 1797 (she was actually in her mideighties when she died, not 105). Her birth name was Isabella Baumfree, though she was often called simply Bell.

One often-neglected historical fact is that emancipation in many Northern states preceded Lincoln's Emancipation Proclamation of 1862 by only a few decades. In 1800, for instance, New York City was second only to Charleston, South Carolina, in the size of its enslaved population. Although New York State had banned the buying and selling of human beings in 1799, the official declaration of freedom didn't come about in that state until 1817, and the process was designed to extend over ten years. Even after the 1827 deadline, children had to remain in servitude until they reached adulthood.

Figure 15.1. Sojourner Truth's gravestone, Oak Hill Cemetery, Battle Creek, Michigan

Northern slave owners tended to own fewer individuals than their Southern counterparts, often only one or two as household servants, though those individuals were at times subjected to the same cruelties as those in the South, enduring beatings and being sold like cattle. Since enslaved people in the North often lived in the master's house, relations could be quite intimate—which often meant sexual intimacy as well.

Such was Isabella's case. Of the five children she had with her husband, Thomas, one had been fathered by the master of the house, a man named John Dumont. While Dumont seems to have been relatively restrained in his treatment of Isabella, Dumont's wife was not, so to avoid tensions at home, Dumont agreed to free Isabella and her children one year before the official 1827 New York emancipation. But at the last minute, Dumont reneged.

"The question in her mind," wrote her biographer, "now was, 'How can I get away?'" Before long, Isabella felt that God had provided her with a plan, so she escaped, carrying only her infant daughter, Sophia, and "a cotton handkerchief containing both her clothes and her provisions."[2] She fled to the home of Isaac and Marie Van Wagenen, acquaintances of Dumont's who, unlike Dumont, were fervent abolitionists.

When Dumont finally managed to track Isabella to the Van Wagenens' house, he confronted her: "Well, Bell, so you've run away from me."

She replied, "No, I did not *run* away; I walked by day-light, and all because you had promised me a year of my time."[3] Enraged, Dumont threatened to take Sophia from her by force if she refused to return.

To ease the tension, Isaac Van Wagenen offered to pay Dumont for the remaining year of Isabella and Sophia's servitude—essentially purchasing them from Dumont, who reluctantly agreed. Still, Dumont took his revenge by selling one of her remaining sons, Peter, to a farmer in Alabama, which meant he had little hope of his ever being freed.

Not long after beginning her new life at the Van Wagenens', Isabella underwent a religious conversion. Although she'd long prayed to a vague, fatherly God, she now came under the influence of some local Methodists and Pentecostals. The Black churches in her part of New York celebrated Pentecost much as Southerners celebrate Mardi Gras, with feasting and indulgent reveling, so in 1827, Isabella was torn between remaining faithful to her new Christian vows and partying with her friends at Pentecost.

In advance of the celebrations, she had a premonition. Dumont, she felt, was coming to take her back. In many ways, she deeply wanted to return and celebrate the holiday with her old friends at Dumont's home, but she also wanted to remain true to her vow to renounce such indulgence. Her feelings were further confused by knowing that three of her children still resided with the Dumonts.

Oddly, Dumont actually did arrive at the Van Wagenens', and with both anticipation and regret, Isabella agreed to return with him. According to her biographer, as she was preparing to place Sophia in his wagon, "God revealed himself to her, with all the suddenness of a flash of lightening, 'in the twinkling of an eye that he was *all over*'—that he pervaded the universe—'and that there was no place where God was not.'" This filled her with terror because she knew that her motives in returning with Dumont amounted to the breaking of her vows, and "she shrunk back aghast from the 'awful look' of Him whom she had formerly talked to. . . . A dire dread of annihilation now seized her."[4] She was overcome by her sense of shame.

Then when she opened her eyes after this terrible realization, Dumont had vanished. As Isabella walked back to the house, confused, she was burdened by an awareness of the vast, uncrossable distance between "herself and an insulted Deity." Desperately, she thought, if only "some one, who was worthy in the sight of heaven, would but plead *for* her in their own name, and not let God know it came from *her*, who was so unworthy, God might grant it."

Then, as her biographer wrote, "a friend appeared . . . and she felt sensibly refreshed as when, on a hot day, an umbrella had been interposed between her scorching head and a burning sun." To her, this person was human, quite touchable, someone she mistook at first for one of her own friends, but upon examination, she realized this was a stranger.

"Who *are* you?" she asked. And just then "the vision brightened into a form distinct, beaming with the beauty of holiness, and radiant with love." She said, "I *know* you, and I *don't* know you." And eventually, "an answer came to her, saying distinctly, 'It is Jesus.' 'Yes,' she responded, 'it is *Jesus*.'"

Up to that point in her life, she had believed that Jesus was simply a famous person of the past, "like a Washington or a Lafayette." But now she viewed him as a personal, tangible, and present friend. In the days that followed, she was startled to learn that others seemed to know him personally as well—for she had thought that he had revealed himself to her alone—and she even experienced some jealousy. When she was told that some people viewed Jesus as God and others as a man, she said, "I only knew as I saw. I did not see him to be God; else, how could he stand between me and God? I saw him as a friend, standing between me and God, through whom love flowed as from a fountain."[5]

Such was Isabella's supremely beautiful, life-altering encounter. "Yes . . . it is *Jesus*."

✳ ✳ ✳

Energized by her new life, she became a force to be reckoned with in the years that followed. She managed to initiate legal proceedings to have her son Peter returned to her from Alabama—the first instance in American history of a Black woman winning a court case to have a family member freed from slavery. In time, she became a prominent speaker on the abolitionist circuit, an outspoken and controversial advocate of equal rights for women and voting rights for African Americans. In 1843, she abandoned the slave name she'd been born with and adopted the name Sojourner Truth, a name that signified her calling to preach God's truth while she was a pilgrim on this earth. The name may have been inspired by a popular spiritual of the time titled "Sojourner," the apt refrain of which is "All along my pilgrim journey, Lord, I want Jesus to walk with me."[6]

By the time she was in her fifties, she was so admired that she was persuaded to dictate her memoirs, titled *Narrative of Sojourner Truth: A Northern Slave* (figure 15.2), to author Olive Gilbert, and the word *narrative* is important here. Her life was nothing if not a remarkable story.

Today, the phrase most often associated with Sojourner Truth is *Ain't I a woman?* but before the Civil War, she was

Figure 15.2. Portrait of Sojourner Truth from the frontispiece of Olive Gilbert's *Narrative of Sojourner Truth: A Northern Slave* (1850)

most closely identified with the words *Is God dead?*—the words that now appear on her tombstone. Both phrases, curiously, are misquotations.

According to Harriet Beecher Stowe, author of *Uncle Tom's Cabin*, Truth once attended a speech by famed abolitionist Frederick Douglass at the Faneuil Hall in Boston. That evening, Douglass gave vent to his grim prognosis regarding the plight of the enslaved people of the United States, "saying that they had no hope of justice from the whites," and at the height of his despair, he told the crowd, "It must come to blood; they must fight for themselves, and redeem themselves, or it would never be done."

Truth, seated at the front of the auditorium, listened to Douglass's screed to the end. The audience, instead of applauding, sat in stunned silence, but according to Stowe, "In the deep hush of feeling, after Douglass sat down, [Truth] spoke out in her deep, peculiar voice, heard all over the house,—'Frederick, *is God dead?*'"

"The effect was perfectly electrical," wrote Stowe, "and thrilled through the whole house, changing as by a flash the whole feeling of the audience. Not another word she said or needed to say; it was enough."[7] Years later, Douglass himself wrote of the incident, "We were all for a moment brought to a stand-still, just as we should have been if someone had thrown a brick through the window."[8]

Because of Stowe's fame, that version of the story took the abolitionist world by storm, especially among those (like Truth in that time and many in our own time) who felt that nonviolence would be more effective in advancing their cause.

But the story is a dramatization. Stowe placed the event in Boston, though it actually took place at a Progressive Friends meetinghouse in Salem, Ohio, and Truth actually challenged Douglass with these words: "Frederick, is God gone?"[9] Her words were intended to remind Douglass that God was not absent, that God cared for the oppressed. After all, she felt she'd met Jesus personally. Stowe's more shocking version suggests that Douglass was so despairing as to think that God was not just absent but dead.

That famous phrase was later superseded by *Ain't I a woman?* when, in 1863, abolitionist and women's rights activist Frances Dana Barker Gage printed a supposed transcription of a speech Sojourner Truth had delivered in 1851—twelve years earlier. Gage reports that in the middle of an extempore talk at a women's convention in Akron, Ohio, Truth said,

> Dat man ober dar say dat women needs to be helped into carriages, and lifted ober ditches, and to have de best place everywhar. Nobody eber help me into carriages, or ober mud puddles, or gibs me any best place. . . . And ar'n't I a woman? Look at me! Look at my arm! . . . I have plowed, and planted, and gathered into barns, and no man could head me! And ar'n't I a woman? I could work as much and eat as much as a man (when I could get it), and bear de lash as well—and ar'n't I a woman? I have borne thirteen chilern and seen 'em mos' all sold off to slavery, and when I cried out with a mother's grief, none but Jesus heard me—and ar'n't I a woman?[10]

To this day, her often-reprinted speech is a powerful statement of the moral courage of Black women, but again, a regrettable and unintentionally racist kind of dramatization has taken place.

First, Truth was raised in the North and spoke only Dutch as a small child. Her adult dialect was not a Black Southern brogue at all. Second, Truth is unlikely to have claimed to have had thirteen children, since she elsewhere reported to have had only five. Gage, writing more than a decade after the event, is clearly trying to heighten the drama for political purposes while the country was in the throes of the Civil War.

This is not to deny the stark power of Gage's transcription, but Truth never seems to have said, "Ain't I a women?" or even "Ar'n't I a woman?" Only weeks after her speech in 1851, another reporter transcribed that same passage this way: "I have as much muscle as any man, and I can do as much work as any man. I have plowed and reaped and husked and chopped and mowed, and can any man do more than that? I have heard much about the sexes being equal, I can carry as much as any man, and can eat as much too, if I can get it. I am as strong as any man that is now."[11]

✳ ✳ ✳

With all this in mind, you can see why my wife and I made our pilgrimage to Sojourner Truth's grave during the run-up to the 2020 general election, at a time when Black Lives Matter protestors were swarming the streets after the death of George Floyd and other unarmed African Americans. Many of the protestors, like Frederick Douglass himself more than a century and a half earlier, were "saying that they had no hope of justice from the whites." America was again confronting its difficult, discordant history. As William Faulkner wrote, "The past is never dead. It's not even past."[12]

Sojourner Truth is a powerful chapter in the history of Black women in this country, a history that includes such figures as Harriet Tubman, who not only escaped from slavery but

Figure 15.3. A photograph of Sojourner Truth taken in 1870. As the epigraph to her *Narrative* reads, "I will rise to noblest themes, for the soul hath a heritage of glory."[13]

returned to guide more than seventy others to freedom; she later led an all-Black unit of soldiers during the Civil War. Tubman too claimed to hear God's voice. Then there's journalist Ida B. Wells, who chronicled the country's lynchings, fought for civil rights and women's suffrage, and was a founder of the NAACP. And there are also women like Fannie Lou Hamer, Ella Baker, Daisy Bates, and Shirley Chisholm, who were leaders in the civil rights movement, and in our time, we have Alicia Garza, Opal Tometi, and Patrisse Cullors, who founded Black Lives Matter.

Our visit to Truth's grave is also moving because it takes place only three days after the death of Supreme Court Justice Ruth Bader Ginsburg (RBG), who was herself a pioneer of promoting equal justice under the law and a staunch defender of voting rights, and like the women just listed, she too redirected the course of history. Today, the strand that connects Sojourner Truth to RBG seems quite short—no farther than the distance between Truth's grave and the anonymous someone who was interred at the African American funeral only a few hundred yards away.

Aside from leaving coins at the base of Truth's marker, another tradition has grown up. Every election day, people come to Oak Hill Cemetery to affix their "I Voted" stickers to her stone . . . a way of remembering what she fought for so tirelessly during her life. It is now just forty-three days until the 2020 general election. Of course, we have no idea what the outcome of that election will be, but we too will return to let Sojourner Truth know "I Voted."[14]

16

REVIVAL FIRES

Lorenzo Dow, Charles Finney, and Joseph Smith

The Burned-Over District . . . that's how historians refer to western and central New York State after a religious frenzy swept through the area in the first half of the nineteenth century. Although the Second Great Awakening had begun earlier and elsewhere, the Burned-Over District became a focal point of a uniquely American brand of revivalist zeal. The region from Buffalo to Syracuse, from Rochester to Binghamton, was largely a wilderness at that time, settled by scattered enclaves of villagers and hearty pioneers, which gave rise to a surprising number of religious movements, offshoots, and sects. Because life on the frontier could be harsh and uncertain, these settlers were ripe for the appeal of evangelizing circuit riders.

For instance, the territory was a breeding ground for the Millerites, followers of Baptist preacher William Miller, who, through a process of biblical calculation, predicted that Christ's second coming would occur sometime in 1843 or 1844. His followers' tracts and newspapers reached millions of readers, and his ideas spread as far as Australia and Europe. Sojourner Truth herself was a devout adherent. After Jesus failed to return on schedule (in what was then called "the Great Disappointment"), much of Miller's theology was adopted by Adventist groups. One of his publications, *Signs of the Times*, is still published by the Seventh-day Adventists.

The Shakers settled there. After arriving from England, Mother Ann Lee found a home for her first American Shaker community in Watervliet, New York, in 1776, and by 1836, three other Shaker communities had been planted in the area, with more than twenty others nationwide. The Oneida Community—a communal, perfectionist, utopian society— originated in the region in 1848, and German Pietists also established the Amana Colony there in the 1850s. So receptive were residents in the area that abolitionists, women's rights advocates, socialists, utopianists, self-improvement gurus, and promoters of the social gospel found appreciative audiences throughout the Burned-Over District.

✳ ✳ ✳

One of the most popular revivalist preachers of the era was Lorenzo Dow. Although now largely forgotten, he was the Billy Graham of the early nineteenth century, and while he was dubbed "an eccentric genius" and a "theological 'knight errant,'"[1] a more apt epithet might be *protohippie*. Possessing only one suit of threadbare clothes, he seldom washed, and he grew his hair and beard long (figure 16.1). Wherever he traveled, crowds gathered to hear his lively, emotionally charged open-air sermons, during which he would shout thunderously, weep, dash back and forth across the platform, wave his arms wildly, and use previously unheard-of evangelism techniques. For example, one time, he told his audience that he had promised

Figure 16.1. The eccentric preacher Lorenzo Dow (lithograph by Childs and Lehman based on a painting by A. T. Lee, 1834)

God to convert at least two souls that night, and if he failed, he would burn the word *liar* into his own forehead with a red-hot brand. Two converts did in fact step forward.

Dow was born in Connecticut in 1777, though his spiritual life began with a spectacular dream at age thirteen while he was wrestling with religious doubts. He dreamed an old man came to him and asked if he prayed. When Dow answered no, the man left. But soon the man returned and again asked, "Do you pray?" And again he said no. At that point, Dow explains,

> I went out of doors and was taken up by a whirlwind and carried above the skies; at length I discovered, across a gulph, as it were, through a mist of darkness, a glorious place in which was a throne of ivory overlaid with gold, and God sitting upon it and Jesus Christ at his right hand, and angels and glorified spirits, celebrating praise. Oh! the joyful music! I thought the angel Gabriel came to the edge of Heaven, holding a golden trumpet in his right hand, and cried to me with a mighty voice to know if I desired to come there. I told him I did. Said he, "You must go back to yonder world, and if you will be faithful to God you shall come here in the end."
>
> With reluctance I left the beautiful sight and came back to the earth again; and then I thought the old man came to me a third time and asked me if I had prayed? I told him I had. Then, said he, "Be faithful, and I will come and let you know again."[2]

Although Dow went through a subsequent period of depression over the fate of his soul and even briefly contemplated suicide, he eventually converted to Methodism. While weighing the possibility of becoming an itinerant evangelist, another vision came to him. One November night in 1795, when he was eighteen years old, he dreamed he saw

> a beautiful stalk about eight feet high . . . covered with beautiful seeds. I heard a voice over my head saying to me, "Shake the stalk that the seeds may fall off, and cover them up: the seed will be of great value to some, though not to thyself, but thou shalt receive thy reward hereafter."
>
> I shook the stalk and beautiful speckled, red seed fell off, and I covered them up with earth and rotten leaves, and went on my way to serve the Lord.
>
> Some time after that, I thought I was there again, and saw a large number of partridges or pheasants, that had been scratching up a great part of the seed. I discovered them and was very sorry and went and drove them away and watched it to keep them away. Then I tho't I began to preach and immediately awaked, when the parable of the sower came into my mind.[3]

The die was cast. Within three years, the Methodist Church licensed him as a circuit-riding preacher, and within a few more years, he was sharing his gospel message before crowds of as many as ten thousand. He was the originator of the American camp meeting movement, and he is thought to have preached before more people than any evangelist prior to Charles Spurgeon fifty years later. Dow's revival tours took him from the Mississippi Delta to the British Isles, from Canada to the West Indies, and between 1802 and 1814, he made frequent stops in the Burned-Over District, where he was phenomenally popular. After he died in 1834, his memoirs, *The Eccentric Preacher*, became a best seller, second only to the Bible itself.

❋ ❋ ❋

Although Dow's legacy faded, that of one of his younger fellow revivalists, Charles Finney, endured—or, in the words of the late televangelist Jerry Falwell Sr., Finney was "one of my heroes, and a hero to many evangelicals, including Billy Graham."[4] Finney is the epitome of what countless American stump preachers have hoped to become (figure 16.2).

Born in rural Jefferson County, New York, in 1792, Finney was raised a Baptist. At the age of twenty-nine, while apprenticing to become a lawyer, he grew uneasy about his faith and earnestly sought, as he said, "to settle the question of my soul's salvation." After he spent two agonizing days at his law office, secretly praying and reading the Bible, "the whole question of Gospel salvation opened to my mind in a manner most marvelous. . . . I then saw, as clearly as I ever have in my life, the reality and fullness of the Atonement of Christ." Inspired, he left the office, and while crossing a nearby street, the question occurred to him, "Will you accept it, *now, today*?" and he replied, "Yes; I will accept it today, or I will die in the attempt."[5]

To make good on this promise, he walked to some nearby woods to pray, but suddenly, he felt spiritually cold, uninspired, unable to form the words of even a simple prayer. Sin, he knew, was the problem. He recalled the words of Jesus: "Then shall ye seek me and shall find me, when you search for me with all your heart,"[6] and holding to that promise "with the grasp of a drowning man," he vowed, "If I am ever converted, I will preach the Gospel."[7]

Comforted by the peace that now washed over him, he returned to his office intending "to pour my whole soul out to

Figure 16.2. The frontispiece portrait from *Memoirs of Rev. Charles G. Finney* (1876)

God." As he walked into the rear office, he found that although he'd not yet lit a fire in the fireplace, the room was somehow "perfectly light." He wrote,

> As I went in and shut the door after me, it seemed as if I met the Lord Jesus Christ *face to face*. It did not occur to me then, nor did it for some time afterward, that it was wholly a *mental* state. On the contrary, it seemed to me that I met Him face to face and saw Him as I would see any other man. He said nothing, but looked at me in such a manner as to break me right down at His feet. . . . It seemed to me a reality that He stood before me and that I fell down at His feet and poured out my soul to Him. I wept aloud like a child, and made such confessions as I could with my choked utterance. It seemed to me as if I bathed His feet with my tears, and yet I had no distinct impression that I *touched* Him, that I recollect. I must have continued in this state for a good while, but my mind was too much absorbed with the interview to recollect scarcely anything that I said.[8]

Returning to the front office, he suddenly

> received *a mighty baptism of the Holy Ghost* . . . that seemed *to go through me*, body and soul. I could feel the impression, *like a wave of electricity*, going through and through me. Indeed it seemed to come in *waves*, and *waves of liquid love*—for I could not express it any other way. And yet it did not seem like water, but rather as *the breath of God*. I can recollect distinctly that it seemed to *fan* me like immense wings; and it seemed to me, as these waves passed over me, that they literally *moved my hair like a passing breeze*.[9]

And so on the evening of October 10, 1821, his conversion was complete. Now that he'd been "justified by faith" and had experienced "present sanctification," sin no longer burdened his soul—to such an extent that when a client arrived the following morning to ask if he'd prepared the legal briefs for their trial that day, Finney replied, "I have a retainer from the Lord Jesus Christ to plead His cause, and I cannot plead yours."[10]

In time, Finney became a circuit-riding fixture in the Burned-Over District. In fact, he was the person responsible for coining the term, though he never meant it as a compliment. So many wildfires of religious ardor had already spread through the region that the people, Finney felt, had grown hardened, jaded. As he wrote, "I found that region of the country . . . 'a burnt district.' There had been a few years previous a wild excitement passing through that region, which they called a revival of religion, but which turned out to be spurious."[11]

Finney became one of the most influential evangelists of the Second Great Awakening. In 1835, while continuing to preach, he became a professor of theology at what would later become Oberlin College in Ohio, and ten years after that, he became the school's president. Due to the abolitionist fervor at the college, Oberlin became "Station 99" on the Underground Railroad, and it was the first college in the nation to accept Blacks and women alongside its white male students. Finney was a towering figure—an institution—by the time he died in 1875.

✳ ✳ ✳

In addition to revivalism and utopianism, the Burned-Over District gave birth to the largest and most influential religious movement to originate in the United States: the Church of Jesus Christ of Latter-day Saints, commonly known as the Mormons, founded by a man who also claimed a vision of Jesus as the source of his authority.

One day in 1820, a fifteen-year-old boy named Joseph Smith walked out into the woods near his home in Palmyra, New York, intending to pray. Like Dow and Finney and so many others before him, he was in the grip of a spiritual crisis. While drawn to Methodism, he was also intensely curious about the many revivals and camp meetings held by other denominations in the area, and he was equally fascinated by the unorthodox practice of "scrying," a method of folk divination that seeks esoteric knowledge by meditating on special stones.

On that day, according to Smith's testimony, he was praying anxiously about which church he should attend—which one was the true church? While kneeling in the woods, he suddenly felt crushed by a terrifying, malevolent darkness, but then, as he explained, "just at this moment of great alarm, I saw a pillar of light exactly over my head, above the brightness of the sun, which descended gradually until it fell upon me. . . . When the light rested upon me, I saw two personages, whose brightness and glory defy all description, hovering above me in the air. One of them spake unto me, calling me by name and said, pointing to the other: 'This is my beloved Son; hear ye Him!'"[12]

These personages he recognized: God the Father and God the Son. In answer to his question about which church to join, they told him that he "should not join any of them, for they were all wrong, and their creeds were an abomination in His sight."[13]

Smith (figure 16.3) later claimed that three years after this startling encounter, an angel directed him to a hill near his home where a stone box lay buried. The angel, named Moroni,

Figure 16.3. Thirty-eight-year-old Joseph Smith, based on a photo taken in Nauvoo, Illinois, in 1843, a year before he was killed by an angry mob

prevented him from uncovering its contents until four years later, when, at age twenty-one, Smith was allowed to retrieve from the box a stack of loosely bound golden plates. They were inscribed with the strange hieroglyphics of a lost language that Smith called "reformed Egyptian." With the use of scrying stones, Smith was given the ability, he believed, to translate the mystifying text, and that book is what we now know as the Book of Mormon.

Within a decade, Smith had established the Church of Jesus Christ of Latter-day Saints and led them to Nauvoo, Illinois. That is where Smith was eventually murdered—or in some people's opinion, martyred—by an angry mob, after which Brigham Young led the Mormon faithful to Salt Lake City.

The Book of Mormon presents a sort of metahistory of a stray group of ancient Hebrews who found their way across the ocean to the Americas, and it describes how Jesus, between his resurrection and ascension, ministered in person to them as well as to the Native peoples, dispensing wisdom and salvation to the New World. Since I've not read more than a smattering of passages, I don't presume to judge the book's character or content. Among my friends is one man, a prolific playwright, who would argue that the Book of Mormon is a sacred document of inestimable value; also among my friends is a woman, a former Mormon, who has written a best-selling book debunking the claims of Mormonism and its founding documents.

My interest, rather, is in the effect that his vision—as well as Dow's and Finney's—had on reshaping the religious culture in America.

✳ ✳ ✳

So what *was* going on in the Burned-Over District? Why were its people at that time so susceptible to spiritual suggestion? How could three men, so different but all inspired by visions of Jesus, succeed in changing the trajectory of American Christianity? The religious world we live in today was shaped, at least in part, by what occurred in that region.

The conventional Christian answer is that God was "troubling the waters," creating an environment ripe for an almost frantic spiritual renewal. But another possibility exists, though not necessarily exclusive of the first. Just as the Protestant Reformers of the sixteenth, seventeenth, and eighteenth centuries resolved their own inner crises of faith, the cognitive dissonances, by creating a non-Catholic kind of mysticism, so too these three American thinkers, on a deeply psychological level, were moved to create a uniquely non-European kind of faith—new wine and new wineskins.

Although their visions differed (Dow's was a dream, Finney acknowledged that his might have been a "mental state," and Smith believed his was an external reality), still, they all hint at something deeper. At that time, the great American experiment was underway, when artists and writers and thinkers were reinventing society, toiling to discern just how this new land differed from Europe, and nowhere was this struggle more deeply felt than in the realm of religion. Dow, Finney, and Smith, immersed as they were in the predominant Protestantism of the area, absorbed the unsettling spiritual tensions of the time.

The Burned-Over District was the cradle of American religious exceptionalism, ripe for an American Renaissance of the soul. The people lived on the fringes of civilization, improvising a practicable culture as they expanded west, clearing the wilderness, tyrannizing and persecuting the First Nations peoples, debating the issue of slavery, and struggling to survive. Western New York represented the often-brutal tensions inherent in the questions, Who are we as Americans? What do we owe to Europe and to the wealthy interests back east? What sort of religion is suited to survival in this as yet unmapped spiritual and geographical territory?

Dow and Finney, and countless other revivalists like them, seized Protestantism from the grip of the hierarchy-based denominations of the east and focused their preaching on the individual—a message that resonated with the independent-minded settlers and pioneers. These evangelists preached that personal holiness was more important than church membership; that personal sanctity was the only true worship; that each individual, burdened by the weight of unbearable sin, must face God's judgment alone, unaided by denominations or traditions. Only that kind of faith could help them survive. As theologian Michael Horton wrote, "Evangelists pitched their American gospel in terms of its practical usefulness to the individual and the nation."[14]

Finney's sermonizing has been the model for preachers to this day. Unlike the Calvinist Puritans of the eighteenth century, who taught that only the elect would reach heaven, Finney preached a fiery, freewill brand of perfectionism—that each person has a choice, moment by moment, to resist sin and seek salvation. By exploiting this sense of conviction, he devised what was called the "anxious seat," a side bench or row of chairs where listeners could sit when they felt crushed by sin. Finney would sometimes even call out people by name and list their shortcomings aloud. The line between preaching and shaming grew thin, and in time, the "anxious seat" evolved into what preachers like Billy Graham and others termed the *altar call*, a technique that has come to define evangelistic outreach.

Joseph Smith went so far as to reinvent Christianity, to remake it from whole cloth, tailoring it specifically to the new nation, a Christianity that threw off its European forerunners and proclaimed that Christ had arrived in person on the shores of the New World.

Dow, Finney, and Smith made their culture's spiritual tensions their own. The Burned-Over District was internal as much as geographic. Each man's encounter with Jesus, which ultimately granted each of them spiritual authority, seems to have been an unconscious means of resolving the question of how to make faith relevant to a revolutionary new country in a revolutionary new era. They were on the cutting edge of making sense of America in the decades after the War of Independence.

The Jesus each man encountered was not so much a vision as a manifestation of the psychosocial dissonance in their own souls.

PART FIVE

MODERNS

17

"KEEP YOUR MIND IN HELL"

Silouan the Athonite

Meet Simeon Ivanovich Antonov—a hard-drinking, hot-tempered, womanizing young carpenter living in the lush forest steppes of western Russia in the late 1880s. Some people say he can drink three bottles of vodka without getting drunk. He loves dancing and singing the popular songs of his native Tambov district to the accompaniment of his own concertina. Were he not an actual historical person, he could easily be mistaken for a character in some drama or other by Anton Chekhov, for Simeon's story is nothing if not Chekhovian.

✳ ✳ ✳

Act One

The curtain goes up one night as Simeon, with concertina in hand, is strolling through the village one festival day, entertaining the revelers who are clustered along the streets. Suddenly, a drunken man, a local cobbler, tries to snatch Simeon's concertina because the drunk is jealous of the attention Simeon is attracting from the young women. In the struggle, Simeon hits the man—hard—and sends him flying halfway across the road. Everyone gasps and grows quiet . . . the villagers think the cobbler is dead. Eventually, he revives, though severely injured.

Later, Simeon has a dream: a snake has slithered down his throat. As he wakes in fright, a woman's voice speaks out of the darkness: "Just as you found it loathsome to swallow a snake in your dream, so I find your ways ugly to look upon."[1] Although mystified at first, he soon decides that the voice must have been that of Mary, the mother of Jesus, attempting to steer him from the dissolute path he's been on. The only reason he couldn't see her, he reasons, is that he was so full of sin. It's a turning point. Even later, Simeon meets a man from his village who has just been released from prison, having been convicted of murder years before, but curiously, the man is joyous and grateful because he found God in prison. Simeon realizes how close he himself came to murdering the cobbler and going to prison. He vows to change his ways.

Soon he's conscripted into the army of Czar Alexander III, where he becomes an exemplary soldier, scrupulous in his duties and beloved by his comrades. One evening, while he is drinking with friends, they ask him why he seems so distant, and he replies, "I'm thinking that here we sit in a tavern, eating, drinking vodka, listening to the band and enjoying ourselves, while at this very hour on Mt. Athos, they are in church for vespers and will be at prayer all night. And I'm wondering which of us will put up the best defense before God's Judgment Seat—them or us?"[2]

His friends laugh and slap him on the back, but a seed has been planted. It grows until Simeon leaves the military, and in 1892, in his twenty-seventh year, he travels to Mount Athos, to the only Russian monastery among the twenty monasteries there, so that he might become a monk—an ascetic like those who are "at prayer all night."

✳ ✳ ✳

Act Two

One night, not long after arriving at the Panteleimon Monastery, Simeon, whose monastic name is now Brother Silouan—earnest, devout, sincere—is alone in his cell when an unearthly light floods the room, radiant and overwhelming. It seems to shine through everything, "even piercing his body so that he saw his entrails." A voice seems to whisper to him, "Accept what you see. . . . It proceeds from grace." An ecstatic incident.

But what seems a divine moment quickly fades into despair. Within days, he's filled with terror as demons begin to haunt his cell nightly, constantly mocking him. Two accusations do the demons repeatedly throw at him: "You are holy now" (in a mocking tone) and "You will not be saved" (in a serious tone). When Silouan demands to know what they mean by these contradictory taunts, they say, "We never tell the truth" (laughing uproariously).[3]

For months, Silouan struggles to defeat the shame that has welled up in his soul because he is now aware of the pride and vanity that his mystical moment has inspired. He fasts, sleeps only an hour or two each night, prays constantly—but the taunts increase. One day, in despair, he cries out, "God will not hear me!"[4]

✳ ✳ ✳

Act Three

But on the same day on which he thought God would never hear him, something happens—unexpectedly, miraculously. Silouan walks to the nearby Church of the Holy Prophet Elijah so he can kneel before the icon of Jesus that hangs beside the entrance. He prays the familiar Jesus Prayer he has prayed thousands, if not tens of thousands, of times before: "Lord Jesus Christ, have mercy upon me, a sinner." "As I uttered these words," Silouan later wrote, "I saw the living Lord in the place where the ikon was, and the grace of the Holy Spirit flooded my soul and my whole body. And so it was I came to know through the Holy Spirit that Jesus Christ is God; and I was filled with a sweet longing to endure suffering for His sake."[5]

Silouan is so overcome that he collapses to the ground unconscious. His biographer explained, "He was lifted out of the world and in spirit transported to heaven, where he heard ineffable words; that at that moment he received, as it were, a new birth from on high."[6] He has experienced a revelation; a vision of Christ; a personal Pentecost; a joyous, devastating, intoxicating baptism of the Holy Spirit.

But even now, despite this rare and affirming vision, the joy and lightness eventually fade, just as they did after the strange light appeared in his cell, and before long, a wave of desperate yearning engulfs him. Why, he wonders, can he not always feel the joy of that rapture? Why can't Jesus always appear to him in that way? And once more, Silouan realizes that his day-to-day struggle is to defeat his own vanity and pride, the sense that he is somehow entitled to a deep, constant communion with the Holy.

Silouan continues to wrestle with his spiritual shortcomings until one day, fifteen years after Jesus appeared to him, he finds that his cell is filled with menacing demons and that an unusually large devil is blocking the icon before which Silouan is kneeling in prayer. "Lord," Silouan prays, "You see that I desire to pray to You with a pure mind but the devils will not let me. Instruct me, what must I do to stop them hindering me?" He was, in a sense, surrendering control of his spiritual life to God.

And then he receives an answer. From somewhere within his own soul, these words spring up: "The proud always suffer from devils. . . . Keep your mind in hell, and don't lose hope."[7]

An odd revelation, but it gave Silouan a focus for his meditations, and he drew several lessons from it. Because of his demons, he felt he was already living in hell—but to have that inner voice also tell him not to despair, that was something new. As the psalmist wrote, "If I make my bed in hell, behold, thou art there."[8] In other words, God can't help us fight our demons unless we are already living among them. Just as Christ was willing to harrow hell for the sake of lost souls, so too we should be willing to confront our pride and vanity, meeting those demons where they live. Silouan recalled the time when he was a novice and the demons had told him that he was holy but would never be saved—but now he realized that instead of being intimidated by them, the correct response would have been to cast them out, to contradict them outright: he was *not* holy, and he *would* indeed be saved anyway.

Next, from this revelation, he realized that his prayers had been focused almost entirely on himself; from that point on, he resolved to pray for others, even to the point of feeling it shameful to pray for his own needs. We need to pray especially for the seemingly hopeless, he felt, because no one was beyond hope, not even the dead who may already be in hell. When one of Silouan's monastic brothers, a hermit, remarked that "God will punish all atheists. They will burn in everlasting fire," Silouan was upset and replied, "Tell me, supposing you went to paradise, and there looked down and saw somebody burning in hell-fire, would you feel happy?"

The hermit said, "It can't be helped. It would be their own fault."

Silouan, grieved at the hermit's heartlessness, said, "Love could not bear that. . . . We must pray for all."[9]

Most of all, this admonition to never lose hope filled Silouan's heart with a deep sense of peace. Love seemed to flood his soul. His life as a monk meant not that he was alone—even though he was an ascetic—but that his life was interwoven with the lives of everyone in the world, that he was to love them and pray for them. One saying that Silouan often repeated was "Our brother is our life."[10]

For the rest of his life, Silouan (figure 17.1) was thought of as one of the holiest and wisest monks on Mount Athos, sought out for his wisdom and clear-sighted devotion to God. He wrote short reflections on inspirational topics. Among his many writings on the spiritual life is this beautiful prayer poem, which seems to summarize his faith:

> Where is your habitation, O humble soul? And who dwells in
>   you; and to what shall I compare you?
> You burn bright like the sun and are not consumed, but with
>   your warmth you give warmth to all.
> The earth is yours, for the meek shall inherit the earth, said the
>   Lord.

Figure 17.1. A photograph of Silouan the Athonite, ascetic and saint, taken in the 1930s, in his final decade

You are like a flowering garden. In the heart of the garden is a fair
    dwelling in which it pleases the Lord to take up his abode.
You are the beloved of heaven and earth.
The apostles, prophets, prelates and holy Father love you.
The angels, the seraphim and cherubim love you.
The most holy Mother of the Lord loves you, O humble soul.
The Lord loves you, and in you does he rejoice.[11]

✳ ✳ ✳

So what do we make of this remarkable monk and his vision of Jesus?

First, Silouan cannot be understood apart from the grand and venerable traditions of Eastern Orthodox mysticism, specifically the meditative practice known as *hesychasm*, a term that comes from the Greek, meaning "quiet" or "stillness." One of the earliest formulators of this spiritual path was the eleventh-century monk and hymnist Symeon the New Theologian (whom we encountered in chapter 9), who perceived God directly as a light that "shines on us without evening, without change, without alteration, without form."[12] Symeon startled the theologians of his time by boldly recounting the details of his own mystical apperceptions of God, and furthermore, he taught that true contemplatives should seek to experience God in those visionary ways. Some of Symeon's writings are included in the *Philokalia*, one of Orthodoxy's most beloved resources for hesychast practice.

Mount Athos itself (figure 17.2), with its twenty Orthodox monasteries, has been the center of hesychast practice almost from the time the first monastery was officially established there. The impressive mountain, six thousand feet high, looks out over the Aegean Sea from a peninsula on the northern coast of Greece. It is one of the holiest sites in the world. When Lord Byron visited there in 1823, he described it as "a quiet refuge . . . / Whence the rapt spirit may ascend to Heaven!"[13]

In its simplest and most popular form, hesychasm is a spiritual discipline in which the practitioner repeatedly recites the Jesus Prayer: "Lord Jesus Christ, Son of God, have mercy upon me, a sinner." It becomes a focal point for meditation, like a

Figure 17.2. A view of Mount Athos as drawn by artist and limericist Edward Lear during a visit in 1856

Hindu mantra or a religious incantation, although the believer repeats the prayer not for the sake of repetition but to focus on the implications and meaning of each word as it is spoken. The goal is to seek a higher level of communion with God.

Often, readers in the West first encounter hesychasm in the various translations of the Russian spiritual classic *The Way of a Pilgrim*. The book is narrated by an anonymous nineteenth-century pilgrim who, inspired by the words of the apostle Paul to "pray without ceasing,"[14] sets out on a quest to learn how that can be achieved. Eventually, he encounters a poor forester who becomes his *staretz*, his spiritual director, and this man encourages him to "have the ceaseless prayer of Jesus in your heart. . . . Set to work, my brother, upon the ceaseless saying of the prayer of Jesus. . . . The prayer will make you feel such lightness and such bliss in your heart that you will be astonished at yourself, and your wholesome way of life will be neither dull nor troublesome to you."[15]

The original manuscript of *The Way of a Pilgrim* first came into the possession of some monks on Mount Athos, and in the mid-1880s, they saw to it that the book was published in Russia. It was a huge success. Silouan himself was still in his teens when the book appeared, and although no evidence exists that he ever read it (he was, in fact, only semiliterate), the book embodies the atmosphere of fervent Russian spirituality at the time that Silouan himself decided to become an ascetic.

In its more complex forms, hesychasm goes beyond the repetition of a simple prayer. While its practice is complex and demanding—and more than can be described adequately here—it basically leads the practitioner through a three-tiered process of spiritual enlightenment, beginning with purification, continuing through illumination, and ending with intimate communion with God.

In the first step, purification, the hesychast (as the contemplative is called) learns through deep prayer how to avoid distractions, which are often embodied as demons, like those encountered by Anthony of Egypt in the fourth century. This is the stage at which Silouan encountered so many difficulties. His pride and vanity were evident at that point because he believed that he had achieved illumination when his room was filled with the radiant light.

In Eastern Orthodox tradition, such experiences are referred to as *prelest*—that is, a misleading spiritual delusion. Such experiences may seem like enlightenment but lead to confusion. Such was Silouan's initial vision of the light filling his room. His overpowering vision of Jesus, which knocked him down and caused him to faint, also led to disappointment, for he spent the next fifteen years trying to recover the joy of that experience, and again he only became more aware of his pride and vanity. The cure for this disappointment is the intense pursuit of humility—or as Silouan said, meekness—so by putting his "mind in hell," he was reminded not to think too highly of himself.

As far as the visions themselves, Silouan in both instances was repeating the Jesus Prayer immediately beforehand. As famed neurologist Oliver Sacks affirms, "Such practices as meditation, spiritual exercises, and ecstatic drumming or dancing can . . . facilitate the achievement of trance states akin to that of hypnosis, with vivid hallucinations and profound psychological changes. . . . Meditative or contemplative techniques (often aided by sacred music, painting, or architecture) have been used in many religious traditions—sometimes to induce hallucinatory visions."[16] Also worth noting is the fact that Silouan had nearly starved himself before his vision of Jesus and was sleeping only one to two hours a night, facts that may well have contributed to his mind-altering experience.

* * *

With Silouan, we have now moved into the modern era. Since he was born in 1866 and died in 1938, he was a contemporary of such great Russian figures as Anton Chekhov, Modernist painter Wassily Kandinsky, and social realist writer Maxim Gorky, or for those who are more familiar with English literature, Silouan was an exact contemporary of W. B. Yeats.

Despite dismissing the demons who mockingly declared him to be holy, Silouan became a saint. He was canonized by the

Orthodox Church in 1987, a distinction he would no doubt have scoffed at because such honors invariably lead to vanity and pride. In fact, I believe Silouan would have found great humor in a comment made by one of his fellow monks decades after Silouan's death. When the aged monk was told of Silouan's elevation to sainthood, he said (in what seems a moment of great Chekhovian irony), "What is all this talk about Staretz Silouan? We would drink tea and vodka every evening, and now Silouan has become a saint?"[17]

18

"O GOD–IF THERE IS A GOD"
Sadhu Sundar Singh

A world-renowned Christian missionary was once asked whether fame ever went to his head. He replied, "When Jesus entered Jerusalem, many people spread their clothing and palm branches on the street to honor the Lord. Jesus was riding, as the prophets foretold, on a donkey. . . . It would have been very stupid of the donkey if she had imagined that she was very important. It was not for her that the people threw their clothes on the street."[1]

These are the words of Sadhu Sundar Singh, an Indian holy man whose vision of Jesus was one of the most remarkable of the twentieth century.

✳ ✳ ✳

In India, the term *sadhu* means "poor man" or "beggar," though it implies far more. Sadhus, like mahatmas, are itinerant holy men, living cultural icons, said to possess nearly divine wisdom. They renounce earthly pleasures—marriage, family, possessions, occupation, home—to spread a message of love and unity and peace, and due to their personal sacrifice and insight, they are universally welcomed and sought out for their counsel. Although most sadhus are Sikhs or Hindus, some have been Christians, a tradition that dates all the way back to the apostle Thomas, who is thought to have been the first Christian missionary to India. Sundar Singh, by a curious reversal of history, was the first Indian Christian who felt called to become a missionary to the West.

Singh was born in 1889 into a wealthy Sikh family in Rampur, in the Punjab region of northern India. Sikhism, native to that region, contains elements of both Hindu and Muslim cultures, though it's a distinct faith in its own right, dating back to the fifteenth century. As the youngest son, he was deeply devoted to his mother, a fervently devout Sikh woman who made sure that he was tutored in the ways of religion by a local guru. His mother said to him, "You must seek peace of soul and love religion, and someday you must become a holy Sâdhu."[2] He is said to have learned the Bhagavad Gita by heart by the age of seven.

Since most Punjabis under colonial rule at the turn of the century felt compelled to learn English, his mother sent him to a Presbyterian missionary school. Although language rather than religion was the focus of his studies, the teachers used the Bible as their primary English textbook—a fact that Singh intensely resented. Sometimes he would shout at the school's staff, accusing them of being "evil doers," and as his biographer wrote, "He would even go so far as to throw stones and dung at them, and he ordered his father's servants to do the same."[3]

When Singh was fourteen, his mother died. He was devastated. Unable to fathom why such a vibrant, loving woman had been torn from his life, he demanded answers from the Sikh elders as well as the ministers at the English school, but their answers left him empty. He was so distraught that he burned a Bible in public, reportedly one page at a time.

Three days after his mother's death, he announced to his family that he planned to kill himself. He went to his room on the night of December 17, 1904, intending to throw himself under the train that passed near his father's house every day at five o'clock in the morning. As he prayed in the hours after midnight, he issued an ultimatum to God: "O God—if there is a God—show me the right way, and I will become a Sâdhu; otherwise, I will kill myself."[4] As was the custom for purification, he bathed himself in the ritual Hindu fashion, and then, hour after hour, he continued to pray. He received no response until

towards half-past four—a great light shone in his little room. He thought the house was on fire, opened the door and looked out; there was no fire there. He closed the door and went on praying. Then there dawned upon him a wonderful vision: in the centre of a luminous cloud he saw the face of a Man, radiant with love. At first he thought it was Buddha or Krishna, or some other divinity, and he was about to prostrate himself in worship. Just then, to his great astonishment, he heard these words . . . "Why do you persecute Me? Remember that I gave My life for you upon the Cross." Utterly at a loss, he was speechless with astonishment. Then he noticed the scars of Jesus of Nazareth. . . . Then the thought came to him: "Jesus Christ is not dead; He is alive, and this is He Himself."[5]

He then woke his father, exclaiming, "I am a Christian!" to which his frustrated father replied, "You're off your head, my boy . . . just now you were going to kill yourself!"

Singh replied, "I have killed myself: the old Sundar Singh is dead; I am a new being."[6]

Among Sikh families, conversions to Christianity are rare and not well received, so relations between Singh and his family grew immediately worse. After a failed attempt at poisoning him, they drove him from their home, and his father disinherited him.

Within days of his startling vision, he was homeless and wandering on the streets. He found his way to a Christian boys' home and then to an Anglican medical mission, where he began to devote himself to Bible study. When he begged the missionaries to baptize him, they told him that since he was only fifteen, he'd have to wait until his sixteenth birthday. Although the priests encouraged him to join a Bible study and read books of theology and devotion, he refused. He wanted only to read the words of the Bible itself.

On his sixteenth birthday, he was baptized. Within a month, he fulfilled his mother's prophetic wish for him to become a sadhu; he donned the traditional saffron-colored robe worn by Indian holy men, and not unlike Francis of Assisi, who also left his father's home as a penniless beggar, Singh set out on an epic, lifelong journey to convert lost souls. He became known as the "barefoot evangelist," traveling from village to village, eating only the food that was given to him, and sleeping outdoors when no other bed could be found. He carried only a Bible, as well as a blanket, which he would sometimes wrap around his head, turban-like, to protect him from the sun. He grew into a tall, stately figure with dark hair and eyes. Some people even said he looked like Jesus himself. (See figures 18.1 and 18.2.)

While traveling on foot throughout northern India, into Kashmir, Afghanistan, Pakistan, and Tibet, where Christian

Figure 18.1. The Sadhu (undated photograph)

Figure 18.2. Singh in Germany, 1922 (from Heiler's *Sadhu Sundar Singh: Ein Apostel des Ostens und Westens*, 1924)

missionaries were not welcome, he experienced persecution, arrest, and stoning—as well as miraculous rescues and conversions. Through it all, he continued to have mystical experiences—though none, he said, that were as tangible as the original visitation from Jesus. Eventually, the "barefoot evangelist" became even better known as the "apostle with the bleeding feet."

Among the many discouragements he encountered, one galled him in particular—the fact that the Christian missionaries he met on his travels, most of whom were from Europe and America, encouraged him to adopt Western dress and customs. Otherwise, they said, he wouldn't be taken seriously. Singh came to believe that such cultural trappings were not just extraneous to preaching the gospel but antithetical to it. And it inspired him to travel to the West . . . as a Christian sadhu.

✳ ✳ ✳

In 1920, when he was thirty-one years old, Singh was greeted with much fanfare when he first arrived in Europe. Initially, people were drawn to him because he so neatly fit the image of what an Indian holy man should look like—a mysterious, almost ethereal figure with a turban, saffron robes, and a dark beard. But as more people heard him speak, they were drawn to him for his forthright spirituality. For a short time, his fame as an evangelist rivaled even Billy Sunday's.

When author Corrie ten Boom was a young woman in the Netherlands, she eagerly went to hear Singh speak, and she was so moved by the story of his vision of Jesus that she approached him after his talk. She told him that she wished more than anything to have a vision like his, but his response surprised her. He said that she was, in fact, already more blessed than he was—because she possessed the invaluable gift of believing without seeing, whereas he only was able to believe because he had seen.[7]

Author Dorothy Sayers too was impressed and even quoted Singh in the preface to her 1943 radio play *The Man Born to Be King*, a reference that would have pleased her friend C. S. Lewis.[8] Twenty years earlier, at the time of Singh's lecture tour of England, Lewis had been attending classes at Oxford. Although the lecture by this strange Indian holy man created a buzz throughout the university, Lewis was, at the time, a somewhat embittered World War I veteran and a confirmed atheist. He most certainly did *not* attend. He was too busy studying for his exams in Greek and Latin literature.

But things change. By 1929, about the same time that Singh disappeared on his final missionary journey to Tibet, Lewis himself had become a Christian. Lewis took an interest in Singh and referenced him in at least two of his books. Singh was most likely the model for the figure of "the Man" in *The Pilgrim's Regress*, Lewis's 1933 allegorical spiritual autobiography. The Man suddenly rescues John, the protagonist, from a deep canyon and just as suddenly disappears. A short while later, the Man reappears to John in a manner that resembles Singh's own nighttime vision of "the face of a Man, radiant with love." Lewis wrote, "Once more the Man came to him [John] in the darkness and said, 'You must pass the night where you are. . . . Your life has been saved all this day by crying out to something you call by many names.'"[9]

Also, in the final novel of Lewis's Space Trilogy, *That Hideous Strength* (1945), one of the characters learns of the existence in India of "the great native Christian mystic whom you may have heard of—the Sura. . . . The Sura had reason to believe, or thought he had reason to believe, that a great danger was hanging over the human race. And just before the end—just before he disappeared—he became convinced that it would actually come to a head in this island."[10] *Sura* is an Arabic word meaning "angel" or "genie," but Lewis seems to have used it as a stand-in for *Sadhu*. Scholar Kathryn Lindskoog even suggests that Singh may have been one of the inspirations for Aslan, Lewis's Christ figure in the Narnia books—because the name Singh means "lion."

The fact that Lewis's Sura disappears mysteriously is also significant. Nine years after his visit to England, Singh, though in very poor health, wanted to make one final missionary journey to Tibet. He set out alone, as always, but this time, he was never heard from again. To this day, the fate of Sadhu Singh is a mystery, though lovers of his writings would assure us that he is with the "Man, radiant with love" who appeared in the center of the luminous cloud.

* * *

But not everyone in the West was as enamored of the Sadhu as Corrie ten Boom and C. S. Lewis were. Even today there are those who insist he was a charlatan. Some German theologians in the 1920s were stung by Singh's suggestion—as much through his humble example as his actual preaching—that Western Christianity had become materialist and hyperintellectual and had thereby strayed from its first love. These theologians dismissed Singh as naive and uneducated, to which

Singh replied, "You must stop examining spiritual truths like dry bones! You must break open the bones and take in the life-giving marrow."[11]

Freudianism was in vogue at that time, so these theologians readily dismissed Singh's famous vision of Jesus as a psychological aberration. In the psychoanalytic opinion of one German theologian, Friedrich Heiler, Singh's vision could have been the result of the "utmost tension of effort, followed by a state of despair and complete cessation from struggle, culminating in a sudden inflow of assurance . . . [and] the influence of the story of Paul's conversion, which is very similar"[12] . . . in other words, the result of unconscious impulses suggested by Singh's reading of the Book of Acts.

Curiously, Heiler himself experienced a change of heart. After scrutinizing Singh's life and writings, Heiler reevaluated his opinion. Concerning Singh's vision, Heiler reasoned that "the religious intuition of the convert alone is able to perceive the Divine reality and the working of Divine grace behind all the historical and psychological processes through which it is revealed. . . . The external form which embodied this inward experience is the Vision of Christ."[13] This is a complicated way of saying (as we've noted several times throughout this book) that simply because a vision is induced by psychological factors doesn't mean that divine grace isn't present.

For me, the best way to understand Singh's unusual experience is found in the following passage from his writings, a passage that hints, beautifully, I think, at the source of not just Singh's vision but many of the other visions described in this book: "God is infinite while we are finite. We can never fully comprehend the infinite, but we do have within us a spiritual sense that allows us to recognize and enjoy God's presence. With the tip of our tongues we can recognize at once that the ocean is salty. We have not understood even a fraction of all there is to know about the ocean, but with our sense of taste we can experience its essence."[14]

19

INNER LOCUTIONS

Mother Teresa

On September 5, 1997, in one of those odd coincidences of history—synchronicity, as some people call it—Mother Teresa died on the same day as the funeral of Lady Diana, Princess of Wales. Five days earlier, Diana had died in a catastrophic high-speed car crash in a tunnel in Paris as she was being hectored by paparazzi on motorbikes. Mother Teresa (figure 19.1) died quietly of heart failure in a hospital bed in Calcutta—or, as one man wrote in a letter to the editor of *Time* magazine, "it is far more accurate to say that at long last she had given all her heart away."[1] These two internationally known women had even met just two and a half months earlier—for the second and final time in their lives.

Another synchronicity, just as curious and perhaps more significant, is that Mother Teresa was born on August 26, 1910, less than two weeks after the death of Florence Nightingale, the mother of modern nursing practice, and just one week after the birth of Anna Muttathupadathu—Saint Alphonsa—the first woman from India to be canonized by the Roman Catholic Church. As a teenager, Alphonsa had a vision in which she

Figure 19.1. President Ronald Reagan, with Nancy Reagan, presents the Presidential Medal of Freedom to Mother Teresa, June 6, 1985 (source: Reagan White House Photographs)

saw the famed nineteenth-century saint Thérèse of Lisieux, the same Thérèse whose name Mother Teresa would one day adopt.

✳ ✳ ✳

Mother Teresa's story is well known. She was born Anjezë Gonxhe Bojaxhiu in an Albanian district of North Macedonia. She felt called to a religious life in her early teens, and at eighteen, she traveled to Ireland to train as a missionary with the

Sisters of Loreto. She arrived in India the following year and took her vows two years later, adopting the name Teresa.

While teaching at a convent school in Calcutta for more than two decades, she became increasingly distressed by the poverty and misery she saw around her in the city. So after a life-changing revelation—a convicting personal conversation with Jesus—in 1946, she determined to serve the poor in a more active way. She asked the Vatican to allow her to form an organization of missionary workers who would serve the poorest of the poor, and within two years, she opened her first hospice for the terminally ill in Calcutta.

In 1979, she was awarded the Nobel Peace Prize for her work, and by the time she died in 1997, her organization, the Missionaries of Charity, had established 610 hospices, hospitals, orphanages, soup kitchens, and schools in more than 120 countries. Pope Francis canonized her in 2016.

Still, many people have argued that she was not the saint she appeared to be. So for a few moments, allow me to play devil's advocate.

❋ ❋ ❋

How often I used the phrase *devil's advocate* before becoming aware of its origin. Within the Roman Catholic Church, the devil's advocate—in Latin, *advocatus diaboli*—is the official title given to the person designated to argue *against* the canonization of a prospective saint—in opposition to the *advocatus Dei*, "God's advocate," whose job is to argue *for* canonization. The idea is to ferret out any previously undisclosed misdeeds that might bar someone from being a saint—a person whom

Catholic believers are permitted to venerate. Major scandal and sainthood don't mix.

One thing puzzles me though: If a nominee had been a covert fraud during his or her lifetime and therefore unworthy of veneration, then wouldn't the person arguing *against* sainthood and *for* the truth really be *God's* advocate? It seems that by designating one person as being on the devil's side and the other as being on God's side sort of stacks the deck in advance.

Be that as it may, the procedure was first established in the late sixteenth century under Pope Sixtus V, who was an energetic though often draconian anticorruption fighter within the church. In 1983, Pope John Paul II diminished the role of the *advocatus diaboli*, though it was revived occasionally when needed, one notable instance occurring in 2003, when the late Mother Teresa was being considered for beatification, the procedural step before canonization.

One wonders why the church would even feel the need to have someone argue against her beatification, since she was then one of the most revered women in the world. A CNN / USA Today Gallup poll in December 1999 found that she was the most-admired person of the entire twentieth century, ranking ahead of Martin Luther King Jr., John F. Kennedy, Albert Einstein, and Helen Keller among the top five.[2]

But despite her popularity, the church knew she was not without her critics—and vehement ones at that. Beginning in the early 1990s, a number of magazine articles began chronicling what appeared to be the less-than-saintly aspects of Mother Teresa's life and ministry, or as the title of one negative magazine article asked, "Who Does She Think She Is . . . Mother Teresa?"[3]

First, many critics in the medical community spoke out. In 1994, the British medical journal the *Lancet* reported that their on-site study of one of Mother Teresa's hospices in Calcutta found that it provided only "haphazard" care at best, with untrained staff making major and sometimes ill-informed medical decisions.[4] A later study by the University of Montreal in 2013 confirmed the *Lancet*'s findings. Many doctors were also stunned by Mother Teresa's refusal to administer painkilling drugs. Since she was a believer in the holiness of Christ's sufferings, she felt that those dying under her care were especially blessed to partake in that suffering. Some critics argued that she'd made a fetish of suffering.

In addition, investigative reporters found that her charity had amassed millions of dollars of undistributed contributions, money that might have been spent directly to aid the poor. Of the funds that did get distributed, much of it was spent on evangelization and promoting the Catholic Church rather than providing for immediate needs like food, medical supplies, clothing, and shelter—all despite the fact that these financial contributions had been solicited under the guise of "serving the poor."

One noted Protestant theologian asserted that "she preached a false religion. In so doing she provides us with . . . an example of deeds of charity and compassion completely separated from the Truth."[5] Other religious leaders were shocked when her private letters were published in 2007, in which she admits to experiencing decades of spiritual drought and even occasional doubts as to God's presence in her life or even God's existence. One prominent evangelist rather boastfully declared that unlike Mother Teresa, she had *never* doubted God for an instant.

After Mother Teresa's death, it came to light that she had personally advocated for the reinstatement of a priest who had been removed from his position in 1993 due to multiple credible accusations of pedophilia. After the priest was reinstated due to her influence, more accusations were brought against him, and he was eventually arrested in 2005.[6]

In 1994, three years before Mother Teresa's death, renowned atheist and cultural gadfly Christopher Hitchens wrote a scathing book called *The Missionary Position: Mother Teresa in Theory and Practice*, in which he was critical of not only her medical practices but her coziness with authoritarian leaders, sketchy politicians, and corrupt businessmen. As Hitchens wrote, she was "a fund-raising icon for clerical nationalists . . . [and] has furnished PR-type cover for cultists and shady businessmen (who are often the same thing). . . . Nor has she ever deigned to respond to questions about her friendship with despots."[7]

Which brings us back to the *advocatus diaboli*—for the Roman Catholic Church actually called on Hitchens to perform the official role of devil's advocate while the beatification of Mother Teresa was being considered. Needless to say, his arguments did not keep her from being beatified in 2003, though it may have delayed her canonization as Saint Teresa of Calcutta for several years, until 2016.

My intention is not to denigrate Mother Teresa. Even if the worst of these stories were true, her organization has most certainly done more good in the long run than all of her critics combined, and many noted scholars have argued just as compellingly in her defense.

My interest is in her encounter with Jesus—the central turning point in her life and the moment that led to the founding of the Missionaries of Charity. That encounter, which took place during an extended train journey, was not exactly a vision but rather what is referred to as an "inner locution"[8] with Jesus—an ongoing internal conversation.[9]

* * *

While teaching in Calcutta as a young nun, Teresa made habit of making an annual retreat to a convent in Darjeeling, a four-hundred-mile train journey north from Calcutta. During one of those trips, on September 10, 1946, she felt overwhelmed by Jesus's presence and heard his voice. As she told British writer Malcolm Muggeridge years later, "It was on that train, I heard the call to give up all and follow him into the slums to serve him among the poorest of the poor. . . . I knew it was his will, and that I had to follow him. There was no doubt that it was going to be his work."[10]

The precise content of her conversation with Jesus that day is unknown, but it revolved around Christ's plea from the cross that he was thirsty.[11] Teresa interpreted his thirst to mean that he was thirsty for souls and desired, more than sustenance itself, to draw the dying and impoverished to himself. For Teresa, this revelation became what she called her "call within a call," and it inspired her with the idea of creating a ministry, which eventually became the Missionaries of Charity, to serve the poor with Christlike compassion and draw them to Jesus. As she explained later, "Jesus is God: Therefore His love, His thirst is infinite. Our aim is to quench this infinite thirst of a God made man. . . . The Sisters, using the four vows of Absolute Poverty, Chastity, Obedience and Charity toward the poor ceaselessly quench the thirsting God by their love and of the love of the souls they bring to Him."[12]

This encounter was not a singular event. Her inner dialogue with Jesus continued for several months. He explained to her in detail the shape her ministry should take: "You will dress in simple Indian clothes," he told her, "or rather like My Mother dressed—simple and poor. . . . I want Indian Missionary Sisters of Charity—who would be My fire of love amongst the very poor—the sick—the dying—the little street children. . . . Ask His Grace [Father Celeste van Exem, Teresa's spiritual director] to give Me this in thanksgiving of the 25 years of grace I have given him." With each new request, Jesus would add, "Wilt thou refuse?"[13]

Although she encountered setbacks as she sought permission to set aside her former vows to the Sisters of Loreto and begin her own new organization with its own rules, she eventually convinced the authorities of the genuineness of her inner locutions and her calling from God. Like Ananias's and Francis's encounters with Jesus, Teresa's was a direct command, a set of marching orders for the future, and it revolutionized the public image of the Catholic Church.

✳ ✳ ✳

To make sense of all this, I'd like to play devil's advocate once again and suggest, bluntly, that she imagined the whole thing. Which I don't mean to be dismissive in the least. That is also the opinion of Mother Teresa's own biographer Brian Kolodiejchuk.[14] Catholic theologians, he explains, distinguish between three types of locutions, or "manifestations of God's thought." The first is an external "auricular locution"—an audible voice. The second is an "interior imaginative locution"—specific words occurring in the mind. The third is an "interior intellectual locution," which is also internal but perceived only as thoughts separate from words. Mother Teresa's locutions were of the second kind—an imaginative experience.

An imagined Jesus, as I've suggested before, isn't necessarily a delusion. Since Teresa's conviction to help the poor was inspired by Jesus's own biblical commands ("If you want to be perfect," Jesus said, "go, sell your possessions and give to the poor, and you will have treasure in heaven"[15]), then her inner dialogue was not so much between her and Jesus but between her and a deeply internalized Jesus part of her. But isn't that the point of Christian faith, that there should be no difference between Jesus himself and the Jesus part within each believer's soul? The day before his crucifixion, Jesus said, "Before long, the world will not see me anymore, but you will see me. Because I live, you also will live. On that day you will realize that I am in my Father, and you are in me, and I am in you."[16] So why should we be surprised when sincere followers of Jesus have an ongoing dialogue with that internalized part of themselves?

In Teresa's case, she may also have been influenced by a highly emotional experience that occurred just a month before her formative train journey. In August 1946, she had witnessed a tragedy on the streets of Calcutta. A violent conflict had broken out between Muslims and Hindus in the city, and in the chaos, more than five thousand people were murdered outright and another eight thousand wounded. During the fighting, the city authorities attempted to impose curfews and lockdowns, but those orders only left the students in Teresa's school without much-needed supplies. So Teresa, a bold thirty-six-year-old nun, disobeyed the orders to venture into the city in a desperate search for food. When the police stopped her, she explained the heartrending situation to them, but instead of arresting her, they agreed to deliver sacks of rice to the school. Although the outcome was positive, the experience left her shaken. She had seen the wounded crying for help at every corner and the corpses rotting by the roadsides.

＊ ＊ ＊

So let me play devil's advocate to the devil's advocates themselves by asking, Do we really expect perfection from the church's saints? Is it normal, or even healthy, that we insist on the absolute purity of our religious heroes? Jerome was, frankly, ill-tempered; Francis was impulsive and a confessed thief. We know that Margery Kempe could be annoying, and I suspect even Hildegard and Julian had their bad days.

Teresa's unsettling experience combined with the love she felt for the poor of Calcutta must have contributed to her inner dialogue. If she was misguided, her intention seems to have been always focused on one thing: a fervent, consistent love for one's neighbor.

Which brings me back to Florence Nightingale. While the founder of modern nursing techniques might well have had the same criticisms of Mother Teresa that many modern medical people do, still, I think she would have recognized that Teresa's motives were deeply founded, if imperfectly, in love. Even when Teresa most doubted God's active presence in her life, she attempted to remain true to what she perceived as God's will from that single conversation with Jesus on the train. Florence Nightingale would have classified Teresa, I suspect, as being among the mystics. This passage from Nightingale's own writings seems to foreshadow the kind of ministry that Teresa would have:

That Religion is not devotion, but work and suffering for the love of God; this is the true doctrine of Mystics—as is more particularly set forth in a definition of the 16th century: "True religion is to have no other will but God's." Compare this with the definition of Religion in Johnson's *Dictionary*: "Virtue founded upon reverence of God and expectation of future rewards and punishments"; in other words on respect and self-interest, not love. Imagine the religion which inspired the life of Christ "founded" on the motives given by Dr. Johnson! . . .

Those who have to work on men and women must above all things have their Spiritual Ideal, their purpose, ever present.[17]

20

TORTILLAS AND TELEVANGELISTS
Maria Morales Rubio and Oral Roberts

On the morning of October 5, 1977, at 6:20 in the tiny town of Lake Arthur, New Mexico, a mile west of the Pecos River . . . something peculiar occurred. A Spanish-speaking Mexican immigrant named Maria Morales Rubio was making breakfast for her husband, Eduardo, and her daughter, Rosy. As Maria stood over the hot griddle pan, called a *comal*, she flipped one of the tortillas over, and as she was preparing to spoon beans onto it, she noticed something odd. The tortilla had a strange scorch mark on it about the size of a half-dollar. She looked at it . . . and looked again. She called Rosy to the kitchen. Did it really look like . . . ? Rosy too was amazed.

The scorch mark seemed to be in the shape of Jesus's face. No mistaking it.[1] To Maria, it seemed like a miracle. Surely, she thought, this was a divine gift.

She took the tortilla to Father Finnigan, the local priest, and though he didn't believe the image was a miracle, he agreed to bless it anyway. Before long, as word spread, scores of locals came to see it, and in the three decades that followed, thousands upon thousands from across the world found their way to the Rubios' home to see the tortilla, which Maria preserved in a small glass shrine called a *capilla* (figure 20.1). Maria and Rosy were guests on *The Phil Donahue Show* in 1994, and in 2005, their story was, in part, the inspiration for the film *Tortilla Heaven*.

One thing was immediately apparent: while many people found the incident inspiring, others found it ridiculous. It became a standing joke on late-night television, fodder for the tabloids, and the source of snickers in Phil Donahue's audience.

Figure 20.1. Maria Morales Rubio and the image of Jesus (Bettmann / Getty Images)

I confess that I snickered as well. To this day, the words *tortilla Jesus* suggest the absurdity of a certain kind of religious enthusiasm—so much so that when I tell people I'm writing a book about visions of Jesus, the first question is often, "Including tortillas?"

The answer is yes, I'm including tortillas. But also no, I no longer snicker. If we're to take the fruits of such appearances seriously, then the Rubios' story is to be valued, if only for the hundreds of people who claimed to have found physical and spiritual healing after praying before the image. Maria herself said the events freed her from long-term depression and cured Eduardo's alcoholism. He took his final drink on the day the image appeared.

Were any of those healings documented? Probably not. Still, those healings don't seem any more or less absurd than Anthony being freed from his demons by a glowing Jesus descending through the ceiling or an equally glowing Jesus appearing at the foot of Margery Kempe's bed to cure her postpartum depression.

Our impulse to laugh, I suspect, has roots in a latent bigotry. For many of us, the face of Jesus on a tortilla seems somehow less spiritual than a Byzantine crucifix in the Church of San Damiano or a blazing icon on Mount Athos. But why would an Italian fabric merchant's son or a former Russian soldier be any more credible than an impoverished Mexican immigrant? They aren't. You see, I find that I'm as intrigued by Maria's tortilla as I am by the crucifix that was held before the face of Julian of Norwich. These things happened to real people, and we are left having to make sense of them.

Which leads to the larger question: Do images of Jesus actually have miraculous powers? Do they cure sicknesses? Let's be clear: Jesus himself provided the most direct answer when he told the blind man whose sight had just been restored, "Your faith has healed you."[2] Faith, not faces, is the miracle.

✳ ✳ ✳

Of course, Maria's tortilla signaled the start of a social phenomenon. Jesus's face began to pop up in the strangest places. If you google the words "Jesus seen in objects" and click Images, you'll find a mind-boggling array of face-like pictures, all of which—with a little imagination—vaguely resemble Jesus. In the past forty years, that face has been perceived in tree bark and wood grain, in wall plaster and peeling paint, on frosted windows and in ultrasound photos, in a half-eaten chocolate bar and a banana skin, in clouds and sunbeams and burnt toast and rusted car bumpers. As suggested by the illustration on the cover of this book, some barista artists have even mastered the art of drawing faces in the foam on the top of lattes—though I've yet to see Jesus's face among them. Give them time.

Curiously, these faces, or at least the most discernible of them, look like the Jesus of classic paintings, whether by Rembrandt or Warner Sallman—that is, with shoulder-length hair, a long beard, an aquiline nose, and a somber expression. In the more obscure cases, anything suggesting eyes, a nose, and a mouth is taken to be Jesus. Of course, none of them are his face. They are merely vague representations of that face as we imagine it—our minds, like small movie projectors, casting images on the screen of the world's random objects.

Psychologists refer to our tendency to perceive faces and other shapes in objects as *pareidolia*. The man in the moon is the most common. (My mother said she always saw a Gibson girls' profile in the moon.) One friend of mine always points out faces in the front grilles of cars, and I even notice emoji-like "wow" faces in the three holes of electrical outlets. I constantly see faces of angels and kings and trolls in the rough chipboard flooring of our barn.

Since childhood, most of us have imagined shapes in the clouds. The most famous incident occurred in the Mexican town of Ocotlán in 1847, when, a day after a devastating earthquake decimated the area, the image of Jesus, standing upright with arms widespread, appeared in a cloud formation that lasted for more than a half hour. It was witnessed by hundreds of people.

Our psychological obsession with faces had an evolutionary value. Our early ancestors needed to distinguish instantly between friend and enemy and to read the mood and intention on their faces: happy . . . pleading . . . loving . . . threatening? As mentioned before, researchers say that each of us has the ability to identify as many as five thousand faces and to read their subtle emotional cues, which is why a card sharp's "poker face" not only misleads the other players but may also be psychologically intimidating by its sheer expressionlessness. Our brains are predisposed to see faces, and reading them accurately has helped our species survive.

※ ※ ※

Maria Morales Rubio was far from being the only religious person to be reduced to a punch line. Over the past half century, some of the most prominent media preachers in America have become laughingstocks for their antics, to say nothing of their corruption. Scandal plagued the ministries of such figures as Jimmy Swaggart, Ted Haggard, and Benny Hinn, and lawsuits alleging fraud or tax evasion were lodged against televangelists like Jim Bakker, W. V. Grant, and Robert Tilton. During the COVID-19 pandemic of 2020, some of the wealthiest megachurches in America claimed millions of dollars earmarked for small businesses, which meant that public tax dollars were going to support religious institutions.[3] One televangelist was even accused of purchasing a private jet with the emergency relief money. Back in 2009, prominent evangelical John MacArthur wrote, "Someone needs to say this plainly: The faith healers and health-and-wealth preachers who dominate religious television are shameless frauds."[4]

Consider Peter Popoff, a popular televangelist who claimed to be a healer and seer. He regularly astonished his audiences by calling out people by name, knowing where they came from, and diagnosing their ailments in detail—information that he claimed to have received directly from God. Throughout the 1970s and early 1980s, he would perform miraculous healings at his revival meetings, asking the sick to throw away their medications and commanding those in wheelchairs to rise and walk—all done dramatically on stage. His ministry was a fundraising powerhouse. At one point, he solicited money for a Bibles-behind-the-Iron-Curtain project, the concept of which was to attach tens of thousands of Bibles to helium-filled balloons so they could float into the Soviet Union.

In 1986, some critics grew skeptical of Popoff's claims. Magician and professional illusion-debunker James Randi, with the help of radio scanning equipment, was able to confirm that Popoff was actually using a wireless radio earpiece so that his wife could transmit information about audience members to him—information gathered beforehand. It was also found that many of those who threw away their pills were just as ill afterward, and the "wheelchair healings" were deceptions;

fully ambulatory audience members were given wheelchairs in advance so they could appear to be miraculously healed. Also, when no evidence of the Bibles-and-balloons scheme materialized, some people began asking what had become of the donations. Apparently, Popoff ordered that his own warehouse be robbed as part of a cover-up to explain the delay.[5] Though insisting on his innocence throughout, Popoff's ministry went bankrupt within two years.

One common denominator in these fundraising schemes is the claim that the televangelist has a special connection to God or Jesus, often hearing their words or seeing them in visions. Pat Robertson, for instance, has regularly claimed to receive prophetic messages from God: God told him that George H. W. Bush would win reelection in a "blowout" in 1992;[6] that a major tsunami would hit the United States in 2006; that in the fall of 2007, there would be "a major terrorist attack in a major city this year. . . . Millions of people may be killed."[7] Needless to say, none of these predictions came to pass. In 2020, God told Robertson that Donald Trump would win reelection,[8] though six weeks after Trump lost the election, Robertson admitted that Trump "lives in an alternate reality" and should "move on."[9]

✳ ✳ ✳

Anyone born after 1960 will remember the story of Oral Roberts, who was probably the most controversial preacher of the last century (figure 20.2). He too had a noted—or notorious—vision of Jesus.

One day in 1947, when he was a poor twenty-nine-year-old preacher, he rushed out the door of his house to catch a bus. As he hastily grabbed his Bible, it flipped open to 3 John 1:2 KJV:

Figure 20.2. Oral Roberts before an evangelistic event in Texas, 1962 (photo by Francis Miller, from the *LIFE* Picture Collection / Getty Images)

"Beloved, I wish above all things that thou mayest prosper and be in health, even as thy soul prospereth." He was astonished. He'd never seen that verse before, but it became a turning point in his life and ministry. While he knew that Jesus embraced poverty, Roberts now came to believe that Jesus intended for his followers to attain—by faith—financial and physical health (despite the fact that John wrote that Bible verse, not Jesus). At the same time, by an odd coincidence, one of Roberts's parishioners happened to be a car dealer, and noticing that Roberts's car was run down, he managed to get Roberts and his wife a Buick at a cut rate.

Roberts, stunned by the possibility of an entirely new direction in his preaching, decided to pray about it. He told his wife that he planned to spend the day at their church until God gave him a clear sign. It came. God told him to get into his new car and start driving, and while he drove, God spoke these words: "From this hour your ministry of healing will begin. You will have my power to pray for the sick and cast out devils."[10]

That was the beginning of his phenomenal rise as a preacher of the health-and-wealth, or prosperity, gospel. He became an internationally known evangelist, with only Billy Graham being more well known. Roberts created the popular *Abundant Life* television ministry in the 1950s, and in 1963, he founded Oral Roberts University in Tulsa, Oklahoma, again claiming it had been a direct command from God.

In 1977, shortly after the tragic death of his daughter Rebecca and her husband, Roberts received a visit from God in a hotel room in California, and Roberts wrote out the words that God had spoken to him. The gist of the message was this: "You must build a new and different medical center for Me. The healing streams of prayer and medicine must merge through what I will have you build. . . . You shall call it the City of Faith."[11] And God even gave him a vision of what the massive structure should look like. From that point on, the God-given mission of merging faith and medical healing became the driving passion in his life.

Roberts set about the task despite opposition from some local bureaucrats and medical professionals who argued that an additional hospital complex in Tulsa was not needed. By 1980, the project, now the tallest structure in Tulsa, was nevertheless only half completed and foundering for lack of funds. So on May 25, 1980, Roberts wrote a letter to his most loyal supporters, describing a vision of Jesus he'd recently had. It read, in part,

> I felt an overwhelming holy presence all around me. When I opened my eyes, there He stood . . . some 900 feet tall, looking at me; His eyes . . . Oh! His eyes! He stood a full 300 feet taller than the 600 foot tall City of Faith.
>
> There I was face to face with Jesus Christ, the Son of the Living God. . . . I have only seen Jesus once before, but here I was face to face with the King of Kings. He stared at me without saying a word; Oh! I will never forget those eyes! And then he reached down, put His hands under the City of Faith, lifted it, and said to me, "See how easy it is for me to lift it!"[12]

At that point, claimed Roberts, he told Jesus that he had done everything possible to complete the project, but resources had evaporated, to which Jesus replied, "I told you at the beginning that you would not be able to build it yourself. I told you that I would speak to your partners and, through them, I would build it!"

Needless to say, this was a *fundraising* letter. He was trying to persuade donors to send more money. The letter reminded them that they needed to obey Christ "by giving a *precious seed* this week to help me pay the bills in September. . . . If you will obey, it will not be difficult to finish the second half of the City of Faith."

When news reports of the letter began to appear, an executive vice president of the Oral Roberts Association assured curious reporters, "What he said he saw, he saw."

The controversy over the City of Faith only grew more intense four years later, when Roberts offered his donors, in return for their continued support, a small statuette of an angel that he claimed had appeared to him. Three years later, in March 1987, as the now finished hospital was still faltering financially because fewer than half its beds were filled, Roberts told the viewers of his *Abundant Life* television program that if he could not raise $8 million for medical scholarships, he'd die. God had told him directly, "I'm going to call you home in one year."[13] His followers panicked, and the unsympathetic media called it crass exploitation.

In 1989, Roberts was forced to close the Oral Roberts University Medical School and sell the City of Faith because the complex was now $25 million in debt. (Oral Roberts didn't die until 2009.)

❋ ❋ ❋

In 1982, when Roberts appeared on *The Phil Donahue Show* in an attempt to restore his reputation after the negative publicity caused by his unusual claims, he told Donahue's audience something about the nine-hundred-foot-tall Jesus that he did not tell his donors in the original fundraising letter: "I saw Jesus with my *inner* eyes—not my physical eyes—I saw him rise up behind the building . . . and I heard him in my heart. In my inner self I could see my savior."[14]

In other words, like Stephen and Jerome and Julian and Charles Finney and so many others, he was aware that his vision was an interior one.

❋ ❋ ❋

Two appearances of Jesus—one scorched onto a tortilla and the other nine hundred feet tall. Both incidents seem bizarre, even disturbing. Both created snickers on Phil Donahue's show. But the contrast between the two is stark.

Roberts lived in a 6,328-square-foot mansion and owned two vacation homes. He owned expensive cars and wore Italian silk suits. He loved "diamond rings and gold bracelets," which were carefully "airbrushed out by his staff on publicity pictures."[15] One major newspaper titled its obituary of Roberts "The Evangelist Preacher Who Worshipped Money."[16]

Maria Morales Rubio, by contrast, refused to accept money from the visitors who came to view the tortilla, and even when they insisted on leaving a donation, she used the money to buy the candles that burned perpetually around the *capilla*. Any money left over was spent on food and clothing for her needy neighbors. To use the money any other way would have been to blaspheme the gift she'd been given. So deeply did she believe in the healing power of the image that she would leave her door open whenever she went out so that no pilgrim would be denied the chance to see it. It was never stolen. She could have taught Oral Roberts a thing or two about wealth and healing and faith.

EPILOGUE
The Face of Faces

So . . . a mystic and a skeptic walk into a bar.

The mystic says, "Hey, you know, I saw Jesus last night."

"How'd you know it was him?" asks the skeptic.

"Well . . . how do you know it wasn't?"

Not very funny, I know. But it sums up my feelings about the stories in this book because I feel as if I'm both the mystic and the skeptic at the same time.

✳ ✳ ✳

As I've tried to make sense of these stories, to search for their fruits, a few patterns have emerged.

1. Each person was predisposed to seeing Jesus. Most were already devoted to him. A few hated him but then had overpowering conversions. Either way, nearly all were absorbed by him beforehand.

2. Most of these visions can be explained by psychological, physiological, or emotional factors—depression, guilt, headache, anxiety, illness, stress, trauma, and so on— though "explained" doesn't necessarily mean "explained away." Those factors don't preclude the Divine.

3. These people were their own first and best interpreters. By telling others about their visions and even writing books, they controlled their own narrative, shaping the meaning they expected others to find. They were often storytellers as much as they were visionaries.

4. Finally, each dream and vision (after the ascension) was, as Charles Finney said, a "mental state." Despite those who claimed that Jesus appeared to them in tangible, physical form, no third-party evidence exists. Except for the tortilla of Maria Morales Rubio, the visions were private, internalized occurrences—and accepted by others only as a matter of faith.

❊ ❊ ❊

So I end much as I began—skeptical but intrigued, baffled but also strangely moved. Even if every one of these stories is untrue, if every vision of Jesus was an aberration, I still find each of these people—both the good and the not so good—fascinating . . . and far more interesting than the people social media has told us we're supposed to find interesting. How miraculous that history has recorded tales of people like Jerome and Hildegard and Francis and Julian and Sojourner Truth and all the rest. How wonderful to realize that such people once walked the earth.

As far as which visions are true and which are counterfeit, I don't know. I have my favorites. Some seem to have borne more fruit than others, and some seem wholly absurd, but I've come to think it doesn't matter. Just as these visions took place in the minds of the visionaries, so too, in reading about them, their visions inhabit my mind as well. They become our own. The mind cultivates that fruit.

I read these stories in much the same way I read poetry. I've never wondered whether Robert Frost really stopped by the woods on a snowy evening, because I trust he was trying to communicate something other—deeper and more truthful—than any literal event. When we read the Gospels, we can't help but imagine the scenes as if they were a beautifully filmed and grippingly scripted movie, and that may, in fact, be why biblical films seem so disappointing. They are never as vivid as the pictures in the mind's eye. Each of us, as we read the Bible, has our own vision of Jesus. We picture him in our mind's eye.

Perhaps the stories in this book are really about each of us, about the mystery of seeking Jesus in our own lives and within our souls. His presence may, in fact, make up our truest self. If we do not see his face, it is because we have not really seen our own. "The first step," as C. S. Lewis wrote, "is to try to forget about the self altogether. Your real, new self (which is Christ's and also yours, and yours just because it is His) will not come as long as you are looking for it. It will come when you are looking for Him."[1] The people in this book managed to see the unrecognized stranger on the road and to feel the burning in their hearts. And with their visions, they are saying to us, "Now it's your turn. . . . What do you see?"

✳ ✳ ✳

If we can catch a glimpse of that Jesus who is our truest self, if we can see his face within, then we are freed to see him reflected in others. Centuries of Christian thinkers—most of whom were *not* mystics—have told us that we see the face of Jesus every day, walking the streets of every city, in the face of every person. Fifteenth-century theologian Nicholas of Cusa wrote, "In all faces is seen the Face of faces, veiled, and in a riddle";[2] eighteenth-century poet William Cowper wrote, "The mind indeed enlighten'd from above / Views him in all"[3]; and twentieth-century theologian Dietrich Bonhoeffer put it most clearly when he wrote, "He comes in the form of the beggar, of the dissolute human child in ragged clothes, asking for help. He confronts you in every person that you meet. As long as there are people, Christ will walk the earth as your neighbor, as the one through whom God calls you, speaks to you, makes demands on you."[4]

And so I end with a story . . . with a vision of my own.

Recently, my friend Sherwood and I were seated at a table at an outdoor café, masked and socially distanced due to COVID-19. As we chatted, a man pulled into the parking lot in a beat-up car. He got out (not wearing a mask), approached us, and explained that he'd driven all the way from Kentucky for a construction job that hadn't panned out, and he now found himself stranded in Michigan with no gas money to get back home. The local relief agencies were willing to give him a bed and a meal but not money.

I was suspicious of his story. His car had a Michigan rather than a Kentucky plate. I asked him about it, and he gave me a confused explanation. When I asked him where in Kentucky he was from, he only added to the confusion.

Still, I thought about all I've experienced in writing this book, so I studied the man, his face and demeanor. All I can remember now is that he seemed weathered, battered by hard times. I asked myself, Can I see *the* Face in that face? Is Jesus in there, "veiled, and in a riddle"? I studied him some more. Yes, I thought, Jesus's face could very well be lurking just behind those pale cheeks and earnest eyes. With darker hair and skin, Jesus could have looked just like this.

To Sherwood's surprise, I pulled out my wallet, fished out a twenty-dollar bill, and handed it to the man. He thanked me and then walked back toward his car.

"I know," I said to Sherwood, "the odds are nine in ten he won't spend the money on gas," and I quickly told him about my idea of trying to see the face of Jesus in every face I see. I quoted for him that line from Nicholas of Cusa.

A short way off, the man was about to get back into his car, so I yelled, "Hey, my name's Bob; I forgot to ask—What's yours?"

He turned and shouted, "Josh!" And then he got into his car and drove off.

Sherwood and I looked at each other. We had precisely the same thought. Joshua is the anglicized form of Yeshua, "the deliverer"—the Hebrew name of Jesus.

✳ ✳ ✳

The skeptic in me says, "How'd you know it was him?"

The mystic in me says, "How do you know it wasn't?"

ACKNOWLEDGMENTS

This book came into being because of the hard work and encouragement of the following people. A simple *thank you* seems so inadequate compared to the gratitude I feel. But *thank you*

- scholar, bookman, writer, and agent Tim Beals of Credo Communications;
- Broadleaf Books editor Emily King; and
- Broadleaf Books copy editor Claire Vanden Branden and the proofreaders at Scribe Inc.

Thank you also to Linda Lambert for your valuable feedback, to Glenn Warners for suggesting the framework for the "Revival Fires" chapter, and to Brian Phipps for opening your library to me and for teaching me about Silouan the Athonite.

Thank you to the many others who contributed to this work, often in ways they might not even know—Sarah Arthur, Sherwood de Visser, Nancy Erickson, James Ernest, Susan Hudson Fox, Terry Glaspey, Sarah Gombis, Julie Gridley, Bob Hartig, Clarence Hogeterp, Abbie Hudson, Molly Hudson, Lili Hudson, George Ray and Barbara Hudson, Pam Keating, Deborah Leiter, Tisha Martin, Brother Jeff and JoEllen Maskow, Kin Millen, Bill and Beth Murphy, Jack Roeda, John Sloan, Ann Spangler, Leonard Sweet, Kim

Tanner, Virginia Tobiassen, Julie Warners, Bryan and Linda Whittemore, and Ed Vander Maas.

And most of all, thank you to poet, musician, and dancer Shelley Townsend-Hudson.

APPENDIX
Visions of Jesus—A List

As mentioned in chapter 1, a virtual history of Christianity could be written focusing only on those who have claimed to have had remarkable dreams or visions of Jesus. Here are just a few of the most famous from the late first century to the early twentieth. They are listed in order of their birth year. (An asterisk indicates that the person is discussed in this book.)

late first century	Alexander I (pope)	540	Gregory the Great (pope)
ca. 251	Anthony of Egypt (ascetic, founder of monasticism)*	ca. 656	Hubert of Brittany (bishop)
ca. 289	Philomena (martyr)	949	Symeon the New Theologian (monk, theologian)*
316	Martin of Tours (ascetic, bishop)*	first half of the tenth century	Wulsin of Sherborne (bishop)
ca. 345	Jerome (theologian, translator of the Vulgate)*	ca. 973	Henry II (Holy Roman emperor)
ca. 347	Porphyry of Gaza (bishop)	1092	Hildegard of Bingen (abbess, writer)*
sixth century	Honoratus of Amiens (bishop)	ca. 1127	Julian of Cuenca (bishop)
sixth century	Trasilla (aunt of Gregory the Great)	ca. 1129	Elisabeth of Schönau (abbess)

ca. 1150	Hermann Joseph (canon regular)	1233	Rose of Viterbo (recluse)
1170	Dominic of Osma (priest, founder of Dominicans)	1242	Christina of Stommeln (lay sister, stigmatic)
ca. 1174	Edmund of Abingdon (archbishop, theologian)	ca. 1244	Agnes Blannbekin (lay sister)
		ca. 1246	Nicholas of Tolentino (priest)
ca. 1181	Francis of Assisi (founder of the Franciscans)*	1248	Angela of Foligno (Franciscan tertiary)
1182	Lutgardis of Aywières (nun)	mid-thirteenth century	Ida of Louvain (nun)
ca. 1185	Hyacinth of Poland (priest, missionary)	1256	Gertrude the Great (nun, theologian)
ca. 1192	Juliana of Liège (canoness)	1268	Agnes of Montepulciano (prioress)
1195	Anthony of Padua (priest)	1277	Christina Ebner (nun, writer)
late twelfth century	Robert of Lyons (student)	1291	Margareta Ebner (nun, writer)
ca. 1200	Hadewijch of Antwerp (lay sister, writer)	ca. 1312	Bridget of Sweden (nun, founder of Bridgettines)*
ca. 1200	Beatrice of Nazareth (nun, writer)	ca. 1343	Julian of Norwich (anchoress)*
ca. 1207	Mechtilde of Hackeborn (lay sister, writer)	1347	Catherine of Siena (lay sister, writer)*
ca. 1232	Ramon Llull (philosopher, writer)	1350	Vincent Ferrer (monk, missionary)
		ca. 1373	Margery Kempe (writer)*

1413	Catherine of Bologna (nun, writer, artist)
ca. 1445	Veronica of Milan (nun)
1449	Osanna of Mantua (tertiary, stigmatic)
1457	Stephana de Quinzanis (nun, stigmatic)
b. 1467	Columba of Rieti (nun)
b. 1474	Angela of Brescia (founder of Company of St. Ursula)
ca. 1491	Ignatius of Loyola (priest, founder of the Jesuits)*
1515	Teresa of Ávila (nun, writer)*
1542	John of the Cross (monk and writer)*
1550	Stanislaus Kostka (novice)
1575	Jacob Boehme (philosopher)*
1586	Rose of Lima (lay nun)
1599	John Engelbrecht (clothier, visionary)
1619	Margaret Parigot (nun, founder of Family of the Child Jesus)
1624	George Fox (founder of Quakers)*
1647	Marguerite Marie Alacoque (nun, promoted Sacred Heart of Jesus)
1647	Benoîte Rencurel (shepherdess)
1660	Veronica Giuliani (nun)
1688	Emanuel Swedenborg (scientist, theologian)*
1726	Gerard Majella (lay brother)
1736	Ann Lee (founder of the Shakers)*
1752	Public Universal Friend (preacher)*
ca. 1754	Seraphim of Sarov (staretz)
1757	William Blake (artist, poet)*
1774	Anne Catherine Emmerich (canoness, stigmatic)
1777	Lorenzo Dow (evangelist)*
1786	John Vianney (priest)
1792	Charles Finney (evangelist)*

ca. 1797	Sojourner Truth (abolitionist, activist)*	1889	Sundar Singh (evangelist, missionary)*
1805	Joseph Smith (founder of the Mormons)*	1890	Josefa Menéndez (nun)
		1890	Maria Pierina de Micheli (nun)
1809	Angelina (abbess)	1897	Maria Valtorta (lay sister, writer)
1816	Marie of Saint Peter (nun, began devotion to Holy Face of Jesus)	1898	Therese Neumann (stigmatic)
1822	Harriet Tubman (abolitionist, activist)*	1902	Marie Rose Ferron (stigmatic)
1829	William Booth (founder of the Salvation Army)	1905	Faustina Kowalska (nun)
		1910	Mother Teresa (founder of Missionaries of Charity)*
1840	Taisiia of Leushino (abbess)		
1841	Marie Martha Chambon (nun)	1915	Roy Gustafson (cofounder of Billy Graham Association)
1850	Marie-Julie Jahenny (stigmatic)		
1863	Mary of the Divine Heart (nun)	1918	Oral Roberts (evangelist)*
1866	Silouan the Athonite (monk)*	1924	Madeleine Aumont (laywoman)
1878	Gemma Galgani (stigmatic)	1942	Vassula Rydén (writer)
1887	Pio of Pietrelcina (priest, stigmatic)		

NOTES

1. You Just Want to See His Face

1. So intense was this woman's story that more than fifty years later, I remember it as something she had experienced herself, but I confess that my memory is vague, and she may have been relating a story about someone else. It is possible that this woman was Esther G. Frye (1914–2011), the most prominent and popular chalk-art evangelist of the time. Then again, I've found pictures of Ms. Frye online, and she looks nothing like the woman I remember seeing decades ago.
2. In the back of this book, see the appendix.
3. John 14:16–17.
4. John 14:18.
5. Matthew 19:14 KJV.
6. John 7:37; 11:43; Matthew 27:46.
7. Revelation 1:10, 15.
8. Revelation 1:16.
9. Matthew 7:29; Mark 1:22; Luke 4:32. The NLT and the NET, among others, used the word *spoke*.
10. Subsequent research by biblical scholar Joan E. Taylor confirmed what the earlier study found. See Joan E. Taylor, *What Did Jesus Look Like?* (London: T&T Clark, 2018).
11. Taylor, 130.
12. The original color photograph of *Mummy Portrait of Young Officer with Sword Belt* was taken by Anagoria and reproduced here under the terms of the GNU Free Documentation License. The photograph was slightly cropped and rendered in black and white for print production. See "User: Anagoria," Wikimedia Commons, last modified August 14, 2020, https://tinyurl.com/276nrgxb.
13. Matthew 17:2; Luke 9:29.
14. Revelation 1:16.

15. John 12:3 KJV.
16. Paul Tillich, *On Art and Architecture* (New York: Crossroad, 1987), 144.
17. Hebrews 11:1 KJV.
18. Matthew 7:15–16 KJV.
19. Quoted in Idries Shah, *The Sufis* (New York: Anchor, 1971), 91. Adapted.

2. The Doubter

1. Charles Dickens, *The Annotated Christmas Carol*, ed. Michael Patrick Hearn (New York: Clarkson N. Potter, 1976), 76.
2. 2 Corinthians 4:18 WNT.
3. John 20:25.
4. John 20:27.
5. John 20:28.
6. John 20:29.
7. Emily Dickinson, *The Master Letters of Emily Dickinson* (Amherst, MA: Amherst College Press, 2002), 32.
8. John 11:16.
9. John 14:2–4.
10. John 14:5.
11. Malcolm Guite, "St. Thomas the Apostle," in *Sounding the Seasons: Seventy Sonnets for the Church Year* (Norwich, UK: Canterbury, 2012), 54.
12. John 14:6.
13. Matthew 10:16.
14. Matthew 7:15–16.
15. Matthew 24:4–5, 23–26.
16. Frankie Schembri, "The Average Person Can Recognize 5000 Faces," *Science*, October 9, 2018, https://tinyurl.com/ymupwn9c.
17. John 20:29.
18. Marvin Meyer, ed., *The Gospel of Thomas: The Hidden Sayings of Jesus* (San Francisco: HarperSanFrancisco, 1992), 23.
19. Matthew 25:40.

3. The Stranger Within

1. Luke 24:4 KJV.
2. Luke 24:4.

3. Luke 24:5–6.

4. Luke 24:25–26.

5. I know that this term, meaning "teacher," is used only in the gospels of Mark and John and not in Luke, but I have allowed myself some poetic license in this case. It's my pageant, after all.

6. Charles Wesley, "Hymn for Easter Day," in *Hymns and Sacred Poems*, ed. John Wesley and Charles Wesley (London: Strahan, 1739), 209–10. Spelling adapted.

7. John 19:25.

8. John 19:25. Some scholars suggest that the phrase "Mary . . . of Clopas" in this passage might mean that Clopas is Mary's father. One scholar has even suggested that Clopas was Joseph's brother who married Mary, the mother of Jesus, after Joseph's death, as was a custom in ancient Israel.

9. Mark Piesing, "The Race to Fingerprint the Human Voice," *Independent*, February 13, 2013, https://tinyurl.com/39b69e54.

10. George Bernard Shaw, *Pygmalion* (New York: Dover, 1994), 39.

11. Luke 24:32.

12. John Wesley and Charles Wesley, *Selected Prayers, Hymns, Journal Notes, Sermons, Letters and Treatises*, ed. Frank Whaling (Mahwah, NJ: Paulist, 1981), 107.

13. Mahalia Jackson, "My God Is Real (Yes, God Is Real)," disc 1, track 2 on *Gospels, Spirituals, and Hymns*, Columbia/Legacy C2K 47083, 1991—based on Kenneth Morris's hymn "Yes, God Is Real" sheet music (Chicago: Martin and Morris, 1944).

14. T. S. Eliot, *The Waste Land and Other Writings* (New York: Modern Library, 2002), 49.

15. Luke 7:37–38.

16. Luke 8:2–3.

17. John 20:11 WYC.

18. John 20:12.

19. Luke 24:4 KJV.

20. John 20:13. Some scholars translate John 20:13 as "*We* don't know where they have put him," indicating that perhaps some of the other women are with Mary. In any case, Mary Magdalene is, among the women, the primary focus of this scene in all four gospels.

21. John 20:16–17.

22. John 20:17 KJV.
23. Matthew Henry, *An Exposition of the Old and New Testaments* (New York: Carter & Brothers, 1856), 4:806.
24. John 21:6.
25. Luke 17:21 KJV.
26. Thomas Merton, *Conjectures of a Guilty Bystander* (Garden City, NY: Doubleday, 1966), 142.

4. "On the Right Hand of God"

1. James 1:27; 2:15.
2. Acts 6:5, 8.
3. Acts 6:11.
4. Acts 7:52.
5. Acts 7:54.
6. Acts 7:56 KJV.
7. Matthew 26:64.
8. Daniel 7:13.
9. Acts 7:55.
10. Acts 7:59–60.
11. Luke 23:34.
12. Acts 7:58.
13. Acts 22:20.
14. Acts 23:6.
15. Thomas Merton, "St. Paul," in *Collected Poems* (New York: New Directions, 1977), 95.
16. Acts 9:1.
17. Acts 9:3–5.
18. Acts 9:11.
19. Acts 9:15.
20. Acts 9:18.
21. Acts 9:20.
22. Romans 16:7.
23. D. Landsborough, "St Paul and Temporal Lobe Epilepsy," *Journal of Neurology, Neurosurgery, and Psychiatry* 50 (1987): 659–64.
24. Oliver Sacks, *Hallucinations* (New York: Knopf, 2012), 161.
25. 1 Corinthians 15:7–8.
26. Galatians 1:12.

5. *VOOM!*

1. G. K. Chesterton, *Orthodoxy* (New York: John Lane, 1909), 29.
2. Charles Spurgeon, quoted in Joseph S. Exell, *The Biblical Illustrator: Anecdotes, Similes, Emblems, Illustrations, Expository, Scientific, Geographical, Historical, and Homiletic, Gathered from a Wide Range of Home and Foreign Literature on the Verses of the Bible* (New York: Anson D. F. Randolph, 1905), 36.
3. Revelation 1:1 KJV.
4. Revelation 1:1 KJV.
5. Revelation 1:7 KJV.
6. Revelation 1:10 KJV.
7. William Blake, *Vala or the Four Zoas*, in *Complete Writings*, ed. Geoffrey Keynes (London: Oxford University Press, 1972), 356.
8. Revelation 1:12–18 KJV.
9. Revelation 1:3.
10. John Milton, *Paradise Lost*, bk. 12, lines 227–29.
11. Revelation 1:12, 16, 17 KJV (emphasis mine).
12. Revelation 1:13, 14, 16, 14, 18 KJV.
13. Revelation 1:16 KJV.
14. Revelation 1:17 KJV.
15. Revelation 1:17 KJV.
16. Revelation 1:1 KJV.
17. Revelation 1:17, 18 KJV.
18. Revelation 1:18 KJV.
19. Revelation 1:15 KJV.
20. Revelation 10:10 KJV.
21. Revelation 18:11–13 KJV.
22. Revelation 21:1–6 KJV.
23. Virginia Woolf, *The Common Reader* (New York: Harcourt, Brace, 1925), 49.
24. W. B. Yeats, "The Second Coming," in *Michael Robartes and the Dancer* (Churchtown, Dundrum: Cuala, 1920), 19.
25. Eliot, *Waste Land*, 49.
26. William Blake, *Milton*, in *Complete Writings*, 532.
27. Revelation 10:2 KJV.

6. Demons and a Dream

1. Ovid, *The Poems of Exile: Tristia and the Black Sea Letters*, trans. Peter Green (Berkeley: University of California Press, 2005), xxiv.

2. William Edward Hartpole Lecky, "The Saints of the Desert," in *History of European Morals from Augustus to Charlemagne* (New York: Appleton, 1869), 2:114.

3. Matthew 19:21, quoted in Athanasius, *The Life of Saint Antony*, trans. Robert T. Meyer, Ancient Christian Writers Series (New York: Newman, 1950), 19. Meyer doesn't quote any version of the verse exactly, but it is quite similar in wording to DRB and KJV.

4. Athanasius, 19.

5. Athanasius, 87.

6. Athanasius, 28.

7. Athanasius, 65.

8. Revelation 16:13–14 KJV.

9. Matthew 4:3 KJV.

10. Matthew 4:8 KJV.

11. Sacks, *Hallucinations*, 34.

12. Sulpitius Severus, *Life of St. Martin*, trans. Alexander Roberts, in *The Nicene and Post-Nicene Fathers*, ed. Philip Schaff and Henry Wace, vol. 11, *Sulpitius Severus, Vincent of Lérins, John Cassian* (New York: Christian Literature Company, 1894), 5.

13. Severus, 11:10.

14. Matthew 25:40. The story of Martin and the beggar is told in Severus, *Life of St. Martin*, 11:5.

15. Lecky, *History of European Morals*, 2:114.

16. Count de Montalembert, *Monks of the West from St. Benedict to St. Bernard* (Edinburgh: Blackwood, 1861), 305–6; language modernized.

17. Augustine, *Confessions*, trans. R. S. Pine-Coffin (London: Penguin, 1961), 149–50.

18. Leonard Sweet, *Soul Salsa: 17 Surprising Steps for Godly Living in the 21st Century* (Grand Rapids, MI: Zondervan, 2000), 162.

19. Arnold Toynbee, "The Desert Hermits," *Horizon*, Spring 1970, 27.

7. God's Grouch

1. Jerome actually revised portions of the Bible from existing translations, checking them for accuracy and improving them. But much of the Vulgate was his own translation from the original languages.

2. Philip Schaff and Henry Wace, eds., "Letter CXXVII," in *The Nicene and Post-Nicene Fathers*, vol. 6, *Saint Jerome: Letters and Select Works* (New York: Christian Literature Company, 1893), 257.

3. Thomas Merton, *Saint Jerome, God's Grouch*, audio recording (Kansas City, MO: Credence Cassettes, National Catholic Reporter, 1988).

4. E. Cobham Brewer, *A Dictionary of Miracles: Imitative, Realistic, and Dogmatic* (London: Chatto & Windus, 1884), 220.

5. Sadeler's and Mostaert's *Saint Jerome* engraving (late sixteenth century), Wellcome Collection, Wellcome Library, no. 5644i. Public domain.

6. Marianne Moore, "Leonardo da Vinci's," in *New Collected Poems*, ed. Heather Cass White (New York: Farrar, Straus & Giroux, 2017), 224.

7. Philip Schaff and Henry Wace, "Letter XXII," in *Nicene and Post-Nicene*, 6:35–36.

8. Charles Christopher Mierow, trans., *The Letters of St. Jerome*, vol. 1, *Letters 1–22* (New York: Newman, 1963), 165.

9. Mierow, 1:165–66. Italics are in the original and find their source in Matthew 6:21 DRB. The DRB is referenced throughout this chapter as the authoritative translation into English of Jerome's Vulgate.

10. John 5:22 DRB.

11. Mierow, *Letters*, 1:166.

12. Mierow, 1:166.

13. Genesis 28:10–17.

14. Daniel 7:13 DRB. Biblical scholar Jeffrey Kranz has created a helpful chart of all the dreams in the Bible: Jeffrey Kranz, "Infographic: Every Dream in the Bible (and What They Mean)," overviewbible.com, July 27, 2018, https://tinyurl.com/497lrcpc.

15. The Apocrypha is replete with interesting dreams, but a full discussion of those is beyond the scope of this book.

16. Matthew 1:19, 23 DRB.

17. Matthew 2:12; 2:13, 19, 22 DRB.

18. Matthew 27:19 DRB.

19. 2 Chronicles 33:6 DRB. "Manasseh" is called "Manasses" in the DRB.

20. Jeremiah 27:9 DRB.

21. Sirach 34:1–2, 7 DRB.

22. Ecclesiastes 5:6 DRB.

23. This discussion of Jerome and mistranslation was inspired by and in large part drawn from two sources: Morton Kelsey, *God, Dreams and Revelation: A Christian Interpretation of Dreams* (Minneapolis: Augsburg, 1991), 136–39; and Robert Moss, "St. Jerome Bewitches Dreams and Dreamwork," Dream Gate, Beliefnet, accessed August 2020, https://tinyurl.com/x5kctbnh.

24. Henry Wace and Philip Schaff, eds., "Rufinus' Apology against Jerome, Book II," in *The Nicene and Post-Nicene Fathers*, vol. 3, *Theodoret, Jerome, Gennadius, Rufinus: Historical Writings, etc.* (New York: Christian Literature Company, 1892), 463.

25. Mierow, *Letters*, 1:244.

26. Quoted in Helen Waddell, *The Wandering Scholars* (London: Constable, 1932), xv.

27. Richard de Bury, *The Love of Books: The Philobiblon of Richard De Bury*, trans. E. C. Thomas (London: de la More, 1902), 85–86.

28. Psalms 130:1; Genesis 1:3; John 19:5, respectively.

29. John 14:19–20.

8. Apocryphal Visions

1. Frederik Wisse, trans., "The Letter of Peter to Philip," in *The Nag Hammadi Library in English* (Hollywood, CA: Gnostic Society Library, n.d.), http://gnosis.org/naghamm/letpet.html.

2. William Hone, Jeremiah Jones, and William Wake, eds., "The Epistles of Jesus Christ and Abgarus King of Edessa," in *The Lost Books of the Bible* (New York: Bell, 1979), 63.

3. Mark M. Mattison, trans., "The Infancy Gospel of Thomas," gospels.net, accessed September 2020, https://www.gospels.net/infancythomas.

4. Mattison.

5. M. R. James, trans., *The Acts of John*, in *The Gnostic Society Library: Gnostic Scriptures and Fragments* (Hollywood, CA: Gnostic Society Library, n.d.), sec. 89, http://www.gnosis.org/library/actjohn.htm.

6. M. R. James, trans., *The Acts of Peter*, in *The Apocryphal New Testament* (Oxford: Clarendon, 1924), sec. 21, https://tinyurl.com/u9htmtm6.

7. Xenophanes, quoted in Constantine J. Vamvacas, *The Founders of Western Thought: The Presocratics* (New York: Springer, 2009), 88.

8. Ron Cameron, ed., "The Apocryphon of James," in *The Other Gospels: Non-canonical Gospel Texts* (Philadelphia: Westminster, 1982), 62.

9. Stephen Emmel, trans., "The Dialogue of the Savior," in *Nag Hammadi Library*, http://gnosis.org/naghamm/dialog.html.

10. Mark M. Mattison, trans., "The Gospel of Judas," gospels.net, accessed August 2020, https://www.gospels.net/judas.

11. Wisse, "Letter of Peter to Philip."

12. Wisse.

13. Thomas à Kempis, *Of the Imitation of Christ*, trans. W. H. Hutchings (London: Rivingtons, 1881), 88.

14. Wisse, "Letter of Peter to Philip."

9. The Shadow of Living Light

1. John Ruskin, "Traffic," in *The Crown of Wild Olive* (New York: Wiley, 1866), 61.

2. Symeon the New Theologian, *The Discourses*, ed. C. J. deCatanzaro and George Maloney, SJ (Mahwah, NJ: Paulist, 1980), 27.

3. Martin Rule, *The Life and Times of St. Anselm* (London: Kegan, Paul, Trench, 1883), 13.

4. C. H. Talbot, trans., *The Life of Christina of Markyate* (Oxford: Oxford University Press, 2008), 4.

5. Documentary discrepancy exists regarding the age at which Hildegard came to live at Disibodenberg with Jutta. Hildegard herself says she was eight, but other evidence suggests that Jutta herself did not come to the monastery before Hildegard was fourteen. Either way, Jutta was a primary influence.

6. Hildegard of Bingen, *Mystical Writings*, ed. Fiona Bowie and Oliver Davies (New York: Crossroad, 1990), 68.

7. 1 Timothy 2:12.

8. Hildegard of Bingen, *Scivias*, trans. Mother Columbia Hart and Jane Bishop (Mahwah, NJ: Paulist, 1990), 59.

9. Hildegard, 161.

10. John 8:12. This verse is identical in nearly every version of the Bible in English, from WYC to NIV.

11. Exodus 33:20 KJV.

12. See, among others, Richard Grossinger, *Migraine Auras: When the Visual World Fails* (Berkeley, CA: North Atlantic Books, 2006); and

Oliver Sacks, *Migraine: Evolution of a Common Disorder* (Berkeley: University of California Press, 1973).

13. Mayo Clinic Staff, "Migraine with Aura: Symptoms and Causes," Patient Care and Health Info, Mayo Clinic, May 30, 2019, https://tinyurl.com/3youcg6v.

14. Oliver Sacks, *Hallucinations*, 128; Sacks is referencing Klaus Podoll and Derek Robinson, *Migraine Art: The Migraine Experience from Within* (Berkeley, CA: North Atlantic Books, 2008).

15. Hildegard, *Mystical Writings*, 68.

16. Evelyn Underhill, *The Mystics of the Church* (New York: Schocken, 1964), 77.

10. "Repair My House"

1. Nicholas Vachel Lindsay, "St. Francis of Assisi," in *General William Booth Enters into Heaven and Other Poems* (New York: Macmillan, 1919), 43.

2. Saint Bonaventure, *The Life of Saint Francis*, trans. E. Gurney Salter (London: Dent, 1904), 14; language modernized.

3. Paul Sabatier, *Life of St. Francis of Assisi*, trans. Louise Seymour Houghton (New York: Scribner's, 1916), 56. Most of the details about Francis's San Damiano experience are from chapter 4 of Sabatier, 53–70.

4. Matthew 19:21.

5. Matthew 10:9–10.

6. Bonaventure, *Life of Saint Francis*, 139–40.

7. Gilbert K. Chesterton, *St. Francis of Assisi* (Garden City, NY: Image, 1957), 204–5.

8. Sabatier, *Life of St. Francis*, 304–5. My own translation of the Italian.

9. Philip Yancey, *What's So Amazing about Grace?* (Grand Rapids, MI: Zondervan, 1997), 233.

10. Micah 6:8.

11. Pierre Teilhard de Chardin, quoted in Eugene Peterson, *Under the Unpredictable Plant: An Exploration in Vocational Holiness* (Grand Rapids, MI: Eerdmans, 1992), 137.

11. "All Shall Be Well"

1. Charles Albert Tindley, "We'll Understand It Better Bye and Bye," in *Living Hymns* (Charlottesville, VA: L. B. Goodall, 1905), 47b.

2. C. S. Lewis, "God in the Dock," in *God in the Dock: Essays on Theology and Ethics*, ed. Walter Hooper (Grand Rapids, MI: Eerdmans, 1970), 244. The essay was originally published in *Lumen Vitae* vol. 3 (September 1948) under the title "Difficulties in Presenting the Christian Faith to Modern Unbelievers."

3. John Milton, *Paradise Lost*, bk. 1, lines 24–26.

4. Modernization of "Dame Jelyan." Margery Kempe, *The Book of Margery Kempe*, bk. 1, pt. 1, ed. Lynn Staley (Rochester, NY: University of Rochester, 1996), line 955. This original-language version is available online as part of the Robbins Library Digital Projects, TEAMS Medieval Text Series: https://tinyurl.com/3r92xdcs.

5. E. L. Watkin, *Poets and Mystics* (London: Sheed & Ward, 1953), 72.

6. The quotations from Julian throughout this chapter are my own modernizations, based on the Middle English Short Text and portions of the Long Text found in Barry Windeatt, *English Mystics of the Middle Ages* (Cambridge: Cambridge University Press, 1994), 184–226. The Long Text is also referenced from time to time at "The Middle English Text Series Online," Robbins Library Digital Projects, accessed March 15, 2021, https://d.lib.rochester.edu/teams/text-online.

7. Julian of Norwich, *The Shewings of Julian of Norwich*, ed. Georgia Ronan Crampton (Rochester, NY: University of Rochester, 1994), pt. 1, lines 40–45, https://tinyurl.com/lly1mwoh. Language modernized.

8. James Sillett, "St. Julian's *Supposed before the Conquest*," 1828, lithograph, Norfolk Museums Collections, used by permission; first published in James Sillett's *Views of the Churches, Chapels and Other Public Edifices in the City of Norwich* (Norwich, UK: Sillett, 1828), lithograph 19, https://tinyurl.com/xfycm5s. Although this rendering of Norwich Church was done four centuries after Julian lived there, the building was largely unchanged.

9. Windeatt, *English Mystics*, 184.

10. Windeatt, 185.

11. Thomas Merton, *Witness to Freedom: The Letters in Times of Crisis*, ed. William H. Shannon (New York: Farrar, Straus & Giroux, 1994), 43–44.

12. Windeatt, *English Mystics*, 185.

13. Windeatt, 185.
14. Windeatt, 186.
15. Windeatt, 190.
16. This answer is transcribed in the Long Text: Julian, *Shewings*, pt. 1, lines 467–70.
17. Julian, chap. 27.
18. Windeatt, *English Mystics*, 195.
19. Windeatt, 209–10.
20. Julian of Norwich, *Revelations of Divine Love Shewed to a Devout Anchoress by Name, Mother Julian*, ed. Henry Collins (London: Thomas Richardson, 1877).
21. Evelyn Underhill, *The Essentials of Mysticism and Other Essays* (London: Dent, 1920), 183.
22. W. B. Yeats, *Yeats's Mask, Yeats Annual No. 19: A Special Edition*, ed. Margaret Mills Harper and Warwick Gould (Cambridge, UK: Open Book, 2013), 24.
23. T. S. Eliot, "Little Gidding," in *The Complete Poems and Plays, 1909–1950* (Orlando: Harcourt Brace, 1967), 138–45.
24. W. H. Auden, "Memorial for the City," in *Nones* (London: Faber & Faber, 1952), 34–40.
25. Merton, *Witness to Freedom*, 43.
26. Merton, *Collected Poems*, 367.
27. Denise Levertov, "The Showings: Lady Julian of Norwich," in *The Stream and the Sapphire* (New York: New Directions, 1975), 50–58; Denise Levertov, "On a Theme from Julian's Chapter XX," in *Stream and the Sapphire*, 75–76.
28. Malcolm Guite, "Julian of Norwich," in *The Singing Bowl: Collected Poems by Malcolm Guite* (London: Canterbury, 2013), 82.
29. Sydney Carter, "Loud Are the Bells of Norwich," in *Worship in Song: A Friends Hymnal*, ed. David Budmen (Carol Stream, IL: Hope Publishing, 1981), 250.
30. Windeatt, *English Mystics*, 235–36.

12. "It Is Full Merry in Heaven"

1. Thank you to Fr. Luke Penkett of the Julian Centre in Norwich, who helped me visualize Julian's cell and its environs.

2. Margery Kempe, *The Book of Margery Kempe*, trans. B. A. Windeatt (New York: Penguin, 1985), 36.
3. Margery Kempe et al., *Dyvers Doctrynes . . . Taken Out of the Lyfe of . . . Saynt Katheryn of Seenes, etc. A Shorte Treatyse of Contemplacyon Taught by Our Lord Jhesu Cryst, or Taken Out of the Boke of Margery Kemp Ancresse of Lynne, etc.* (London: Henry Pepwell, 1521). The unique copy of this book is housed in the British Library.
4. Kempe, *Book of Margery Kempe*, trans. Windeatt, 41–42.
5. Kempe, 42.
6. Kempe, 51–52.
7. Kempe, *Book of Margery Kempe*, ed. Staley, line 955.
8. Kempe, *Book of Margery Kempe*, trans. Windeatt, 76.
9. Kempe, 76.
10. Kempe, 77.
11. Kempe, 78.
12. Kempe, 78–79.
13. My daughter Abigail Hudson, MSW, assisted me in this section.
14. Michelle Davidson, "Postpartum Psychosis," Postpartum Support International, September 5, 2017, https://tinyurl.com/1sfecye7.
15. Davidson.
16. Merton, *Witness to Freedom*, 43.
17. William Blake, "The Marriage of Heaven and Hell," in *Complete Writings*, 150.
18. Kempe, *Book of Margery Kempe*, trans. Windeatt, 46.

13. Quakers, Shakers, and Groundbreakers

1. George Fox, *The Journal of George Fox: Being an Historical Account of His Life, Travels, Sufferings, and Christian Experiences* (London: Headley Brothers, 1902), 109–10.
2. Fox, 6.
3. Evelyn Underhill, *Mysticism: A Study in the Nature and Development of Man's Spiritual Consciousness* (New York: Dutton, 1912), 213.
4. Lawrence Ferlinghetti, "I Am Waiting," in *A Coney Island of the Mind* (New York: New Directions, 1958), 52.
5. Jacob Boehme, *Aurora: That Is, the Day-Spring*, trans. John Sparrow (1656; Internet Archive, 2009), 2, https://tinyurl.com/4w8detxv.
6. Boehme, 103.

7. Psalm 36:9.

8. Jacob Boehme, *The Confessions of Jacob Boehme*, ed. W. Scott Palmer (London: Methuen, 1920), 1–2.

9. John Wesley, *The Journal of the Rev. John Wesley* (London: J. Kershaw, 1827), 359.

10. David Masson in his *Life of John Milton*, quoted in Ariel Hessayon, "Jacob Boehme and the Early Quakers," *Journal of the Friends' Historical Society* 60, no. 3 (2005): 192.

11. Boehme, *Aurora*, 30.

12. Fox, *Journal*, 127.

13. John Woolman, *The Journal of John Woolman*, ed. John G. Whittier (Boston: Houghton, Mifflin, 1882), 61.

14. Herbert A. Wisbey Jr., *Pioneer Prophetess: Jemima Wilkinson, the Publick Universal Friend* (Ithaca, NY: Cornell University Press, 1964), 12. Public Universal Friend rejected the use of gender-specific pronouns after the indwelling of Jesus. When writing of that experience later, the Friend used female pronouns to describe the person before that experience. I have tried to follow that preference in my own short synopsis.

15. Wisbey, 13.

16. Wisbey, 12.

17. Wisbey, 206.

18. Genesis 1:27 KJV.

19. F. W. Evans, *Ann Lee (the Founder of the Shakers): A Biography* (London: Burns, 1858), 21–22.

20. Evans, 22–23.

21. Lars Bergquist, *Swedenborg's Secret: A Biography* (London: Swedenborg Society, 2005), 190.

22. Blake, "Marriage of Heaven and Hell."

23. Ralph Waldo Emerson, *Representative Men: Seven Lectures* (London: Routledge, 1850), 60.

24. Helen Keller, *How I Would Help the World* (West Chester, PA: Swedenborg Foundation, 2011), 49.

25. Jorge Luis Borges, "Emanuel Swedenborg," in *Selected Poems*, ed. Alexander Coleman (New York: Penguin, 1999), 209.

26. Robert Frost, *The Collected Prose of Robert Frost*, ed. Mark Richardson (Cambridge, MA: Belknap, 2007), 200.

27. Teresa of Ávila, *The Life of S. Teresa of Jesus . . . Written by Herself*, trans. David Lewis (London: Burnes, Oates, 1870), 219.

28. John Milton, *Paradise Lost*, bk. 10, lines 63–67.

29. Matthew 7:14 KJV.

30. John Bunyan, *The Pilgrim's Progress as John Bunyan Wrote It*, facsimile reproduction of the first edition (1678; London: Elliot Stock, 1895), 3, 11.

14. To Imagine Is to See

1. Thomas Bailey Aldrich, "In Westminster Abbey," in *Poems* (Boston: Jefferson, 1915), 74.

2. William Blake, "Jerusalem: The Emanation of the Giant Albion," in *Complete Writings*, 717.

3. Sir Joseph Ayloffe, "Account of the Body of Edward the First," in J. S. Forsyth, *An Antiquaries Portfolio* (London: Whightman, 1875), 155.

4. William Blake, *On Homer's Poetry [and] On Virgil*, relief-etched broadsheet, in *Complete Writings*, 778.

5. Alexander Gilchrist, *Life of William Blake, "Pictor Ignotus"* (London: Macmillan, 1863), 18.

6. Gilchrist, 342, 7.

7. Blake, *Complete Writings*, 576–77.

8. In Blake's day, the north doors were the main entrance, not the west doors as today.

9. Torrigiano's *Head of Christ* later came into the possession of the Wallace Collection, London. It is not known exactly when the sculpture disappeared from the abbey, though it was sometime in the late eighteenth century. I cannot be 100 percent sure that Blake ever saw it, but the evidence is strong that he saw either it or similar images of Florentine Christs at that time. My hunch is that the Torrigiano piece was a specific inspiration.

10. Mary Ellen Reisner, "William Blake and Westminster Abbey," *Man and Nature* 1 (1982): 185–98.

11. Robert Blair, *The Grave: A Poem* (London: R. H. Cromek, 1808), frontispiece—engraved by Luigi Schiavonetti based on illustrations by Blake. Cromek disliked Blake's own engravings of his illustrations for the book, so he hired Schiavonetti to execute them.

12. Blake, *Complete Writings*, 606.

13. Blake, 605–6.

14. Samuel Taylor Coleridge, *Biographia Literaria: Or Biographical Sketches of My Literary Life and Opinions* (London: Rest Fenner, 1817), 295–96.

15. "I Know You, and I Don't Know You"

1. Emily Dickinson, "I Felt a Funeral, in My Brain," in *Emily Dickinson's Poems: As She Preserved Them*, ed. Cristanne Miller (Cambridge, MA: Belknap, 2016), 179.

2. Olive Gilbert, *Narrative of Sojourner Truth*, ed. Nell Irvin Painter (New York: Penguin, 1998), 28.

3. Gilbert, 29.

4. Gilbert, 44.

5. Gilbert, 44–45.

6. "I Want Jesus to Walk with Me," in *African American Heritage Hymnal: 575 Hymns, Spirituals, and Gospel Songs*, ed. Delores Carpenter and Nolan E. Williams (Chicago: GIA, 2001), hymn 563.

7. Harriet Beech Stowe, *The Writings of Harriet Beecher Stowe* (Boston: Houghton, Mifflin, 1896), 4:326–27.

8. Nell Irvin Painter, *Sojourner Truth: A Life, a Symbol* (New York: Norton, 1996), 162.

9. Gilbert, *Narrative*, 162.

10. Gilbert, 92.

11. Sojourner Truth, "Women's Rights Convention," *Anti-slavery Bugle*, June 1, 1851, 160, from Chronicling America, Library of Congress, https://tinyurl.com/1205hlo1.

12. William Faulkner, *Requiem for a Nun* (1951; New York: Vintage, 2011), 73.

13. From the epigraph on the title page of Olive Gilbert, *Narrative of Sojourner Truth: A Northern Slave Emancipated from Bodily Servitude by the State of New York, in 1828* (Boston: printed privately by the author, 1850).

14. We did indeed return to Truth's grave site on November 23, 2020, three weeks after the election. The gravestone was plastered with "I Voted" stickers. We did not add any, since we voted by mail from home and obtained no stickers.

16. Revival Fires

1. Lorenzo Dow, *The Eccentric Preacher: Or a Sketch of the Life of the Celebrated Lorenzo Dow* (Lowell, MA: E. A. Rice, 1841), 87, iii.

2. Dow, 10–11.

3. Dow, 18. The parable of the sower is found in Matthew 13:1–30.

4. Quoted in Michael Horton, "The Disturbing Legacy of Charles Finney," Monergism, 2018, https://tinyurl.com/rud5gs73. My take on Finney's legacy is largely shaped by this excellent overview by theologian Michael Horton.

5. Charles G. Finney, *The Original Memoirs of Charles G. Finney*, ed. Garth Rosell and Richard A. G. Depuis (Grand Rapids, MI: Zondervan, 2002), 10, 11–12.

6. Finney, 13. The verse is Finney's own paraphrase of Jeremiah 29:12–13. The KJV renders it this way: "Then shall ye call upon me, and ye shall go and pray unto me, and I will hearken unto you. And ye shall seek me, and find me, when ye shall search for me with all your heart."

7. Finney, 14.

8. Finney, 16.

9. Finney, 16.

10. Finney, 18, 19, 20.

11. Finney, 61.

12. Charles W. Carter, *Organization of Jesus Christ of the Church of Latter-Day Saints and Their Belief* (Salt Lake City: Utah Lithographing, 1897), 8.

13. Carter, 8.

14. Horton, "Disturbing Legacy."

17. "Keep Your Mind in Hell"

1. Archimandrite Sophrony, *St. Silouan the Athonite* (Crestwood, NY: St. Vladimir's Seminary Press, 1999), 15. Most of the details of Silouan's life in this section are from this work.

2. Sophrony, 17.

3. Sophrony, 24.

4. Sophrony, 25.

5. Sophrony, 458.

6. Sophrony, 26.

7. Sophrony, 42; language modernized.

8. Psalm 139:8 KJV.

9. Sophrony, *St. Silouan*, 48.

10. Sophrony, 47.

11. Sophrony, 306; language modernized.

12. Symeon, *Discourses*, 27.

13. Lord Byron, *The Works of Lord Byron: Poetry* (London: John Murray, 1904), 3:18–19.

14. 1 Thessalonians 5:17 KJV.

15. R. M. French, trans., *The Way of a Pilgrim and the Pilgrim Continues His Way*, with an introduction by Huston Smith (New York: Quality Paperback Book Club / HarperCollins, 1998), 34.

16. Oliver Sacks, *Hallucinations*, 247.

17. John Sanidopoulos, "The Russian Monk Who Drank Tea and Vodka Daily with Saint Silouan the Athonite," Mystagogy Resource Center, August 12, 2019, https://tinyurl.com/1bsvk8kz.

18. "O God—If There Is a God"

1. Sundar Singh, quoted in Corrie ten Boom, *Clippings from My Notebook* (Nashville: Nelson, 1982), 71.

2. Friedrich Heiler, *The Gospel of Sâdhu Sundar Singh*, trans. Olive Wyon (London: Allen & Unwin, 1927), 38.

3. Heiler, 40.

4. Heiler, 42.

5. Heiler, 42–43.

6. Heiler, 43–44.

7. This story is told in Kathleen White, *Corrie ten Boom* (Bloomington, MN: Bethany House, 1991), 31.

8. All the details in this chapter about Singh's influence on C. S. Lewis come from Kathryn Lindskoog's "Links in a Golden Chain: C. S. Lewis, George MacDonald, and Sadhu Sundar Singh," in *Surprised by C. S. Lewis, George MacDonald, and Dante* (Macon, GA: Mercer University Press, 2001), 63–74. I dedicate this chapter to the memory of Kathryn Lindskoog (1934–2003), whom I had the great privilege of befriending as I edited two of her books for Zondervan: *Creative Writing: For Those Who Can't Not Write* and *Fakes, Frauds and Other Malarkey*.

9. C. S. Lewis, *The Pilgrim's Regress* (New York: Sheed & Ward, 1944), 184–85.

10. C. S. Lewis, *That Hideous Strength (a Modern Fairy-Tale for Grown-Ups)* (London: Bodley Head, 1945), 137.

11. Kim Comer, ed., *Wisdom of the Sadhu: Teachings of Sundar Singh* (Farmington, PA: Plough, 2000), 187.

12. Heiler, *Gospel*, 45.

13. Heiler, 46–47, 48.
14. Comer, *Wisdom of the Sadhu*, 57–58.

19. Inner Locutions

1. Michael Clark, "Letters," *Time*, October 6, 1997, 12.
2. Frank Newport, "Mother Teresa Voted by American People as Most Admired Person of the Century," Gallup News Service, December 31, 1999, https://tinyurl.com/f3ahqypb.
3. "Who Does She Think She Is . . . Mother Teresa?," *Door*, March/April 1996, 11.
4. Robin Fox, "Mother Teresa's Care for the Dying," *Lancet* 344 (1994): 807–8.
5. Tim Challies, "The Myth of Mother Teresa," *@Challies* (blog), November 2, 2003, https://tinyurl.com/55lm8syb.
6. Peter Jamison, "Tainted Saint: Mother Teresa Defended Pedophile Priest," *SFWeekly*, January 11, 2012, https://tinyurl.com/gqm0kfj1.
7. Christopher Hitchens, *The Missionary Position: Mother Teresa in Theory and Practice* (New York: Verson, 1995), 98.
8. Brian Kolodiejchuk, *Mother Teresa: Come Be My Light; The Private Writings of the "Saint of Calcutta"* (New York: Image Doubleday, 2007), 44.
9. Kolodiejchuk, 54.
10. Mother Teresa, quoted in Malcolm Muggeridge, *Something Beautiful for God: Mother Teresa of Calcutta* (London: Collins, 1971), 85–86.
11. John 19:28.
12. Kolodiejchuk, *Mother Teresa*, 41.
13. Kolodiejchuk, 48–49.
14. Kolodiejchuk, 368.
15. Matthew 19:21.
16. John 14:19–20.
17. Sir Edward Cook, *The Life of Florence Nightingale, in Two Volumes* (London: Macmillan, 1914), 2:233, 235.

20. Tortillas and Televangelists

1. The details of the tortilla story are drawn from three articles: R. H. Ring, "Tortilla with Face of Jesus Remains Enshrined while Family Struggles,"

Arizona Daily Star, July 27, 1983, https://tinyurl.com/wmdd2um8; Angelica Rubio, "Christ on the Comal," Eater, April 23, 2019, https://tinyurl.com/8n81zmxo; and Uriel J. Garcia, "'Tortilla Miracle' Brought Hope and Mockery to N. M. Family," *Santa Fe New Mexican*, July 10, 2017, https://tinyurl.com/1uq29x55.

2. Luke 18:42.

3. Andrew L. Seidel, "Inevitable Magachurch Abuse of PPP Funds Is Coming to Light—Private Jet Included," *Religion Dispatches*, December 15, 2020, https://tinyurl.com/cmag2zkf.

4. John MacArthur, "A Colossal Fraud," *Grace to You* (blog), December 7, 2009, https://www.gty.org/library/blog/B091207.

5. The information about Peter Popoff is gleaned from Wikipedia, s.v. "Peter Popoff," last modified February 19, 2021, 13:09, https://en.wikipedia.org/wiki/Peter_Popoff. For more details, see James Randi, *The Faith Healers* (Amherst, NY: Prometheus Books, 1989).

6. "Robertson Says God Told Him Bush Would Win Reelection in a 'Blowout,'" *Church and State*, February 2004, https://tinyurl.com/1v9y6xu9.

7. Pat Robertson, quoted on *Fox and Friends* in Liz Cox Barrett, "We Report (What Pat Robertson Said God Told Him), You Decide," *Columbia Journalism Review*, January 3, 2007, https://tinyurl.com/1fmr46aq.

8. Josh Peter, "Televangelist Pat Robertson Predicts Trump Win, Then Chaos, Then the End of the World," *USA Today*, October 20, 2020, https://tinyurl.com/gzlyrqgg.

9. Joshua Bote, "Televangelist Pat Robertson No Longer Thinks Trump Can Win Reelection: 'It's Time to Move On,'" *USA Today*, December 22, 2020, https://tinyurl.com/1ge9paq7.

10. David Edwin Harrell Jr., *Oral Roberts: An American Life* (Bloomington: Indiana University Press, 1985), 67. Other details of this story are from Christopher Reed, "Oral Robert Obituary," *Guardian*, December 15, 2009, https://tinyurl.com/4eqw8rll.

11. Harrell, *Oral Roberts*, 333.

12. This and the following quotations from the fundraising letter are quoted in "Oral Roberts Tells of Talking to 900-Foot Jesus," *Tulsa World*, October 16, 1980, https://tinyurl.com/1ji3vkpr.

13. Gil Broyles, "Oral Roberts Says He's Been Given a Money-or-Death Ultimatum," AP News, January 19, 1987, https://tinyurl.com/2rbwzbih.

14. David Averill, "Oral Roberts Says 900-Foot Jesus Appeared before 'My Inner Eyes,'" *Tulsa World*, May 7, 1982, https://tinyurl.com/1byeegl3 (emphasis mine).
15. "Evangelist Preacher Who Worshipped Money," *Irish Times*, December 19, 2009, https://tinyurl.com/yhcxf6p2.
16. "Preacher Who Worshipped Money."

Epilogue

1. C. S. Lewis, *Mere Christianity* (1952; San Francisco: HarperSanFrancisco, 2001), 226.
2. Nicholas of Cusa, *On the Vision of God* (New York: Cosimo Classics, 2007), 26.
3. William Cowper, *The Task: A Poem in Six Books* (London: Joseph Johnson, 1785), 102.
4. Dietrich Bonhoeffer, *God Is in the Manger: Reflections on Advent and Christmas*, trans. O. C. Dean Jr. (Louisville, KY: Westminster John Knox, 2010), 2.

SELECTED BIBLIOGRAPHY

Alexander, Bishop, and Natalia Bufius. *The Life and Teachings of Elder Siluan.* Translated by Anatoly Shmelev. La Canada, CA: Holy Trinity Orthodox Mission, n.d. https://tinyurl.com/2a6hawnr.

Athanasius. *The Life of Saint Antony.* Translated by Robert T. Meyer. Ancient Christian Writers Series. New York: Newman, 1950.

Bergquist, Lars. *Swedenborg's Secret: A Biography.* London: Swedenborg Society, 2005.

Blake, William. *Complete Writings.* Edited by Geoffrey Keynes. London: Oxford University Press, 1972.

Boehme, Jacob. *Aurora: That Is, the Day-Spring.* Translated by John Sparrow. 1656; Internet Archive, 2009. https://tinyurl.com/4w8detxv.

Bonaventure. *The Life of Saint Francis.* Translated by E. Gurney Salter. London: Dent, 1904.

Brown, Raphael, ed. *The Little Flowers of St. Francis.* Garden City, NY: Image, 1958.

Canaday, John. "Albrecht Dürer." *Horizon*, Summer 1964, 16–31.

Canton, William. *A Child's Book of Saints.* London: Dent, 1906.

Carter, Charles W. *Organization of Jesus Christ of the Church of Latter-Day Saints and Their Belief.* Salt Lake City: Utah Lithographing, 1897.

Chesterton, G. K. *St. Francis of Assisi.* Garden City, NY: Image, 1957.

Clissold, Stephen. *The Wisdom of St. Francis and His Companions.* New York: New Directions, 1978.

Comer, Kim, ed. *Wisdom of the Sadhu: Teachings of Sundar Singh.* Farmington, PA: Plough, 2000.

Cook, Christopher C. H. *Hearing Voices, Demonic and Divine: Scientific and Theological Perspectives.* Abingdon, Oxfordshire: Routledge, 2019.

Cook, Sir Edward. *The Life of Florence Nightingale, in Two Volumes.* Vol. 2. London: Macmillan, 1914.

Dow, Lorenzo. *The Eccentric Preacher: Or a Sketch of the Life of the Celebrated Lorenzo Dow.* Lowell, MA: E. A. Rice, 1841.

Evans, F. W. *Ann Lee (the Founder of the Shakers): A Biography.* London: Burns, 1858.

Farrar, Frederick W. *Saintly Workers.* London: Macmillan, 1878.

Finney, Charles G. *The Original Memoirs of Charles G. Finney.* Edited by Garth M. Rosell and Richard A. G. Depuis. Grand Rapids, MI: Zondervan, 2002.

Fox, George. *The Journal of George Fox: Being an Historical Account of His Life, Travels, Sufferings, and Christian Experiences.* London: Headley Brothers, 1902.

Fox, Matthew. *Illuminations of Hildegard of Bingen.* Santa Fe: Bear, 1985.

French, R. M., trans. *The Way of a Pilgrim and the Pilgrim Continues His Way.* With an introduction by Huston Smith. New York: Quality Paperback Book Club / HarperCollins, 1998.

Furlong, Monica. *Visions and Longings: Medieval Women Mystics.* Boston: Shambhala, 1996.

Garcia, Uriel J. "'Tortilla Miracle' Brought Hope and Mockery to N. M. Family." *Santa Fe New Mexican*, July 10, 2017. https://tinyurl.com/1uq29x55.

Gilbert, Olive. *Narrative of Sojourner Truth.* Edited by Nell Irvin Painter. New York: Penguin, 1998.

Gilchrist, Alexander. *Life of William Blake, "Pictor Ignotus."* London: Macmillan, 1863.

Harrell, David Edwin Jr. *Oral Roberts: An American Life.* Bloomington: Indiana University Press, 1985.

Heiler, Friedrich. *The Gospel of Sâdhu Sundar Singh.* Translated by Olive Wyon. London: Allen & Unwin, 1927.

Hessayon, Ariel. "Jacob Boehme and the Early Quakers." *Journal of the Friends' Historical Society* 60, no. 3 (2005): 191–223.

Hildegard of Bingen. *Mystical Writings*. Edited by Fiona Bowie and Oliver Davies. New York: Crossroad, 1990.

———. *Scivias*. Translated by Mother Columba Hart and Jane Bishop. Classics of Western Spirituality Series. Mahwah, NJ: Paulist, 1990.

Hitchens, Christopher. *The Missionary Position: Mother Teresa in Theory and Practice*. New York: Verso, 1995.

Hone, William, Jeremiah Jones, and William Wake, eds. *The Lost Books of the Bible*. New York: Bell, 1979.

Hudson, David. *History of Jemima Wilkinson: A Preacheress of the Eighteenth Century*. Geneva, NY: S. P. Hull, 1821.

Jerome. *The Letters of St. Jerome*. Vol. 1, *Letters 1–22*. Translated by Charles Christopher Mierow. Ancient Christian Writers Series. New York: Newman, 1963.

Juliana of Norwich. *Revelations of Divine Love*. Translated by M. L. Del Mastro. Garden City, NY: Image, 1977.

Kelsey, Morton T. *God, Dreams and Revelation: A Christian Interpretation of Dreams*. Minneapolis: Augsburg, 1991.

Kempe, Margery. *The Book of Margery Kempe*. Translated by B. A. Windeatt. New York: Penguin, 1985.

King, Ursula. *Christian Mystics: Their Lives and Legacies throughout the Ages*. Mahwah, NJ: Hidden Spring / Paulist, 2001.

Kolodiejchuk, Brian. *Mother Teresa: Come Be My Light; The Private Writings of the "Saint of Calcutta."* New York: Image/Doubleday, 2007.

Lindskoog, Kathryn. *Surprised by C. S. Lewis, George MacDonald, and Dante*. Macon, GA: Mercer University Press, 2001.

McColman, Carl. *Christian Mystics: 108 Seers, Saints, and Sages*. Charlottesville, VA: Hampton Roads, 2016.

Merton, Thomas. *Mystics and Zen Masters*. New York: Farrar, Straus & Giroux, 1967.

Meyer, Marvin, ed. *The Gospel of Thomas: The Hidden Sayings of Jesus.* San Francisco: HarperSanFrancisco, 1992.

Morris, Adam. *American Messiahs: False Prophets of a Damned Nation.* New York: Liveright, 2019.

Moss, Robert. "St. Jerome Bewitches Dreams and Dreamwork." Dream Gate. Beliefnet. Accessed December 2020. https://tinyurl.com/x5kctbnh.

Muggeridge, Malcolm. *Something Beautiful for God: Mother Teresa of Calcutta.* London: Collins, 1971.

Nicholas of Cusa. *On the Vision of God.* New York: Cosimo Classics, 2007.

Painter, Nell Irvin. *Sojourner Truth: A Life, a Symbol.* New York: Norton, 1996.

Parker, Mrs. Arthur. *Sadhu Singh: Called of God.* Lawton, OK: Trumpet, 2013.

Reichardt, Mary R., ed. *Catholic Women Writers: A Bio-bibliographical Sourcebook.* Westport, CT: Greenwood, 2001.

Reisner, Mary Ellen. "William Blake and Westminster Abbey." *Man and Nature* 1 (1982): 185–198.

Ring, R. H. "Tortilla with Face of Jesus Remains Enshrined while Family Struggles." *Arizona Daily Star*, July 27, 1983. https://tinyurl.com/wmdd2um8.

Roberts, Oral. *Expect a Miracle: My Life and Ministry, an Autobiography.* Nashville: Thomas Nelson, 1998.

Robinson, Paschal. *The Writings of Saint Francis of Assisi.* Philadelphia: Dolphin, 1906.

Rubio, Angelica. "Christ on the Comal." *Eater.* April 23, 2019. https://tinyurl.com/8n81zmxo.

Sabatier, Paul. *Life of St. Francis of Assisi.* Translated by Louise Seymour Houghton. New York: Scribner's, 1916.

Sacks, Oliver. *Hallucinations.* New York: Knopf, 2012.

Schaff, Philip, and Henry Wace, eds. *The Nicene and Post-Nicene Fathers.* Vol. 6, *Saint Jerome: Letters and Select Works.* New York: Christian Literature Company, 1893.

————, eds. *The Nicene and Post-Nicene Fathers.* Vol. 11, *Sulpitius Severus, Vincent of Lérins, John Cassian.* New York: Christian Literature Company, 1894.

Sophrony, Archimandrite. *St. Silouan the Athonite.* Crestwood, NY: St. Vladimir's Seminary Press, 1999.

Symeon the New Theologian. *The Discourses.* Edited by C. J. deCatanzaro and George Maloney, SJ. Mahwah, NJ: Paulist, 1980.

Taylor, Joan E. *What Did Jesus Look Like?* London: Bloomsbury T&T Clark, 2018.

Thoules, Robert H. *The Lady Julian: A Psychological Study.* London: Society for Promoting Christian Knowledge, 1924.

Toynbee, Arnold J. "The Desert Hermits." *Horizon,* Spring 1970, 22–27.

Trevor-Roper, H. R. "Four Faces of Heresy." *Horizon,* Spring 1964, 8–17.

Underhill, Evelyn. *The Essentials of Mysticism and Other Essays.* London: Dent, 1920.

————. *Mysticism: A Study in the Nature and Development of Man's Spiritual Consciousness.* New York: Dutton, 1912.

————. *The Mystics of the Church.* New York: Schocken, 1964.

Wace, Henry, and Philip Schaff, eds. *The Nicene and Post-Nicene Fathers.* Vol. 3, *Theodoret, Jerome, Gennadius, Rufinus: Historical Writings, etc.* New York: Christian Literature Company, 1892.

Watkin, E. I. *Poets and Mystics.* London: Sheed & Ward, 1953.

Wiebe, Phillip H. *Visions of Jesus: Direct Encounters from the New Testament to Today.* New York: Oxford University Press, 1997.

Windeatt, Barry, ed. *English Mystics of the Middle Ages.* Cambridge: Cambridge University Press, 1994.

Wisbey, Herbert A., Jr. *Pioneer Prophetess: Jemima Wilkinson, the Publick Universal Friend.* Ithaca, NY: Cornell University Press, 1964.

Woolman, John. *The Journal of John Woolman.* Edited by John Greenleaf Whittier. Boston: Houghton, Mifflin, 1882.